# Modern Critical Interpretations

*Modern Critical Interpretations*

Ken Kesey's
*One Flew Over the Cuckoo's Nest*

*Edited and with an introduction by*
Harold Bloom
Sterling Professor of the Humanities
Yale University

CHELSEA HOUSE PUBLISHERS
Philadelphia

Printed and bound in the United States of America

10  9  8  7  6  5  4  3  2  1

∞ The paper used in this publication meets the minimum
requirements of the American National Standard for
Permanence of Paper for Printed Library Materials,
Z39.48-1984

Library of Congress Cataloging-in-Publication Data

Ken Kesey's One flew over the cuckoo's nest / edited and with an
introduction by Harold Bloom.

    p. cm.— (Modern critical interpretations)
    Includes bibliographical references and index.
    ISBN 0-7910-6339-9   HC 0-7910-7118-9 PB
    1. Kesey, Ken. One flew over the cuckoo's nest.
2. Psychiatric hospital patients in literature. 3. Mentally ill in
literature.
I. Bloom, Harold. II. Series.

PS3561.E667 O5328 2001
813'.54—dc21                                          2001042306


Chelsea House Publishers
1974 Sproul Road, Suite 400
Broomall, PA 19008-0914

The Chelsea House World Wide Web address is
http://www.chelseahouse.com

Series Editor: Matt Uhler

Contributing Editor: Aaron Tillman

Produced by Publisher's Services, Santa Barbara, California

# Contents

# Editor's Note

My Introduction reflects upon the literary phenomenon of "period pieces," and then offers an estimate of Kesey's place in the Period Piece Pantheon.

Terry G. Sherwood examines the clear relation between *One Flew Over the Cuckoo's Nest* (1962) as a novel popular with post-hippy anti-Establishment non-readers and its source in "comic strip principles." The late Tony Tanner—the most distinguished critic anthologized in this volume—also sees the comic strip element, but follows Tom Wolfe in apprehending the sadness of Kesey's science-fiction–like adventure in consciousness.

For Raymond M. Olderman, *One Flew Over the Cuckoo's Nest* collapses into the mystery of the self unknown within one, while Bruce E. Wallis explores Kesey's analogue between McMurphy and Christ, so that the frontal lobotomy and ultimate death becomes a crucifixion. Wallis rejects the analogy, since the McMurphy-Kesey pride contrasts with the humility of Jesus.

Stephen L. Tanner finds *One Flew Over the Cuckoo's Nest* to have formalist aesthetic virtues, after which John Wilson Foster is troubled by the possibility that the hustler has an authentic visionary purpose, akin perhaps to that of the Buddha.

To Barry H. Leeds, *One Flew Over the Cuckoo's Nest* is both spiritually and formally admirable, while M. Gilbert Porter centers upon Bromden, McMurphy's chief disciple, who survives to continue the master's vision.

Stephen L. Tanner and Porter both return, the first to emphasize the wide popular appeal of book, play, and movie, the second to emphasize the role of song in Kesey.

In this book's final essay, the carnival-formalism of Mikhail Bakhtin is turned into an analysis of *One Flew Over the Cuckoo's Nest*, rather as if Ken Kesey were Rabelais or Dostoevsky or Cervantes. Though there seems a certain disproportion here, I myself would ascribe the flaw to the overvalued Bakhtin, rather than to Goluboff.

# Introduction

The "Period Piece" is necessarily an involuntary genre, and I find it always causes rage—in some—when I nominate a particular work of enormous popularity to the Period Piece Pantheon. I do not judge *One Flew Over the Cuckoo's Nest* to be worthy of that pantheon, even though I see that my paperback copy is part of printing 88. My personal treasury of period pieces includes *To Kill a Mockingbird*, *Catcher in the Rye*, *A Separate Peace*, *All Quiet on the Western Front*, several *Rabbits*, *Beloved*, *Nineteen Eighty-Four*, *Lord of the Flies*, *Tobacco Road*, *The Grapes of Wrath*, *The Jungle*, *The Old Man and the Sea*. Kesey's books palpably are not of that caliber: they sort better with *On the Road*, *The World According to Garp*, all the Harry Potter books—I forebear continuing, though Tolkien is the Emperor of inferior period pieces, perhaps never to be dethroned.

Rereading *One Flew Over the Cuckoo's Nest*, the comic strip genre begins to contaminate me, and I start to tell myself the tale from the stance of Big Nurse, the nightmare projection of the male fear of female authority. Nurse Ratched should be compared, in her function, to Vergil's Juno, not a comparison that writers far stronger than Kesey could sustain. I entertain myself with the wild notion of rewriting the *Aeneid* from Juno's perspective, but the prospect becomes phantasmagoric, and so I cease.

What is the utility of period pieces? In furniture, sometimes in costume, sometimes in songs—they can achieve, when rubbed down by time, something of an antique value. Alas, literature does not work that way, and the rubbing process leaves only rubbish, vast mounds of worn words, like *The Fountainhead*. The Nineteen Sixties benefit from a general nostalgia, compounded by political correctness and the sad truth that the erstwhile Counter-culture has become Establishment-culture, visible upon every page of *The New York Times*. Dumbing-down is hardly a new phenomenon, and ideological cheerleading, before it took over the universities, had made its way through the churches, the corporations, the unions, and all our technologies. Readers of Ken Kesey or of the Harry Potter saga might risk the cure of carefully reading *Adventures of Huckleberry Finn*.

1

TERRY G. SHERWOOD

# One Flew Over the Cuckoo's Nest
## *and the Comic Strip*

Although first published in 1962, Ken Kesey's *One Flew Over the Cuckoo's Nest* still enjoys a wide readership. Kesey's "hippy" reputation and the book's unusual expression of anti-Establishment themes, ranging from rebellion against conformity to pastoral retreat, would explain its current popular appeal. The critics' response to the book is less understandable. A warm reception by reviewers has been followed by relatively little critical interest. The book deserves more attention as an imaginative expression of a moral position congenial to an important segment of the American population and as a noteworthy use of Popular culture in a serious novel. This essay will demonstrate the central importance of the nexus between Kesey's aesthetic, informed by comic strip principles, and his moral vision, embodying simple, elemental truths. Kesey's references to comic strip materials are not just casual grace notes but clear indications of his artistic stance. Significantly, the importance of the comic strip to Kesey has been confirmed by Leslie Fiedler, the one major critic discussing the novel at length, although he neither affirms such a high degree of artistic consciousness in Kesey nor examines certain essential details.

The climactic ward party ends with reference to the comic strip hero, the Lone Ranger. Harding asks to be awakened for McMurphy's escape. "I'd like to stand there at the window with a silver bullet in my hand and ask

From *Critique* 13, no. 1. (1970) © 1970 by *Critique*.

'Who wawz that'er masked man?' as you ride—." The insightful Harding clearly recognizes that McMurphy, like the comic strip savior, whose silver bullet annihilates Evil, has freed the inmates from the clutches of the monster Big Nurse. The Lone Ranger reference underlines an aesthetic set out clearly in the novel. Briefly, Kesey's method embodies that of the caricaturist, the cartoonist, the folk artist, the allegorist. Characterization and delineation of incident are inked in bold, simple, exaggerated patterns for obvious but compelling statement. As in the comic strip, action in Kesey's novel turns on the mythic confrontation between Good and Evil: an exemplary he-man versus a machine-tooled, castrating matriarch ever denied our sympathies. Both are bigger than life; both are symbolic exaggerations of qualities; neither is "realistic." Bromden's description of the inmates' and ward attendants' stylized behavior is instructive. "Like a cartoon world, where the figures are flat and outlined in black, jerking through some kind of goofy story that might be real funny if it weren't for the cartoon figures being real guys." Characters and incidents are types, bound by set characteristics, before they are uniquely individual. In demonstrating the centrality of such comic strip elements, I will indicate first how they are reinforced by other materials from Popular culture sharing similar techniques, then more explicitly how they shape character and incident, and finally how Kesey's failure to heed the dangers of his mode is symptomatic of the book's moral flaws and central to critical evaluation.

Kesey draws from one form of Popular culture, the folk song, in his initial characterization of McMurphy. We hear lines from "The Roving Gambler" and "The Wagoner's Lad" in McMurphy's exuberant solo on his first morning in the asylum. Both songs treat a typical opposition between the wanderer and society in terms of romantic love. With characteristic bravado the gambler McMurphy sings, "She took me to her parlor, and coo-oo-ooled me with her fan"—I can hear the whack as he slaps his bare belly— "whispered low in her mamma's ear, I luh-uhvv that gamblin' man." The townbred girl is inevitably drawn to the rover living by the uncertainties of the card game, not the genteel, stability and sexual constriction of the matriarchal parlor. Despite McMurphy's resonating exuberance, the second song is more darkly intoned, with the harshness of farewell and the settled community's stony resistance, thereby predicting McMurphy's unalterable battle with Big Nurse. The lad's poverty and way of life ensure parental disapproval. "Oh, your parents don't like me, they say I'm too po-o-or; they say I'm not worthy to enter your door——Hard livin's my pleasure, my money's my o-o-wn, an' them that don't like me, they can leave me alone." Like the comic strip, a method of the folk song is presentation of simple, typical behavioral patterns, while eschewing introspection and highly subtle characterization. Simple details express typical patterns. The town girl's fan cools the heat of the wanderer's movement, and the wagoner's lad expresses proud opposition to economic bigotry by refusing the girl's offer of hay for his horses. Murphy's brief medley is self-characterization—foot-loose virility, uncompromised independence, gambler's whim, acceptance of harsh physical effort, and resistance to society worked out within the easily understood boundaries of folk art.

Kesey further mines Popular culture in frequent references to McMurphy as the cowboy hero. When McMurphy approaches to break the nurses' window, Bromden says, "He was the logger again, the swaggering gambler, the big redheaded brawling Irishman, the cowboy out of the TV set walking down the middle of the street to meet a dare." Elsewhere, McMurphy speaks in his "drawling cowboy actor's voice." The television "western" intersects the Lone Ranger and folk song references to emphasize frontier values. Kesey uses the stereotyped cowboy hero for precisely the reasons he is often attacked: unrelenting selfhood and independence articulated with verbal calmness and defended by physical valor and ready defiance of opposition. Stock "western" formulae constitute a convenient reservoir of popular literary associations for depicting McMurphy in easily definable terms.

Kesey's mode of simplification voices a moral vision rooted in clear-cut opposition between Good and Evil, between natural man and society, between an older mode of existence honoring masculine physical life and a modern day machine culture inimical to it, between the Indian fishing village and the hydroelectric dam. Modern society standardizes men and strait-jackets its misfits; it causes the illness which it quarantines. The spiritual residue of the American Old West opposes the machine culture; but the West, as such, is doomed like McMurphy. For Kesey, Popular culture's hardened simplicity of detail expresses continuing American values and problems, etched deeply in the American consciousness. Modern machine culture is the most recent manifestation of society's threat to the individual, perhaps the most threatening.

Thus, Kesey turns to the comic strip, a more recent aspect of Popular culture, for his literary materials. Here he finds the method of exaggeration basic to his aesthetic. In *The Electric Kool-Aid Acid Test* Tom Wolfe delineates Kesey's attention to comic strips. For Kesey, the comic book superheroes (Captain Marvel, Superman, Plastic Man, the Flash, *et al.*) were the true mythic heroes of his contemporary adolescent generation. Kesey was interested significantly in this comic strip world during his Stanford University, Perry Lane days, the gestation period of *One Flew Over the Cuckoo's Nest*. He realized this interest most spectacularly later in Merry Prankster days by affecting the superhero's costume to image transcendent human possibility (witness his Flash Gordon-like garb at a Viet Nam teach-in in 1965 and his cape and leotards at the LSD graduation in 1966). The longevity of his interest, antedating his first novel and lasting after his Mexican exile, affirms its personal significance. Wolfe's book colors in the authorial consciousness behind the Lone Ranger reference and Bromden's belief that McMurphy, despite his wardmates' fear of his self-aggrandizement, was a "giant come out of the sky to save us from the Combine." The Lone Ranger's mask mysteriously separates him from other men, his origin is uncertain, and his silver bullet has supernatural powers; that is, he has divine characteristics. Bromden's vision of McMurphy as a saving giant recalls air-born superheroes like Superman and Captain Marvel, miraculously aiding others in one fell swoop; also, we are hereby conditioned for the depiction of McMurphy as Christ, sacrificed on the cross-shaped electroshock table on behalf of the ward. For Kesey, the heavenly Christ and the supernatural comic book hero stand on common mythic ground as images of human potential. McMurphy's self-regarding and independent pursuit of physical pleasure, inspirited by defiant laughter and gambler's unconcern for security, make him superior to other men and free him from society; his power of miracle is transmitting his traits to others. He can do the impossible by executing the fishing trip against Big Nurse's wishes and healing sick men with his fists. He has the superhero's efficacious physical power but, like Christ, the magnitude of his threat to society forces his crucifixion.

The comic strip also inspires the characterization of Big Nurse. The Combine, a machine culture which harvests and packages men, is modern Evil; and Big Nurse, its powerful agent. She shares the comic strip villain's control over modern technology; her glass enveloped nurses' cubicle is the ward's electronic nerve center, and she punishes on the electroshock table. She is Miss Ratched—the ratchet—essential cog in ward machinery (also the ratchet wrench, adjusting malfunctioning inmates?). Her gigantism is expressed in her nickname, Big Nurse, and frequently in descriptions of her. "She's too big to be beaten. She covers one whole side of the room like a Jap statue. There's no moving her and no help against her." "Her nostrils flare open, and every breath she draws she gets bigger, as big and tough-looking's I seen her get over a patient since Taber was here—I can smell the hot oil and magneto spark when she goes past, and every step hits the floor she blows up a size bigger, blowing and puffing, roll down anything in her path." Kesey scales her to match the giant of the sky, McMurphy. Like the comic strip villain, she never enjoys our sympathies, even when rendered voiceless and physically weak by McMurphy's uncavalier assault following Billy Bibbit's suicide.

Our lack of sympathy is tied to her static nature as a principle, not a human being. The comic strip is essentially a pictorial representation of stereotyped moral and psychological truths for unsophisticated readers. The Lone Ranger's mask, the image of his mysterious separateness, and Freddy Freeman's crutch, the image of his mortal half, pictorially express constants in their natures. Kesey's characterizations of McMurphy and Big Nurse emphasize similar repeated details. In McMurphy's motorcyclist's cap we see the stereotyped antisocial belligerence of cycle gangs; in his scarred fists, his ready valor and worker's energy; in his red hair, the Irishman's volatility; in the scar on his nose, an emblem of wounds bravely received in aggressive assertion of self; in his white whale underpants, his untamed and socially destructive natural vitality. A hard shell of plastic, starch, and enamel incase Big Nurse's humanity. The impenetrable surface of her "doll's face and doll's smile" iconographically represents her stunted feelings. The militaristic, stiff nurse's uniform constrains the sexual and maternal potential of her admirable bosom. She is part of a machine attempting to level even sexual differences. The stable lines in Kesey's characterization of the two antagonists stress their essential natures.

Imaginative variations of comic strip principles show Kesey's sophisticated manipulation of his mode, as in Bromden's metamorphosis through McMurphy's influence. Bromden's rejuvenation is the gauge of McMurphy's savior's power and is Kesey's promise of hope. Bromden escapes, not McMurphy. The modern world cannot accommodate the freewheeling Irishman. The freedom of the Old West is gone; its spirit resides only in myth; the Irish minority has been assimilated. McMurphy is hounded into a prison farm and, despite delusions of freely choosing the asylum, drawn fatalistically into the showdown with Big Nurse. Gradually, he understands his Messianic role: "We made him stand and hitch up his black shorts like they were horsehide chaps, and push back his cap with one finger like it was a ten-gallon Stetson, slow, mechanical gestures—and when he walked across the floor you could hear the iron in his bare heels ring sparks out of the tile." He cannot remain in a conformist world in which men no longer share the ecstasy of violence and the gambler's defiance of fate; but, by sacrificing himself, he can infuse the spirit of rebellion and selfhood into those able to combine it with other strengths. His diminishing strength transfers to Bromden. McMurphy cannot lift the tub room control panel, but, possessing the "secret" power of "blowin' a man back up to full size," can empower Bromden to make the symbolic gesture of throwing the panel through the asylum wall, of turning the machine upon itself. The doomed giant can create another giant. Shazam. The six foot, eight inch "Vanishing American," the first man in the ward, has been deflated by a racist society which bulldozes its Indian villages and, after using the tribesmen to fight crippling wars, incarcerates them in asylums to clean floors for white inmates. Kesey looks to dormant Indian values, represented *in potentia* by Bromden's size, for answers to problems of modern culture. Residual Indian pastoralism and regard for physical life, plus a yet strong sense of community, represent a possibility for life in defiance of the Combine; but these values need inspiration, inflation by McMurphy's Spirit. Kesey's central image is the superhero's metamorphosis from mortal weakness to supernatural strength.

The relationship between the white McMurphy and the Indian Bromden is further delineated in Kesey's strategic Lone Ranger reference. Bromden is McMurphy's Tonto, the silent but loyal Indian companion under auspices of his white spiritual guide. Equation of McMurphy and the "masked man" not only stresses McMurphy's savior role in "western" terms, but also sums up the previous relationship between McMurphy and Bromden in order to overturn the traditional expectation of Indian subservience. The Lone Ranger and Tonto become, respectively, the sacrificial Christ and his independent disciple, a writer of Holy Scripture carrying Good News composed of both men's values. Only Tonto leaves the asylum: Bromden's Indian values imbued with McMurphy's Spirit are Kesey's final answer to the questions asked by the book. Strategic use of the Lone Ranger, just before McMurphy's demise and Bromden's complete metamorphosis, crystalizes the book's pivotal racial relationship before redefining it. Again, a skillful hand adapts the comic strip materials.

Different kinds of comic strips serve the author's purpose. Although the showdown with Big Nurse most obviously expresses modern man's resistance against a crippling society, she expresses only locally a general condition delineated in part by strokes of Kesey's animal cartoonist's pen. As noted earlier, Kesey borrows frequently from other forms of Popular culture, using techniques similar to the comic strip's. He modulates between forms with considerable finesse. Appalled by the predatory group therapy, McMurphy discusses this "peckin' party" with the ineffectual Harding. The discussion takes its cue from McMurphy's homespun metaphor. Despite his fastidious complaint about McMurphy's metaphorical mixture ("bitch," "ballcutter," "chicken") Harding spins out variations on the animal imagery to articulate his latent antagonism against Big Nurse. Initial denial that she is a "giant monster of the poultry clan, bent on sadistically pecking out our eyes" yields to his own categorization of her as wolf and the men as rabbits. "All of us here are rabbits of varying ages and degrees, hippity-hopping through our Walt Disney world." Animal metaphors depicting static human traits, a common device in folk literature, are frequent in the novel, e.g., Williams, the black attendant, "crawls" to Big Nurse "like a dog to a whipping." To invoke Disney is to translate the animal metaphors into modern cartoon terms especially appropriate to a modern standardized world. Harding's remark at the end of the book—"No more rabbits, Mack" —is to be seen in this more appropriate modern context.

Bromden's first extended description of the conformist ward weds the cartoon to similar literary forms. After depicting the ward inmates and attendants as cartoon figures "flat and outlined in black" locked irrevocably into set behavior and speaking "cartoon comedy speech," he shifts to a similar mode. "The technicians go trotting off, pushing the man on the Gurney, like cartoon men—or like puppets, mechanical puppets in one of those Punch and Judy acts where it's supposed to be funny to see the puppet beat up by the Devil and swallowed headfirst by a smiling alligator." The puppet show reaches out with one hand through the alligator image to Kesey's animal metaphors and with the other to the "dreamy doll faces of the workmen" in Bromden's hallucination and the doll faces of Billy Bibbit and Big Nurse. (The standardized world includes even Big Nurse, who in her stunted emotional development, is victim as well as victimizer.) Kesey deftly shifts from the cartoon to the puppet show to toys, changing terms within his aesthetic frame without altering it.

The same principle governs in a less obvious way McMurphy's white whale underpants, a gift, he tells us, from a co-ed "Literary major" who thought him a "symbol." This is one of the few times when Kesey goes beyond popular culture per se, but Melville is readily adaptable for his purpose. We are reminded that McMurphy is not a "realistic" character, but a representation of certain qualities shared by Moby Dick—natural vitality, strength, immortality, anti-social destructiveness. However, this is a caricature white whale, emblazoned on the Irishman's black underpants to emphasize his sexually intoned vitality, and bearing a devilish red eye linked to McMurphy's red hair and volatile Irish nature. This is a cartoon Moby Dick, minus the cosmic horror and mystery, precise in its suggestions and domesticated for Kesey's purposes.

Designating McMurphy a "symbol" is a clear statement of Kesey's aesthetic, as are the "flat and outlined" cartoon men. But to demonstrate the presence of this aesthetic, as done hereto, is not to elucidate its ultimate moral significance for Kesey. In this regard, Harding is absolutely central for through him Kesey guides our response to important elements in the novel. Harding has concealed his homosexuality, at least bisexuality, behind insincere sexual bravado and, more importantly, behind his considerable learning. He is the modern intellectual avoiding simple realities. Unlike the co-ed, who could appreciate McMurphy's vitality and sexuality while labeling him with terms from her academic vocabulary, Harding initially rejects

McMurphy's homely "analogy" of the "peckin' party," clouding the truth with modern psychological cant. Yet, besides Bromden, he is the most aware character and not prevented by snobbish scorn of McMurphy's "TV-cowboy stoicism" from seeing in McMurphy's deliberate affectation of cowboy drawl an affirmation of "western" values. McMurphy instructs him, not *vice versa*, and his identification of McMurphy and the Lone Ranger is a final measure of new knowledge, expressed significantly in Popular cultural terms. No longer "Perfessor Harding" defeated in the symbolic blackjack game by another queen, he has the vision of wisdom to see Big Nurse as Evil Monster.

Harding is closest to the intended reader, college educated and uprooted from moral values of Popular culture by academic prejudices. Like the reader, he can recognize the comic strip aesthetic but is unwilling to admit its moral truths. The novel offers simple truths in a simplified mode, taunting the reader for his literary condescension and related moral weakness. Like McMurphy we must turn to our "cartoon magazine" and television "westerns" for a rudimentary vision of human values, and away from a specious notion of moral complexity in the modern world. Kesey encourages anti-intellectualism, at least anti-academicism. Significantly, Harding is not cured of homosexual impulses, just his fear of admitting them; far removed from the springs of fully realized physical existence, the intellectual can learn self-consciously from those who drink directly. Harding's change is paradigmatic for the intended effect on the educated reader aware of the nature of Kesey's aesthetic, but lacking the moral perception lying behind it.

Of course, given that moral problems tend toward more complexity and not less, this necessary link between moral vision and literary mode causes us uneasiness. The book lures us in the wrong direction. Even the reader recognizing the self-indulgence in exaggerating the modern world's complexity may deny that moral problems are simple or that a frontier defiance dependent upon physical courage and raw individuality can solve them. McMurphy lacks the introspective self-irony and spiritual wisdom which could enrich and humanize his readiness to act in a physical world. In my judgement the book's major weakness lies partially in a wavering treatment of McMurphy as "symbol." Kesey rejects the profounder symbolism of Melville, frightening in its incomprehensible mysteriousness, for the delimited symbolism of the comic strip superhero. Our sympathy with these "unrealistic" and superhuman heroes is always reserved. We cannot expect psychological fullness from them. Kesey wishes to shorten partially this aesthetic distance to increase our sympathy with McMurphy, the human opposite to the plastic monstrosity Big Nurse. Kesey risks the simplification of his statement. Unfortunately, he does not manage to have it both ways: as he rounds out the character McMurphy, we rightly expect a fuller range of human response than necessary for a "symbolic" representation of masculine physical vitality. But our expectations remain unsatisfied. The rebel McMurphy resembles the prankish schoolboy against the schoolmarm or the naughty boy against the mother. Although the book recommends laughter as necessary therapy against absurdity, there is a euphoric tone of boyish escapism and wish-fulfillment to McMurphy's humor too often reminiscent of the bathroom or locker room. The euphoria at times embarrasses, as in the maudlin, communal warmth of the fishing boat trip and the ward party. In sum, the novel too often shares the wish-fulfillment of the comic strip without preserving the hard lines of its mythic representation.

Admittedly, other attempts to humanize McMurphy also reveal Kesey's awareness of the problems posed by his "symbolic" characterization, however unsuccessful his solutions. The brawler McMurphy uncharacteristically paints pictures and writes letters in a "beautiful flowing hand." His upset caused by a return letter suggests an emotional softness complementary to more typical behavior, as does his sensitivity to the personal loss necessitated by his savior's responsibilities. The visit to McMurphy's old home emphasizes his fatigue and "frantic" anticipation of that loss. The dress flapping in the tree commemorates his first act of love, freely given by the nine-year-old "little whore," and thereby keynotes his loving but defiantly anti-social relationships with his prostitute lovers. We are asked to believe that the sensitive and anguished letter writer, the energetic lover, and the tavern warrior are at bottom the same character apotheosized in his savior's role; his "psychopathic" sexuality and violence are really the human feeling and zest for life in which his Calling is grounded. As the Lone Ranger acting outside Society on behalf of humanity, he protects those qualities from extinction in others. Accordingly, his self-sacrifice is consistent with the lesson in gratuitous love taught by his childhood lover. Despite these attempts to fill in the simple comic strip outline of McMurphy's character, such details are too incidental, too hastily appended, to modify substantially our more limited version of him.

Kesey's handling of sex suffers from a failure to consider all implications of his materials, comic strip included. According to Leslie Fiedler, the love between McMurphy and Bromden expresses mythically an escape from the values of a white civilization ruled by women; but Fiedler overlooks the inadvertent blurring of Kesey's mythology caused by the unclear status of sex, both before and after McMurphy's death. The "symbolic" McMurphy is the blatantly sexual doctor of "whambam" seeing the inmates' sexual inadequacies as important expressions of psychological debility. Bringing prostitutes into the asylum is saving therapy which, contrary to Kesey's intents, fails to save. Neither of the Irishman's two principal disciples, Harding and

Bromden, is fully heterosexual. Sefelt's prodigious sexual powers are merely adjunct to his epilepsy and Billy Bibbit's sexual initiation brings suicide. Despite McMurphy's joking estimate of Bromden's sexual potential, the Indian is asexual; he embraces only the lobotomized body of McMurphy in defense of the Spirit; this murderous act of love could even be seen as homosexual in nature if it were not for the book's overt heterosexuality. Bromden's sexuality simply is not restored with his physical power. McMurphy's Spiritual influence is unsexed further by its comic strip ties: the superhero lives in a boys' escape world in which sexuality is released in muscular athleticism or violence; the Lone Ranger and Tonto are above sexuality, if not innocently homosexual; likewise the TV cowboy is rarely sexual. The meaning of McMurphy's physical assault on Big Nurse a public exposure of inherent femininity in a figurative rape of machine morality, is eroded by Kesey's failure to free McMurphy from such inadvertent implications of asexuality in the comic strip charaterization, and by the failure to provide a convincing heterosexual disciple for McMurphy. The book seems at times an unwitting requiem for heterosexuality, most ironically sounded in the innocent child's embrace of McMurphy and the prostitute Sandy after the ward party. However, we must conclude only that Kesey fails to harness the potential allusiveness of his materials.

We are left with a somewhat sentimentalized over-simplification of moral problems. Admittedly, Kesey's opposition of Good and Evil is less bald and the victory of Good less clear than might seem. The superhero McMurphy is sacrificed to the machine culture and Big Nurse remains in the ward. There is little hope that the Combine can be defeated. Only limited defiance is possible, for Harding by accepting his homosexual inclinations, for Bromden by escaping from the asylum. Moreover, such defiance is perhaps imaginary: Bromden begins his narration *in* the asylum, recalling *past* events concerning McMurphy and breaking a long held silence. "But, please. It's still hard for me to have a clear mind thinking on it. But it's truth *even if it didn't happen*" [my italics]. Perhaps Bromden's story is like the comic strip, a world only as it ought to be. After all, McMurphy must die and Bromden's interpretation of his future is euphoric, without convincing evidence of further satisfaction. Whether he finds his fellow tribesmen (perhaps drunk or widely disseminated) or fishes atop the hydrolectric dam (that others do so is only hearsay) or flees to Canada (also Combine territory?), he must remain outside Combine society. Perhaps the only escape from modern life is the tenuousness of hallucination. Kesey's irony compromises the victory of Good, suggesting that things may be more difficult than they seem.

However, these notes in a minor key do not really discolor the euphoric ending. The book's beginning is too easily forgotten and we are pushed along by Bromden's optimism. We are to hope, not despair, and, more importantly, not define the line between. Kesey believes in the comic strip world in spite of himself. This is the moral ground on which critical faultfinding must begin. Kesey has not avoided the dangers of a simplistic aesthetic despite his attempts to complicate it. He forgets that the comic strip world is not an answer to life, but an escape from it. The reader finds Kesey entering that world too uncritically in defense of the Good.

TONY TANNER

# Edge City (Ken Kesey)

'Because always comes the moment
when it's time to take the Prankster
circus further on toward Edge City.'

*The Electric Kool-Aid Acid Test*
—Tom Wolfe

While Norman Mailer has been defining his own position on the edge in the eastern part of America, another writer has been moving towards his own kind of edge on the West Coast. One might think that it would be hard to find a contemporary American writer more different from Mailer than Ken Kesey, and certainly Kesey's North-Western origins and Californian odyssey are quite different from anything in Mailer's upbringing and subsequent adventures and explorations. Nevertheless, despite the fact that they seem to derive their experience from two different Americas, their work reveals certain shared preoccupations and parallel perceptions which suggest it might be possible to generalize about an American vision without ever wishing to minimize the rich variety of individual talents.

At first glance Kesey has all the marks of a peripheral figure, even an eccentric. Born in Oregon, he attended creative writing classes at Stanford in the late 'fifties. While he was there he volunteered to be a guinea-pig in some

From *City of Words: American Fiction 1950–1970.* ©1971 by Tony Tanner.

experiments with psychomimetic drugs. One of these was LSD; this took Kesey into a realm of consciousness in which everything was perceived in an entirely new way. With the proceeds of his successful first novel, *One Flew Over the Cuckoo's Nest* (1962), he set up an establishment in La Honda, California, where with a group of like-minded friends he experimented with LSD (not then illegal). They tried supplementing and extending 'the experience' with all sorts of audio-visual aids. More people gravitated to the group, and in time they held more public parties and trips (or 'acid tests'). This in turn led to acid-rock, light shows, psychedelic posters, and the vast gatherings of young people at places like the Fillmore Auditorium and Avalon Ballroom in San Francisco, and later in halls all over America. As the law tightened up, Kesey duly found himself in trouble with the police and he became a famous fugitive in Mexico in 1966. He returned to San Francisco where he was caught and finally sentenced to ninety days in a work camp. Before serving the sentence he held a strange inconclusive ceremony which was supposed to mark the 'graduation' from acid—to what he did not say. At present Kesey is living quietly in Oregon, while speculation about his doings and intentions is still quite alive on the West Coast. He may thus seem a somewhat odd figure with which to conclude a study of American fiction during the last two decades. Yet the strange thing is that his work and life seem effectively to summarize a number of the issues which have arisen in connection with the other American writers discussed in this book, and to push certain possibilities and paradoxes we have noted to their extreme conclusions. Just how he does this, and what his significance is, I shall attempt to suggest in this chapter.

*One Flew Over the Cuckoo's Nest* is about a mental hospital (Kesey worked in one while writing it). It is dominated by Big Nurse, a female of dread authority. She is the servant, or rather the high priestess, of what is referred to as the 'Combine' or 'system', another version of the notion that society is run by some secret force which controls and manipulates all its members, which is so common in contemporary American fiction. Big Nurse keeps the patients cowed and docile, either by subtle humiliations or punitive electric shock treatment. In a crude way she embodies the principles of Behaviorism, believing that people can and must be adjusted to the social norms. Into her ward comes a swaggering, apparently incorrigible character called Randle McMurphy. He is outraged to see how Big Nurse has reduced the men to puppets, mechanically obeying her rules. He tries to inculcate by example the possibilities for independent action, for the assertion of self against system. By the end Big Nurse finds an excuse to have him lobotomized, but her authority has been broken and most of the inmates break free of the institution. The opposition is intentionally stark. Big Nurse speaks for the fixed pattern, the unbreakable routine, the submission of individual will to mechanical, humourless control. McMurphy speaks an older American language of freedom, unhindered movement, self-reliance, anarchic humour and a trust in the more animal instincts. His most significant act is to persuade a group of the inmates to accompany him on a one-day sea voyage. Most of the men are frightened to venture outside at first (they are mainly self-committed to the institution). It is this fear which keeps them cowering inside Big Nurse's routines. But McMurphy persuades the men to come with him, and he duly leads them to the edge of the land—where the ocean starts. The voyage they then embark on is one of very unconcealed significance: it affords the various pleasures of sex, drink, fishing, and the authentic joy and dread of trying to cope with the immense power of the sea. McMurphy has brought them all out of the System, and into—'Reality'.

It may be objected that such a parabolic simplification of American life is excessively schematic. McMurphy is like a cliché hero in a cartoon-strip, a Captain Marvel or Superman; while Big Nurse is a cartoon horror—like Spider Lady, who drew her victims into an electrified web (cf. the electric shock treatment meted out by Big Nurse). I think this is deliberate. Comparisons with cartoons are made throughout, so Kesey is hardly unaware of his technique. Someone calls McMurphy a TV-cowboy; a girl gives him some underpants with white whales on them because "'she said I was a symbol.'" He is addicted to comic-strips and TV which have in turn nourished his stances and speeches. You could say that he is acting out one of the most enduring and simple of American fantasies—the will to total freedom, total bravery, total independence. Big Nurse is a projection of the nightmare reverse to that fantasy—the dread of total control. Wolfe in *The Electric Kool-Aid Acid Test* (1968) records Kesey talking about 'the comic-book Super-heroes as the honest American myths', and Kesey may be defying us to distinguish comic-book clarity from mythic simplicity. In the contemporary world as he portrays it, to be a hero you have to *act* a hero (it is a discovery in his next novel that while weakness is real, strength has to be simulated: 'you can't ever fake being weak. You can only fake being strong.'). McMurphy has had to base his act on the only models he has encountered, in cartoons and movies. He is, if you like, a fake, a put-together character with all the seams showing. But, the book suggests, such fakery is absolutely necessary, unless you want to succumb to authentic weakness and the mindless routine supervised by Big Nurse. It is McMurphy's fakery and fantasy which lead others out into reality. In time, it would be Kesey's.

What makes the novel more interesting than just another cartoon, or John Wayne film, is that Kesey understands the need or compulsion to fantasize which is prior to the emergence of such apparitions as McMurphy and

Big Nurse. As some of the men in the institution realize, they are really
driving McMurphy to play out the role of heroic rebel. When he finally
moves to attack Big Nurse, the act which gives her the excuse to have him
lobotomized, the narrator recalls: 'We couldn't stop him because we were
the ones making him do it. It wasn't the nurse that was forcing him, it was
our need that was . . . pushing him up, rising and standing like one of those
motion-picture zombies, obeying orders beamed at him from forty
masters.' Fantasies of the weak converge upon him; one of the burdens
McMurphy is carrying (and he is exhausted by the end) is the number of
wish-fulfilment reveries which are secretly, perhaps unconsciously,
projected on to him by the inmates. The clichés he acts are the clichés they
dream. It is worth remembering that he was committed to the institution
as a psychopath: the psychopath as hero is not a new idea in America.
Robert Musil, in *The Man Without Qualities*, made a profound study of the
psychopath in the figure of Moosbrugger and added the suggestive
comment: 'if mankind could dream collectively it would dream Moosbrugger.' The inmates of the asylum in Kesey's novel are American and as
such they have a particular popular culture determining their most elemen-
tary fantasies. If they could dream collectively they would dream
McMurphy. From one point of view that is exactly what they do.

But we must read McMurphy, then, in two ways. In a sense he is an
authentic rebel who steps to the music that he hears; yet there is a sense in
which he is marching to the music of the fantasies projected on to him and,
as such, in his own way a kind of 'zombie' too, a servitor of the versions
imposed on him. Perhaps Kesey intends us to understand that McMurphy's
heroism is in realizing this second truth, and nevertheless continuing with
the imposed role. He is a singular man inasmuch as not many people would
be able to support the fantasies of strength and independence projected
on to him; the majority are more likely to submit to the controlling plot
and imposed pictures of the Combine and step to the mechanical music of
Big Nurse.

But how we react to McMurphy necessarily depends on our sense of
the narrator, since his version of things is the only one to which we have
access—and he is a giant, schizophrenic Indian called Big Chief. He is a
rather notional Indian, a representative of the towering vitality of the original life of the American continent, now tamed to terrified impotence by all
the mechanical paraphernalia of the white man's institutions. McMurphy
teaches him to regain the use of his strength and at the end of the novel he
is running away from the hospital and towards the country of his ancestors.
This is all fairly obvious. What is unusual is the brilliant way in which Kesey
has recreated the paranoid vision of a schizophrenic in the narrating voice.

Big Chief's vision of the hospital as a great nightmare of hidden machinery, wires, magnets, push-buttons, and so on, is utterly convincing. He is sure that the powers in the institution have fabricated a completely false environment: 'they' can accelerate or decelerate time, the windows are screens on which they can show whatever movie they want to impose as reality, they have fog machines which fill the air with a dense scummy medium in which Big Chief gets utterly cut off from everything and lost. They can do whatever they like with individuals because they have installed automative devices inside them (such as Indwelling Curiosity Cutout). It is a very Burroughs-like vision. This coherent paranoid fantasy extends to the world outside the hospital ward, for that world too is being 'adjusted' by Big Nurse and her like. What others would call factories and suburban housing developments, Big Chief sees as evidence of the spreading power of the Combine, which works to keep people 'jerking around in a pattern'. What the Combine is spreading is another version of entropy—all individual distinctions and differences erased and nature's variety brought down to the deadly uniformity of a mechanically repeated pattern. Some people may want to get 'out', or protest, but any such deviants are sent to the hospital where special machines can adjust them. (One interesting point is that a simple man may escape the Combine—'being simple like that put him out of the clutch of the Combine. They weren't able to mold him into a slot.' This sense of the special value of simplicity is recognizably American, and it is related to the detectable anti-intellectualism in Kesey's work.)

For Big Chief, McMurphy is the man who demonstrates that the Combine is not all-powerful: McMurphy makes the fog go away and enables him to see things clearly; he makes the pictures imposed on the windows vanish, so that when Big Chief looks out he sees the actual world. He gives Big Chief the sense of what it is to be an individual; he restores reality to him, and restores him to reality. At one point Big Chief writes: 'I still had my own notions—how McMurphy was a giant come out of the sky to save us from the Combine that was net-working the land with copper wire and crystal.' The importance of people's 'notions' of other people, and reality, looms large for Kesey.

His second novel, *Sometimes a Great Notion* (1964), concerns a logging family in Oregon. The novel centres on the mainstay of the family, Hank Stamper, a tough and stubborn individualist cast in the same mould as McMurphy, and nourished in his childhood on the same Captain Marvel comics. He is the strongest man in the book when it comes to any physical deed of bravery, effort or endurance. He is a Paul Bunyan type, and, in holding out against the coercive group pressure of a union in a local logging dispute, Hank is asserting a kind of American individualism which Kesey clearly admires. But there are aspects of his relationships with his wife, Viv, and his brother, Lee, which suggest that he suffers from being sealed off in his heroic role. He is more at home confronting the elements, as, for instance, on the dangerous logging run down river on which he has just embarked when the book concludes.

Not that nature in this book is benevolent. There are few pastoral moments in Kesey's sombre Pacific north-west. Through a series of very powerful and evocative descriptions one is made aware of a continual background process of dissolution and erosion: the endless rains, the turbulent rivers, the changing sea, the heavy clouds, the penetrating fog, all make this particular part of America seem like a dream world of endless decay, on which man can never hope to leave any 'permanent mark'. It is a lush and fecund land, but it is also a land 'permeated with dying'. The slow death by drowning of a man trapped in a rising river, described in very poignant detail, serves to focus the more general dread of obliteration, and the absolute certainty of it, which permeates the lives of all who live there. The ubiquitous sense of all things flowing steadily away is responsible for the underlying fear which pervades the community in Kesey's account.

Since logging is the livelihood of the community, some contact with this awesomely flowing nature is inevitable. But there are degrees of removal. Lee Stamper has gone east to study at a university, and has become a neurotic intellectual (much of the plot is concerned with what happens when he returns to Oregon). The union official, Draeger, is a man who believes he has reality neatly contained in his own system of definitions and maxims. He lives in the 'dream of a labeled world', and operates in a verbal world of disputes between workers and management. Hank has little time for this world and prefers to be out in the forests doing the actual cutting. He does not sentimentalize nature. It is something which has to be fought, and fought with machines too. But the direct encounter with nature provides an experience of reality which cannot be had in the protective structures of society. Hank is another American who prefers to move out to the edge. "'It's the part of the show I like best, this edge, where the cutting stops and the forest starts.'" He likes to get to that point at which the contact with untouched nature has to be resumed. It is shown that life in this area can be very dangerous; but at least it is pure. One is beyond categories and, somehow, into the thing itself. In this connection the location of the Stamper house is very suggestive. It stands nearest to the threatening and ever-widening river from which all the other inhabitants have moved back for fear of being washed away. For all its exposed position, it has nevertheless preserved its identity longer than the other houses—'a two-storey monument of wood and obstinacy that has neither retreated from the creep of erosion nor surrendered to the terrible pull of the river.' This suggests that perilous point, somewhere between the social edifice (to which the population has 'retreated') and the unselving flow of elemental natural forces, which so many recent American authors and their heroes seem to be seeking. Right at the edge, but not over it. Mailer's parapet makes an obvious comparison.

As a study of a certain mode of heroic individualism the book has surprising power and authority; but it is another aspect of the book which I want to touch on here. The book is framed by an encounter between Draeger and Viv in a bus depot. Draeger has come to ask her to explain her husband Hank to him. She in turn refers him to a photograph album she has with her, covering the family history of the Stampers. At the end Viv gets on a bus, leaving behind the photographs as she is leaving Hank and Lee and the whole area. Throughout this meeting it is raining very heavily. This juxtaposition of the photographs and the rain seems to me to point to a more profound tension in the book between fixed images and flowing forces. At bottom Kesey's novel is a meditation on themes implicit in this conjunction.

Photography can be seen as an activity which treats people as objects, a substitute for conducting a living relationship. In the novels considered in the course of this study there are many figures who find it easier to photograph other people than to try to establish relationships with them. The last words of Malamud's *A New Life* are '"Got your picture!"'—the revealing cry of the impotent Gilley who can now only take photographs. As we have seen, the dread of being involved in some imposed film version of reality is pervasive. Photographs and films catch and 'fix' the individual, disregarding the full dimensions of his living uniqueness. This brings me back to Kesey's novel, and Viv, whose name, like her temperament, suggests just the mysterious quality of 'life' itself.

Both Hank and Lee in their differing ways 'love' Viv; at the same time Kesey makes it clear that each tries to impose his own version of her. From the start of their marriage Hank has told her how to cut her hair, what to wear, how to behave, turning her into his idea of a mate without wondering what was going on inside her. Lee's love seems to be more sympathetic and sensitive, but he gives himself away when he asks to be allowed to take away a photograph of her which is, we learn later, an early photograph of his own mother. The implication is that he has never seen the real Viv, but only the image he has projected on to her. Thus in differing ways, Viv has been made to fit into the brothers' reality pictures, while her own reality has remained unperceived and thus unloved. This is not depicted as cruelty; if anything it is one of the sad results of that loss of ability to recognize and communicate with other people's reality which more than one American novelist has portrayed.

Before she marries Hank, Viv takes one last look in her mirror and kisses her reflection goodbye. The meaning of this gesture is brought out by one of her later thoughts. 'It means this is the only way we ever see ourselves; looking out . . .' Viv is the one character who has had the ability to move beyond narcissism and look *out* at other people and really see them, and their needs, and this is the only way that true vision—of self and others—can be reached. In some ways, Hank and Lee are still operating within the images they project. It is appropriate that at the end Viv leaves both brothers, for despite the generosity of her love she cannot devote her whole self simply to being what other people need her to be. She gets on the bus simply to move on, with no destination in mind. It is a bid to escape from the images that have been imposed on her, and leave the photographs behind. Almost her last words are—'"I'm just going."' Just so, life itself flows away despite all attempts to hold it.

Photographs are like art and human identity in the one respect that they offer a temporary extrapolation from the flow, a holding of some fragment of the flux of nature in fixed outlines. A novelist has to work with outlines, and Kesey's own novel is the verbal equivalent of a family album. At the same time, the timeless ongoing truth of nature's flow must not be forgotten, and Kesey does what he can to remind us of it: 'the Scenes Gone By and the Scenes to Come flow blending together in the sea-green deep while Now spreads in circles on the surface.' This is what lies behind the narrative strategy of the book which involves a dissolving of chronological time so that past and future events swim into each other, and during the fictional present we move without transitions from place to place, person to person. The intention seems to be to achieve the illusion of temporal and spatial simultaneity in which 'everything is at once'. (As in his first novel, it is possible that Kesey drew on LSD-induced sensations for his narrative strategy.)

The novel suggests that although human perception necessarily deals with particular configurations of reality, we must beware of identifying these temporary arrangements and fixities with the 'whole Truth'—whether we are thinking of reality arrested in photographs or arranged in verbal conceptual systems. We must always be willing to look round the edge of the fixed image to the flow behind it. We must also be aware, as Viv is, that, *'There are bigger forces . . . I don't know what they are but they got ours whipped sometimes.'* One chapter has as a heading a little story about a squirrel who lived in a davenport. He knew the inside so well that he could always avoid being sat on. However, the outside got worn out and it was covered with a red blanket. This confused him and undermined all his certainties about the inside. Instead of trying to incorporate this blanket 'into the scheme of his world', he moved to a drainpipe and was drowned in the next fall of rain—'probably still blaming that blanket: damn this world that just won't hold still for us!' It is a neat reminder that we must keep our schemes of reality flexible so that they can be expanded to incorporate any new phenomenon which the outside world may present. Our notions are only our notions, while the flow is more than we can ever know.

Having depicted two fictional heroes who created themselves on the lines of the available archetypes to be found in cartoons and other such repositories of the more vital popular mythologies, Kesey took a step further. His third hero was Ken Kesey. He moved beyond literature into life, and acted out the kind of fantasies he had previously only described. At this point let me summarize one of the basic themes encountered in the American writing considered in this study. We have found a pervasive fear of control and all suspected methods of conditioning; these can range from the brutal manipulative adjustments administered by Big Nurse to the subtler control of consciousness which is exerted over the individual by the social relationships he has to negotiate, the concepts he is taught to think with, the language he is forced to employ. Because he is uncertain of the sources of power, the American hero is as fascinated with it as he is paranoid about its modes of operation. Related to all this is a feeling that we live inside externally imposed versions of reality, somehow cut off from reality itself. We are trapped in roles that have been forced upon us, we are fixed in a falsifying social structure, we are caught up in a vast movie which some unnamed power insists is reality. There is a strong desire to step out of all this into some kind of free space: at the same time, it is not certain what would happen to the individual if he did manage to break out of all these versions, roles, structures. We have found another pervasive dread of ceasing to have an identity and flowing into something as shapeless as protoplasm, jelly or mud. It has been a constant preoccupation among the writers we have examined to see whether some third area can be found, beyond conditioning but not so far into the flux as to mean the end of the individual altogether. All these issues have been confronted by Kesey, partially in the fictions he wrote, but even more in the fiction that he lived. To see how this is so we have now to turn to Tom Wolfe's chronicle of the experiments of Kesey and his friends, the Pranksters,—*The Electric Kool-Aid Acid Test*.

Three of the key words that recur in Wolfe's account of the adventures of Kesey and the Pranksters are 'games', 'movies' and 'flow'. In Kesey's view, people are always trying to get you into their game or their movie. We have seen how writers as various as Burroughs and Bellow share this idea that other people are always trying to recruit you to their version of what is real; and that apparent reality is only a film has been a recurring proposition.

Kesey and the Pranksters explored the implications of this idea and lived out their reactions to it. In their eyes, most people, 'are involved, trapped, in games they aren't even aware of ', taking part in other people's movies. For instance, when Kesey was in jail he listened to the prisoners talking, and he says that he realized that '"it isn't their language, it's the guards', the cops', the D.A.'s, the judge's."' When you speak someone else's language you are in their movie, playing their game. Kesey was out to resist this. For instance, when he was asked to speak at a Vietnam War Protest he noticed that one of the speakers looked exactly like Mussolini and realized that the protestors were in fact using the language of the military. '"You're playing their game,"' he declared, and, refusing to participate in the dominant rhetoric, played 'Home on the Range' on an old harmonica, introducing deliberate incongruence into the protest 'movie'. A similar motive was behind a lot of the Pranksters' 'pranking'. It became their delight temporarily to foul up other people's movies—hence their far-out clothes, their multi-coloured bus, and their weird antics on the roof of it. As they drove down a suburban street they shocked people because they were not assimilable into the suburban movie. Kesey knew very well how upset people can become when their reality picture is disturbed, but he acted on the assumption that such a disturbance is beneficial. Another of their words was 'fantasy'. Everybody lives in some kind of fantasy; where a lot of those fantasies coincide there is an agreement to identify the fantasy as reality. To avoid the danger of getting drawn into other people's fantasies Kesey and his followers decided it was essential to create fantasies of their own, just as they played their own games, made their own movies, and created their own roles. This was one of the motives behind all the dressing up they went in for. Choose your fantasy. Kesey in particular could 'rise up from out of the comic books' and become Captain Flag, Captain America, Captain Marvel: when the police were moving in on him he countered by acting the role of Pimpernel. The group fantasy was that they could all be 'Superheroes'.

By driving round America taking an endless movie of everything, as Kesey and the Pranksters did, they were making a gesture of putting America into *their* movie before the more usual reverse process happened. And because they had room for everything in their movie—their aim was total unselective assimilation—they were less vulnerable than the ordinary citizens who live in a rather narrow movie with a great deal framed out. Later they delighted in drawing other groups—the Hell's Angels, a Unitarian Church conference—out of their own particular movie and into the Prankster movie. At one point near the end they felt they had 'got the whole town into their movie by now, cops and all'. There are indications in this of the possibility of delusions of grandeur and somewhat megalomaniac dreams of total power.

At the same time we may remember Blake, who built his own system so that he wouldn't be imprisoned in any other man's.

But clearly there is room for a further step. It is possible to become trapped in your own movie: the very metaphor is bound to engender dreams of getting beyond movies altogether. This occurred to Kesey. He gave his followers a talk on the time lag between perception and reaction. "'The present we know is only a movie of the past, and we will never be able to control the present through ordinary means. That lag has to be overcome some other way, through some kind of total breakthrough.'" In seeking for the absolute now, the pure present, Kesey is re-activating a strangely persistent American aspiration, articulated by writers from Emerson to Norman Mailer. It is this desire to pass beyond *all* structurings of reality (including your own movie, though that is preferable to anyone else's) into reality itself—sheer unmediated participation—which is behind the LSD experiments Kesey made. LSD gave hints of that breakthrough: it opened the mind to a world which 'existed only in the moment itself—*Now!*', a world which consciousness coincided with exactly, so that subjective and objective ceased to have much meaning. In the view of Kesey and the Pranksters it was important not to try to structure and programme the LSD experience—hence their emphasis on spontaneity, play, improvization: any attempt to plan, or write a script, 'locked you out of the moment, back in the world of conditioning'. It is quite common to come across the paradox of the writer who is suspicious of all plots and patterns nevertheless having to plot and pattern his own novel. Kesey has attempted to explore just how far beyond planning, composition, orchestration—in a word, structure—one can go, leaving novel-writing behind and moving out of all movies and into the flow.

'Go with the flow.' This is one of the key Prankster slogans which recurs throughout Wolfe's account. It is hardly necessary at this stage to point out how often the notion of 'flow' has occurred, in novels as various as *Cabot Wright Begins, Herzog, Slaughterhouse-Five, Sometimes a Great Notion*, and many more. And of course the feeling for the tidal flow of nature is very deeply rooted in American literature. It is, for instance, ubiquitous in the work of Whitman in which everything is part of an oceanic flow. When the poet looks at the world, says Emerson, he sees 'the flowing or Metamorphosis'. 'The Universe is fluid and volatile'; 'this surface on which we now stand is not fixed but sliding'—such statements by Emerson could be easily supplemented by assertions from other Transcendentalists, and American writers in general have shown less sense of the solidity of the social edifice than European writers, and more sense of some underlying flow. (The music of Charles Ives seems to exemplify this feeling, for there is often an unbroken background stream of sound which flows on, quietly and imperceptibly modulating, while more assertive and distinct foreground noises come and go.) Even Henry James's habitually socialized characters often find themselves, through metaphor, in flowing waters. Whether a writer feels that one should try to go with the flow or hold back from it will obviously depend on his whole world view.

For Kesey the idea of going with the flow expresses, on one level, the fairly traditional longing to escape the imprisoning, limiting structures of society which screen out so much of reality: 'transcending the bullshit' as one of his followers concisely puts it. It also points to the attempt to get out of the subtler entrapments of language. Kesey is quoted as saying that writers are 'trapped in syntax' and artificial rules; more generally it appears that he saw people increasingly living in language as a kind of shadowy substitute for life, distracted by any number of symbols from the thing itself. It is a central belief of the Pranksters that the most important aspects of their experience cannot be labelled. Hence some of their speech habits; for instance the indiscriminate use of 'thing' to refer to anything at all—a return to deliberate imprecision as if to counter the illusion of definitions and distinctions which language propagates.

The flow, then, is all that reality which is felt to lie on the other side of the screens and networks of society and language. There are at least two very different attitudes which can be taken towards this notional flow. The loss of all distinction and differentiation involved in the flow could be a stage in that entropic process which will one day bring life to one great level lake of sameness. It can be the ultimate nightmare, as for instance in the work of Pynchon. But the attainment of such a state from a more Eastern point of view might be called nirvana, that final state of universal quietude which is the goal of existence and which *also* betokens the end of all distinction, differentiation, individuation. So far from being a nightmare this is felt to promise the ultimate bliss. Embarking on the path of spiritual progress which leads to a comprehension of the abiding reality of nirvana, and which transforms 'common people' into 'Saints' is known as 'Entrance into the stream'. The path being explored by Kesey and the Pranksters was intended to turn ordinary American youths into 'Superheroes', and their cry was, 'Go with the flow.' Kesey specifically ruled out any ideas of adopting Buddhist tenets and attitudes; this is where he differs completely from Timothy Leary whom Kesey sees as avoiding the real American present and facing the past. Nevertheless one feels that Kesey's wild bus was headed more for nirvana than Entropyville. It was intended as a joyous ride, and Kesey and his friends aimed to go with 'the whole goddam flow of America', assimilating and 'grooving' with everything, finding everything instantly significant without the interpretative super-structures offered by books or theologies. That this may indeed be too much for some people is indicated in the fate of one mentally unstable girl who broke down while they were making their trip around America. Tom Wolfe's summary is appropriately ominous. 'She had gone with the flow. She had gone stark raving mad.'

There was also a more metaphysical aspect to the flow for Kesey and the Pranksters. They accepted that man may well be caught up in some vast pattern far beyond his power to alter or resist. 'But one could see the larger pattern and move with it—*Go with the flow!*—and accept it and rise above one's immediate environment and even alter it by accepting the larger pattern and grooving with it.' Kesey certainly has that common American sense of being controlled. 'We're under cosmic control and have been for a long long time . . . And then you find out . . . about Cosmo, and you discover he's running the show . . .' Obviously for some people Cosmo might be God or the Devil, as in the work of Mailer. For Kesey he seems to be some sort of Nietzschean power, beyond good and evil, some Shavian life-force. His image for the relation of the individual to Cosmo is a cable containing many intertwined strands of wire; the wires are the individuals, Cosmo vibrates all of them. If you cut across the cable you have the illusion of separately functioning individuals; but if anyone can break through and grasp the total pattern, and tune into it, and go with it, then the power of the whole cable passes through him; more than that, such a person will be able to start to control the flow, or at least wield it and divert its force.

Such a notion could lead to extreme fantasies of power and manipulation. Part of the honesty of Wolfe's book is the way it records a growing feeling that Kesey became obsessed with control, with playing power games, with organizing other people's trips. Some people later came to regard him as a sort of Elmer Gantry, even as a leader with distinct fascist tendencies. Obviously he had the charisma for such a role. However, it could be argued that his interest in control was based on the recognition that the more we can become aware of the forces operating on and through us, the more chance we might have to exert some control over our lives. Kesey's desire to grasp the pattern behind all patterns is in fact very American. Cosmo is the 'main party' which a superhero must try to deal with. (One corollary of believing in Cosmo is that if one's wonder turned to fear it could become a fear of vast proportions. Kesey's paranoia when he was on the run in Mexico was clearly on a cosmic scale. Perhaps a superhero is never far from feeling himself a supervictim. Arguably it might be out of a deep basic paranoia that the need to believe one can control the controller first arises.)

Trying to put the Kesey phenomenon in a larger context, Wolfe points to the visionary experiences recorded by various religious leaders, sect-founders and mystics. In many cases they are similar to the experience described by Kesey on LSD, the barriers between ego and non-ego vanishing, consciousness and environment starting to merge, self and world starting to flow together in a way which releases an intense feeling of enhanced powers. One significant aspect of this is the desire to get beyond individuality, as if personal identity were another of those false structures that have to be left behind if the breakthrough is to be made. Again there are precedents for this feeling in American literature. Emerson's comment on the poet's attraction to all kinds of narcotics, for instance, seems uncannily appropriate. 'These are auxiliaries to the centrifugal tendency of a man, to his passage out into free space, and they help him to escape the custody of that body in which he is pent up, and of that jail-yard of individual relations in which he is enclosed.' And Whitman clearly felt that identity and even individual physiognomy were distractions to be discarded. (See for instance the poem 'To You' which starts:

> Whoever you are, I fear you are walking the walks of dreams,
> I fear these supposed realities are to melt from under
> your feet and hands,
> Even now your features, joys, speech, house, trade, manners,
> troubles, follies, costume, crimes, dissipate away from you,
> Your true soul and body appear before me . . .)

There are also many precedents for this feeling in Buddhism in which the annihilation of individual identity and the voiding of all sense of ego are the objects of prolonged exercises. 'Self' is a fiction which has to be expunged. Now in most contemporary American fiction we find a desperate desire to achieve and protect an individual identity against whatever forces might threaten to dissolve it away; *not* to have or be an authentic self is the great dread for the majority of writers and their heroes. Once again Kesey seems to have turned towards a more Eastern or Transcendentalist mode of vision. At the same time the very active immersion of the Pranksters into the material here and now is very different from the passive renunciation of the passing show which is the ideal of the Buddhist. And, as it appears from Wolfe's account, no less important than the merging of 'I' into 'it', was the merging of 'I' into 'we'.

It is quite clear that Kesey and the Pranksters came to feel themselves to be in some ways a group consciousness, 'all one brain'. 'Intersubjectivity' (or 'combinations of mutual consciousness') was cultivated; for instance by 'rapping' which is a group monologue sustained by free associations, not unlike jazz improvisation. The 'all-in-one' feeling became very important and Kesey's statement that, '"You're either on the bus . . . or off the bus,"' refers, among other things, to the fact that the individual had to sink his individuality into the group experiment if he was to stay with them wherever they were going. Anyone drawing back into the protective and defensive armature of his own precious individuality, with all the anxiety and suspicion and guardedness that usually entails, was by definition off the bus. He would have cut himself off from the group consciousness, the 'all-one'. We can find in Edward Conze's description of the Buddhist exercises which consist of 'reducing the boundary lines between oneself and other people', a relevant parallel to what the Pranksters were practising. But once again it would be wrong to detect a specifically religious dimension to Kesey's idea of group consciousness. Although Wolfe describes the vaguely religious atmosphere which was generated by the group, it is clear that Kesey specifically wanted to avoid any programming in the orthodox sense: there were to be no systematic steps of initiation, no laid-down lines of spiritual progress, no body of secret lore gradually to be learned, no fixed rituals, no fore-ordained definition of the state of enlightenment and faith to be achieved. All that was connected with old movies, as it were, behaviour patterns of past religions. Kesey's bus was simply aimed forward, bearing the one-word creed 'FURTHUR' [*sic*], into the absolute now. The only programme was to see how far they could get 'into the pudding'. The light-hearted inadequacy of just such phrases was itself symptomatic of their determination to leave behind the more portentous terminologies of previous religions as they set out to explore a world of new perceptions, new relations. They were to be pranksters not monks.

Wolfe mentions three books that were of particular interest to Kesey and the Pranksters, and in connection with this desire to leave individual identity behind they have some interesting notions in common. Herman Hesse's *Journey to the East* is about a communal pilgrimage towards the East, the symbolic location of the home of light, everything that the human spirit and imagination have yearned to reach. The narrator describes how, after their leader vanished, the pilgrimage disintegrated and he returned to a prosaic bourgeois life devoid of spiritual aspiration. He subsequently discovers that the pilgrimage did not disintegrate; rather *he* lost faith and so automatically isolated himself from the true questers. In a word, he got off the bus. At the end he is restored into the mysterious sect which maintains the pilgrimage and is received by the lost leader, Leo. One condition of his reacceptance is that he must go and see what the sect's archives say about him. Coming to his name he draws a curtain and sees no words but only a model of two figures joined at the back. Inspecting them he sees that one face is his own in a state of decay and diminution, while the other is that of Leo, strong and radiant. Looking closer he sees that inside the figures there is a 'continuous flowing or melting . . . something melted or poured across from my image to that of Leo's.' At the end the narrator lies down and goes to sleep and one feels that his essence has passed into Leo, into the sect; the individual body has been left behind for a larger spiritual existence—the artist has passed into his own work of art. Hesse's novel has many meanings and implications which are not relevant here. The important image is that of the individual fading and merging into something larger, a leader, a corporate group, a visionary pilgrimage.

Turning to the two science-fiction novels favoured by the Pranksters we can find some comparable images. Robert Heinlein's *Stranger in a Strange Land* (1961) has enjoyed an increase in popularity on the West Coast in recent years. It concerns one Mike Smith, a human who was brought up on Mars, and thus initiated into a non-earthly way of regarding reality, gaining at the same time supra-human powers. On returning to Earth he starts a new religion based on more Martian attitudes, a good deal more hedonistic and pacific than most earthly religions. At the end he is torn to pieces by outraged humans: crucified, no doubt Heinlein means us to feel. In our present context the most interesting aspect of this somewhat turgid book is one of the Martian practices that Smith introduces to his human followers. It is called 'grokking' and it is the basis of his new religion. One explanatory gloss is this: 'the mutually merging rapport—the grokking—that should exist between water brothers'. A more detailed explanation is given by the expert on Martian affairs, Mahmoud, '"Grok" means "identically equal". "Grok" means to understand so thoroughly that the observer becomes a part of the observed—to merge, blend, intermarry, lose identity in group experience.'" 'Grokking' and 'going with the flow' have much in common; the Pranksters adopted the term and Kesey clearly has the charisma to be a leader such as Mike Smith (or Leo).

Arthur Clarke's *Childhood's End* has possibly been even more influential. This is a novel about the end of the world—due not to some humanly caused catastrophe, but because the human race achieves a total breakthrough into pure mind. It happens to all the children under ten, who suddenly cease to be individuals and become a vast group mind endowed with extraordinary powers. Jan, the last man on Earth and spectator of its final hours, watches the children; 'their faces were merging into a common mold.' One of the Overlords (strange creatures from another planet who serve the Overmind) explains that '"possibly what we have called the Overmind is still training them, molding them into one unit before it can wholly absorb them into its being."' As an early test of their powers the children strip a landscape bare by a communal act of mental will, a foreshadowing of how they will later return the Earth into Non-Being. Jan watches these last moments, giving an account for the benefit of the Overlords who have withdrawn to their own planet.

'Something's starting to happen. The stars are becoming dimmer
. . . There's a great burning column, like a tree of fire, reaching
above the western horizon. It's a long way off, right round the
world. I know where it springs from: they're on their way at last,
to become part of the Overmind. Their probation is ended:
they're leaving the last remnants of matter behind.'

The notion of the Overmind is distinctly Shavian, to go no further back,
and it is appropriate that Clarke should refer to *Back to Methuselah* in the
course of his book. For there too it is indicated in Lilith's final speech that
matter is the encumbering junk which will have to be left behind so that
'life' can disentangle itself and '"press on to the goal of redemption from
the flesh, to the vortex freed from matter, to the whirlpool of pure intelli-
gence . . ."' What was perhaps of added interest to Kesey was that Clarke's
description of the last hours of the Earth reads like an account of the most
spectacular light show ever devised, with unbelievable colour combinations
and formations following one after the other until the Earth turns transparent and everything starts to dissolve into light. Life on Earth has gone
with the cosmic flow leaving temporary configurations such as human
identity and material locations to dissolve behind it. It reads curiously like
the ultimate LSD trip.

Some kind of flowing out of self is, then, envisaged in each of these
novels, and that is what Kesey and the Pranksters were trying to live out,
consciously setting off in 'a fantasy bus in a science fiction movie'. Clearly,
just as expanding the mind with LSD might precipitate breakdown in
unstable individuals, so also this experiment in group consciousness could
interfere seriously with the more orthodox forms of familial relationships.
It isn't always clear in Wolfe's account who was minding the children, and
no matter how much one might believe in communal mating, instead of
hunting in pairs, there are the inevitable risks of unwanted pregnancies
and unforeseen jealousies. As Wolfe's account makes clear, there was quite
a lot of inter-personal tension as well as inter-subjectivity on the bus.
These are some of the risks inevitably incurred in any attempt to leave all
the usual forms behind. But, it might still be asked, though it is clear what
they were trying to leave behind, just what or where were they trying to
reach, once you discount the science-fiction fantasies and metaphors?
Kesey and the Pranksters would refuse to define their destination in social,
moral or religious terms—indeed, 'terms' were among those things they
were leaving behind. Perhaps the most explicit thing they would have said
was that they were 'heading out toward . . . Edge City', a recurring phrase
in their group monologue.

Since it was part of the fantasy they were living out that they should move beyond language, one risks missing the spirit of the whole enterprise by trying to define it. However, we may tentatively surmise that Edge City is where the movies end and the flow begins, or where definitions and versions give way to the thing itself. It points, perhaps, to a point at which the structurings of society, language, accustomed habits of perception, individual identity, begin to fall away. The old Buddhists used trance to reach what Edward Conze describes as 'a station where there is *neither perception nor non-perception*. Consciousness and self-consciousness are here at the very margin of disappearance.' That could also be called Edge City. But whereas within the structure of the Buddhist religion the achievement of such a station was part of a system of enlightenment and so could be experienced as a meaningful ecstasy, Kesey's Edge City stands at the margin of the very idea of 'structure'. There is no guiding theology or creed, and a look over the edge can be 'scary' as Wolfe's account makes clear. It is one thing to slough off notions of self under the guidance of an ancient religion; it is another thing to get in a wildly coloured bus and drive at top speed towards the perimeters of consciousness with no sense of what may lie beyond. Perhaps it would be bliss, 'Freedomland', that final emancipation from all definitions and limits which we have seen is such an abiding American dream: but perhaps it would be insanity, chaos, a nightmare which could not be controlled. Only men who, like Kesey, believe that 'a man should move off his sure center out into the outer edges' and 'test the limits of life' are likely to find out.

If we regard Edge City as being poised between social identity and dissolution, a sort of third area *between* structure and the flow, then it becomes a place many American heroes have sought to find, since few of them are content to remain within given boundaries. Their movements are habitually centrifugal, and we have had plenty of occasion to observe that a large number of American novels are about one sort of approach or another to some kind of edge. But most American authors conduct this venture to the periphery in their imaginative writings: for them Edge City is to be found in the City of Words. Just so, Kesey *imagined* McMurphy leading the inmates out to their adventurous voyage on the ocean, and wrote a book about it. Kesey's singularity lies in his subsequent attempt to 'move beyond writing' and set out for Edge City in person. (Norman Mailer could perhaps be said to have made an attempt to get beyond writing when he ran for the office of Mayor of New York.) You could regard the multicoloured bus as Kesey's third novel, only this time he was inside it and at the wheel. Some people may find it easier to regard him as a deluded maniac in this undertaking; but there is an attractive courage in his willingness to stake himself on his beliefs, to forego writing and risk an approach to the thing itself.

One important aspect of the Kesey adventure which Wolfe brings out very well is that it is very much connected with the actual clutter and appurtenances of modern American life, particularly in the West where there are fewer reminders of history and the past than there are in the East. The gadgets and clutter, the freeways, pylons, lights, and cars, all the modernity and movement which make up the Californian panorama—these are the important setting for Kesey's experiment in moving to the edge; indeed they are partially the source of it. Where Timothy Leary and his followers felt that they could sink solemnly back into the Indian past, Kesey and his Pranksters felt that they were already soaring into the great circus of the American future. There is a significant split between East and West Coast attitudes in America today, and Wolfe helps to clarify this split by distinguishing between the Buddhist direction and 'the Kesey direction . . . *beyond catastrophe* . . . like, picking up anything that works and moves, every hot wire, every tube, ray, volt, decibel, beam, floodlight and combustion of American flag-flying neon Day-Glo America and winding it up to some mystical extreme carrying to the western-most edge of experience.'

This direction points to a mysticism arising out of modernity, not in repudiation of it. In this connection the work of Gary Snyder, the West Coast poet, is very relevant. He is specifically interested in Buddhism, but he is seeking for a formulation of it which will embrace life in contemporary America. In his prose book *Earth House Hold* he too talks about 'breaking through the ego-barrier' and getting beyond our usual notions of self and society. One idea in particular that he takes from archaic beliefs is that 'all teach that beyond transcendence is Great Play, and Transformation.' The capitalized words could mean many things, of course, but it might help to understand part of the Kesey experiment if we see him as someone who, far from turning his back on modern America, accepts and relishes its most recent productions and manifestations. But instead of being trapped among all these proliferating things he makes them part of a game and turns everything to sport. To follow the Kesey direction out to the western-most edge should mean deliverance from the stifling world of conditioned action into a realm where all is Great Play and Transformation. It does not always work out this way, and the newspapers keep us plentifully informed of the horrors which may be connected with taking LSD. Nevertheless, despite what one may think about the use of LSD, and however one reacts to the inconclusive, even pathetic conclusion to the whole Kesey venture ('"WE BLEW IT"' is his own comment as recorded by Wolfe), I think one should be aware of the significance of his journey. There is something in the American spirit which has always tended to move towards that western-most edge, and in retrospect it may turn out that Ken Kesey is far from being the least memorable in a great tradition of pioneers.

Obviously to go right over the edge into the flow would mean death; the point about Edge City is that it is a place, a state of consciousness, an experience, in which one may learn something new about the relationship of individual identity to the flow—and from which one can return, perhaps to tell the tale, perhaps to have the tale told, as Wolfe tells it about Kesey. At one point in Kurt Vonnegut's novel, *Player Piano*, the rebel Finnerty explains to the uncertain conformist Proteus why he has given up his job and why he refuses to see a psychiatrist. "'He'd pull me back into the center, and I want to stay as close to the edge as I can without going over. Out on the edge you see all kinds of things you can't see from the center . . . Big, undreamed-of things—the people on the edge see them first.'" It was in a similar spirit, perhaps, that the Pranksters put up a large sign reading HAIL TO ALL EDGES, and so many American heroes in the books we have considered have sought out their own particular edge.

Kesey believes that 'our concept of reality is changing' and that a new generation is coming along which will take up different attitudes to life, adopt different priorities and values. Just what these will amount to he can hardly say, just as it is not clear what he envisaged by the idea of going beyond acid and graduating from the 'Garden of Eden' to which acid opens the door. But by aiming to live at the edge he identifies himself as one of those who hope to see more things, and see them first. The garb in which he made his move to the edge may seem strange, or merely eccentric; necessarily any bid to move out of familiar patterns must take an unfamiliar form, and not even Kesey can predict where his own direction will take him. One possibility is that literature and the values of clear utterance would be left behind and one may well feel that such a tendency should be resisted. The attempt to depart from the City of Words once and for all could involve unforeseen deprivations and might well lead to a notable impoverishment of consciousness. Be that as it may, for anyone interested in trying to appreciate what was going on in both American literature and society in the late 'sixties, Kesey is a figure who has to be understood and, it seems to me, respected. Whatever one's verdict on the final value of Kesey's work and example, that sign put up by his Pranksters is a reminder once again of the relevance and truth of Browning's words—'Our interest's on the dangerous edge of things.'

RAYMOND M. OLDERMAN

# The Grail Knight Arrives: Ken Kesey,
# One Flew over the Cuckoo's Nest

Randle Patrick McMurphy sweeps into the asylum waste land of Ken Kesey's *One Flew over the Cuckoo's Nest* like April coming to T. S. Eliot's waste land: "mixing / Memory and desire, stirring / Dull roots with spring rain." He literally drags the unwilling asylum wastelanders out of the tranquillized fog that protects them—a fog that is forever "snowing down cold and white all over," where they try to hide "in forgetful snow, feeding / A little life with dried tubers." And, by dragging them from their retreat, he cures the Fisher King, Chief Bromden—a six-foot-eight giant from a tribe of "fish Injuns," who is wounded, like all other wastelanders, in his manhood. The cure takes hold most dramatically on a fishing trip when McMurphy supplies the Chief and eleven other disciples with drink for their thirst, a woman for their desires, stimulation for their memories, and some badly needed self-respect for their shriveled souls—and all this despite the fact that the Chief "fears death by water." ("Afraid I'd step in over my head and drown, be sucked off down the drain and clean out to sea. I used to be real brave around water when I was a kid.") The silent Chief's voice is restored and he becomes the prophet who narrates the tale, while the false prophet, the enemy, the Big Nurse, Madame Sosostris, who has the "movement of a tarot-card reader in a glass arcade case," is deprived of her voice in the last moments of the book.

From *Beyond the Wasteland: A Study of the American Novel in the Nineteen-Sixties.* © 1972 by Yale University.

The tale takes place in the ward of an insane asylum where an iron-minded, frost-hearted Nurse rules by means of one twentieth-century version of brutality—mental and spiritual debilitation. Her patients are hopeless "Chronics" and "Vegetables," or they are "Acutes" who do not, according to McMurphy, seem "any crazier than the average asshole on the street." McMurphy comes to the asylum from a prison work farm. He has been a logger, a war hero, a gambler, and generally a happy, heavily muscled, self-made drifter and tough guy. A contest develops between McMurphy (whose initials R. P. M. urge us to note his power) and the Big Nurse (whose name, Ratched, tips us off about her mechanical nature as well as her offensive function as a "ball-cutter"). The implications of the contest deepen; it becomes a battle pitting the individual against all those things that make up the modern waste land, for the Nurse represents singly what the institution and its rules really are. The drama of the battle is intense, and the action seesaws as McMurphy gradually discovers he must give his strength to others in order to pry loose the Big Nurse's hold on their manhood. As they gain in health, McMurphy weakens, and his ultimate victory over the Big Nurse is a mixed one. He is lobotomized, a "castration of the frontal lobes," but he gives his lifeblood to Chief Bromden who breaks free and leaves behind in the Nurse and the Institution not a destroyed power but a shrunken, silent, and temporarily short-circuited one. Beautifully structured, the novel provides us with both a brilliant version of our contemporary waste land and a successful Grail Knight, who frees the Fisher King and the human spirit for a single symbolic and transcendent moment of affirmation.

The world of this waste land is mechanically controlled from a central panel, as the narrator sees it, so that everything in it is run by tiny electrical wires or installed machinery. People are often robots or are made of electric tubing and wiring and springs, as the "adjusted" ones seem to be. The Big Nurse is only one agent of a "Combine" which rules all things including time and the heart and mind of man. *Combine*, as the word implies, is not just an organization; it is a mechanism, a machine that threshes and levels; its ends are Efficiency and Adjustment. According to Chief Bromden, the Combine had gone a long way in doing things to gain total control,

> things like, for example—a *train* stopping at a station and laying a string of full-grown men in mirrored suits and machine hats, laying them like a hatch of identical insects, half-life things coming pht-pht-pht out of the last car, then hooting its electric whistle and moving on down the spoiled land to deposit another hatch.

Those are the adjusted ones. The ones who cannot adjust are sent to the asylum to have things installed so that the Combine can keep them in line.

> The ward is a factory for the Combine. It's for fixing up mistakes made in the neighborhoods and in the schools and the churches, the hospital is. When a completed product goes back out into society, all fixed up good as new, *better* than new sometimes, it brings joy to the Big Nurse's heart; something that came in all twisted different is now a functioning, adjusted component, a credit to the whole outfit and a marvel to behold. Watch him sliding across the land with a welded grin, fitting into some nice little neighborhood.

He is a "Dismissal," spiritually and morally empty, but "happy" and adjusted. If you do not fit, you are a malfunctioning machine—"machines with flaws inside that can't be repaired, flaws born in, or flaws beat in over so many years of the guy running head-on into solid things that by the time the hospital found him he was bleeding rust in some vacant lot." That is what is called a "Chronic." Some people do escape in a way. People like McMurphy who keep moving, and people like Pete Bancini who are just too simple, are missed by the Combine, and if they are lucky, they can get hidden and stay missed.

All this is only the view of the narrator, a paranoid Indian. But there is enough evidence in the way the world around Chief Bromden runs to make his terms more and more acceptable as the novel progresses. Among the few characters on the "Outside" that Kesey takes the time to describe is one of the insulting loafers who taunt the patients while they wait to board their boat for the fishing trip. The man is described as having "purple under his eyes," the same kind of purple that appears under the eyes of all the Ward's finished, lobotomized products. There is, at least for a moment, a frightening suggestion that the Combine's inmates may truly be everywhere. For Chief Bromden it is no madman's logic—after seeing the actual persecution of his father, family, and tribe by the U.S. Department of Interior—to posit a large central organization that seeks the doom of all things different.

The waste land of the asylum is characterized not only by mechanization and efficiency but by sterility, hopelessness, fear, and guilt. The inmates are aimless, alienated, and bored; they long for escape; they "can connect / Nothing with Nothing," not even picture puzzles; they are enervated and emasculated; their dignity is reduced to something less than human. Most of all, they are run as the Asylum is run—by women; it is a "Matriarchy," and behind almost every ruined man is a grasping, castrating female whose big bosom belies her sterility but reveals a smothering momism. So, McMurphy perceives almost immediately that Big Nurse Ratched is pecking at their "everlovin' balls." But the same has been true of Harding's wife, and Chief Bromden's mother, and Billy Bibbit's mother—and these are just about the only women you see in the novel, except a couple of sweet whores named Candy and Sandy. However, what is more startling about this terrible world is its leveling sense of order and its rules. In one incident McMurphy wants to brush his teeth before the proper teeth-brushing time. He is told that the toothpaste is locked up. After questioning the Aide about what possible harm anyone could do with a tube of toothpaste, he is advised that the toothpaste is locked up because it is the rules, and rules are rules. After all, what would happen if everyone just started brushing his teeth whenever he had a mind to. Kesey's point by this time is clear; the true madness, the real dry root of the waste land is not the patient's irrationality, but the deadly order, system, and rationality of the institution. What is normal is perverted and reason becomes madness, while some small hope for salvation lies in the nonrational if not the downright irrational.

All of what the institution means and its effect on humanity come together in the single person of the Big Nurse, who causes the patients' hopelessness, their inadequacy, fear, anxiety, and alienation. She is the institution itself, the waste land personified. White and starched stiff, she suggests Melville's plunge into the dreadful ambiguity and possible evil that could live in the heart of what is white. (McMurphy wears fancy shorts with white jumping whales on them, given to him by an Oregon State co-ed who called him a "symbol.") But with the Big Nurse the ambiguity is only superficial and thrives only on the name of respectability—her real villainy is clear. She is the enemy, the "Belladonna," obstacle to the Grail Knight. She enervates her patients by playing upon their fears, guilts, and inadequacies. She and all other castrators are "people who try to make you weak so they can get you to toe the line, to follow their rules, to live like they want you to. And the best way to do this, to get you to knuckle under, is to weaken you by gettin' you where it hurts the worst." She is relentless in her crippling pity and capable of using any weapon in order to preserve her control. She has handpicked her aides, three shadowy and sadistic black men who are hooked to her by electrical impulses of hate. They have been twisted by white brutality, and their response is savage. As weapons in the Big Nurse's arsenal, they serve as symbols of the force of guilt which she uses to torment her patients. Guilt and the black man twine identities in the white mind to cut deeper into its already vitiated self-respect.

The Big Nurse is continually pictured in images of frost or machinery, or as a crouching swelling beast. She is described as a collection of inert materials, plastic, porcelain—any of modern America's favorite respectable synthetics. "Her face is smooth, calculated, and precision-made, like an expensive baby doll, skin like flesh-colored enamel, blend of white and cream and baby-blue eyes, small nose, pink little nostrils—everything working together except the color on her lips and fingernails, and the size of her bosom." She is sexless and cold enough to halt McMurphy's lecture on how a man can always win out over a woman; she is "impregnable" in almost every sense, even by so vaunted a "whambam" as McMurphy.

> What she dreams of there in the center of those wires is a world of precision efficiency and tidiness like a pocket watch with a glass back, a place where the schedule is unbreakable and all the patients who aren't Outside, obedient under her beam, are wheelchair Chronics with catheter tubes run direct from every pant-leg to the sewer under the floor.

She controls clock time, has all the rules on her side, and uses insinuation like a torture rack. Fear, cowardice, and timidity are all she sees in man. She sums up all that is debilitating to the individual about a modern world of massive institutions. In waste land terms, she is the keeper of the keys, the false prophet; for not only is she the cause of enervation and division, but she also perverts the holy words that are the key to coping with the waste land. When she gives she emasculates; when she sympathizes she reduces; and when she controls she destroys. McMurphy, the Grail Knight, the savior, not only must contest her power, but must listen to, learn how to live by, and restore the true meaning of the holy words from "What the Thunder Said": Give, Sympathize, Control.

The narrative movement of the novel is built around McMurphy's growth in knowledge and his progress toward curing Chief Bromden. As he learns to give and to sympathize, he moves toward death while the Chief moves toward rebirth, "blown-up" to full size by McMurphy's sacrifice and gift of self-control. At the beginning we are given two images foreshadowing McMurphy's fate: Ellis, the patient who stands like an empty Christ, arms outstretched in tortured crucifixion, fixed that way by an electric shock machine used as a weapon of the institution; and Ruckly, blanked of all but mindless, obscene answers and beaten by the trump card of the institution—lobotomy—beaten as a means of dealing with his rebellion. McMurphy will also be personally beaten, crucified, and lobotomized because there is no final victory over the Big Nurse and her waste land; she will continue just as Eliot's waste land continues after the rain that falls.

She's too big to be beaten. She covers one whole side of the room like a Jap statue. There's no moving her and no help against her. She's lost a little battle here today, but it's a minor battle in a big war that she's been winning and that she'll go on winning . . . just like the Combine, because she has all the power of the Combine behind her.

But the little battle she loses is enough to cure the Chief and bring a little rain to a parched land.

Ironically, McMurphy enters the asylum supposedly on a request for "transfer" to get "new blood" for his poker games, but from that very entrance, as he laughs, winks, and goes around shaking limp hands, it is he that does the transferring and the giving of blood. The first foretelling of his effect on Chief Bromden comes as McMurphy seizes the Chief's hand: "That palm made a scuffing sound against my hand. I remember the fingers were thick and strong closing over mine, and my hand commenced to feel peculiar and went to swelling up out there on my stick of an arm, like he was transmitting his own blood into it. It rang with blood and power. It blowed up near as big as his." He brings contact, the human touch, to a place sterilized of all but inverted relationships. His giving and his sacrifice are not, however, a continuous unbroken process, but are correlated to his learning. He launches into full battle with the Big Nurse and begins pulling the patients out of their tranquillized fog. His first assault reaches its peak in the contest over TV privileges.

McMurphy strengthens the other men enough to rebel in unison against the Big Nurse, and he does it by the symbolic gesture of attempting to lift a massive "control panel." It is a symbol of his resistance and willingness to keep trying even when he is going to be beaten, even when he *knows* he is going to be beaten. The strain on him is balanced by his effect on the men and on Chief Bromden in particular. The Chief asserts himself for the first time. He raises his hand to join the vote against the Big Nurse and recognizes that no external power is controlling him—he himself had lifted his own arm expressing his own decision. This first sign of self-control, inspired by McMurphy's struggle with the control panel, leads the Chief out of his fog and out of his safety; he ceases to be the blind, impotent Tiresias and literally begins to see again. Waking up late at night, he looks out a window and sees clearly, without hallucination—something he has been unable to do since he has been in the asylum. What he sees, on another level, is that McMurphy has succeeded in being himself, that it is possible to be yourself without hiding and without the Combine getting you. But just as the Chief makes this discovery McMurphy learns what it really means to be "committed" in this asylum, and he faces the temptation that is hazard to any Grail Knight—the temptation to quit.

Learning that most of the patients are "voluntary," that he is one of the few "committed," and that the duration of his commitment is to be determined by the Big Nurse, McMurphy becomes "cagey" (an ominous word in this mechanized world). He promptly ceases giving and he ceases sympathizing. The immediate result is an assertion of the waste land—Cheswick, one of the patients dependent on McMurphy, drowns himself. Without resistance from the Grail Knight, the waste land perverts water, the symbol of fertility, into the medium of death.

But the demands made on McMurphy by the weaker inmates determine his return to battle, for the weak are driven to the waste land by "Guilt. Shame. Fear. Self-belittlement," while the strong are driven by the needs of the weak. As the Chief ultimately realizes, McMurphy is driven by the inmates, and this drive "had been making him go on for weeks, keeping him standing long after his feet and legs had given out, weeks of making him wink and grin and laugh and go on with his act long after his humor had been parched dry between two electrodes." To signal his renewed challenge to the institution and his acceptance of commitment, McMurphy stands up at what looks like the Big Nurse's decisive victory, strides mightily across the ward, "the iron in his boot heels cracking lightning out of the tile," and runs his fist through the Big Nurse's enormous glass window, shattering her dry hold as "the glass comes apart like water splashing." McMurphy knows where his gesture will lead; he was told in the very beginning that making trouble and "breaking windows" and all like that will lead him to crucifixion on the shock table and destruction by lobotomy.

What McMurphy has learned is the secret of "What the Thunder Said," for, as one critic of Eliot's poem explained it,

> If we can learn to give of ourselves and to live in sympathetic identification with others, perhaps we may also learn the art of self-control and thereby prepare ourselves to take on the most difficult of responsibilities: that of giving directions ourselves, of controlling our destinies and perhaps those of others, as an expert helmsman controls a ship.

McMurphy as helmsman leads his twelve followers, including Chief Bromden, aboard a ship and on to a fishing trip where, through his active sympathy, he gives them the gift of life so that they may gain control of their own destinies. The fishing trip—considering the fish as the traditional mystical symbol of fertility—is the central incident in McMurphy's challenge to the waste land. What he gives to the men is drained from his own lifeblood, and the path of his descent to weariness is crossed by Chief Bromden "pumped up" to full size, the cured Fisher King. And at that point, we are told "the wind was blowing a few drops of rain." "*Damyata:* The boat responded / Gaily, to the hand expert with sail and oar."

McMurphy gives the men not only self-confidence and a renewed sense of virility, but also what Kesey sees as man's only weapon against the waste land—laughter. There has been no laughter in the asylum; McMurphy notices that immediately and comments, "when you lose your laugh you lose your *footing*." By the end of the fishing trip McMurphy has everyone laughing "because he knows you have to laugh at the things that hurt you just to keep yourself in balance, just to keep the world from running you plumb crazy." In effect, he teaches the men to be black humorists, and it is the vision and the balance of black humor that Kesey attempts to employ as a stay against the waste land. To Kesey, being human and having control means being able lo laugh, for the rational ordered world has done us in, and only an insurgence of energy from the irrational can break through the fear and sterility that have, paradoxically, made the world go mad. It is ultimately their laughter that the men cram down the Big Nurse's maw in their brief moment of victory.

In the final section of the book, McMurphy works with growing fatigue and resignation toward his inevitable sacrifice. He battles with the Nurse's Aides, gets repeated shock treatments, has a chance to capitulate to the Big Nurse and refuses, returns from the cruelty of the shock table to the ward where he is faced with the charge of mixed and ulterior motives, and finally holds his mad vigil in the upside-down world of the Chapel Perilous. But madness here is antiorder, and so a sign of health. The scene is the night of Billy Bibbit's lost virginity. McMurphy and his followers run wild, completely subverting the order of the Big Nurse's ward and violating the sanctity of all rules. Billy's entrance into manhood symbolizes their initiation into the final mysteries of life and fertility. All this is as it should be during and following a vigil in the Chapel Perilous. But, as we already know, you cannot beat the Big Nurse. She regains her power by cowing Billy with shame and forcing him to betray his deliverer. Billy, broken again, slits his throat, and the Big Nurse attempts one last time to turn guilt against McMurphy. His response is the ultimate sacrificial gesture; he rips open her dress, exposing her mountainous and smothering breasts, and chokes her— not able to kill her, but only to weaken and silence her. The contest ends in violence, the individual's last offense against the immensities that oppress him. Kesey, like John Hawkes, finds something ultimately necessary and cleansing about violence.

At McMurphy's fall "he gave a cry. At the last, falling backward, his face appearing to us for a second upside down before he was smothered on the floor by a pile of white uniforms, he let himself cry out: A sound of cornered-animal fear and hate and surrender and defiance." It was the only sound and the only sign that "he might be anything other than a sane willful, dogged man performing a hard duty." His madness is all the salvation the twentieth century can muster, for to give and to sympathize in our kind of waste land is itself a sign of madness. McMurphy is lobotomized, and in the final moments of the book Chief Bromden snuffs out the life of the body connected to that already dead spirit, and with his gift of life, seizes the huge "control panel" McMurphy had blown him up to lift, and spins it through the asylum window. "The glass splashed out in the moon, like a bright cold water baptizing the sleeping earth." The Fisher King is free. Although the waste land remains, McMurphy the redheaded Grail Knight has symbolically transcended it through his gesture of sacrifice, and at least allowed others to "Come in under the shadow of this red rock."

*One Flew over the Cuckoo's Nest* is a modern fable pitting a fabulous kind of good against a fabulous kind of evil and making use of many of the traditional devices of American romance which were mentioned in the Introduction. For example: it emphasizes plot and action (not character), and it employs myth, allegory, and symbol. There are equally obvious points of contact between the themes of this book and traditional American themes: for example, the rebellion against old orders and old hierarchies, and the need for communal effort in the face of an alien and overwhelmingly negative force. This book is more closely tied to American tradition than any other book we will deal with, and yet there is much in it that offers a paradigm for what is different about the characteristic vision in the American novel of the 1960s. It does not return to the past, gaze toward the future, or travel to the unknown to get its "romance" setting. The setting is the static institution which sums up both the preoccupation of our age with the mystery of power, and the substitution of an image of the waste land for the image of a journey between Eden and Utopia. It is shot through with the vitality of its use of the here and the now. We are constantly shocked into discovering how the book is really tied to the recognizable, not to the distant or strange, but to our very own—to technology we know of, to clichés we use, to an atmosphere possible only in the atomic tension of our times. Just as no one can confidently say who is mad and who is not in Kesey's novel, no one can say in what sense his story is real and in what sense it is fiction. The narrator sounds a note that echoes everywhere in the sixties: "You think this is too horrible to have really happened, this is too awful to be the truth! But, please. It's still hard for me to have a clear mind thinking on it. But it's the truth even if it didn't happen." The romance elements in the book are not based on devices that whisk us away to some "theatre, a little removed from the highway of ordinary travel," and then whisk us back fueled up with truth. We suspect with horror that what we are seeing very possibly is our highway of ordinary travel, fantastic as it may seem.

The romance elements in *One Flew over the Cuckoo's Nest* are inspired by a world vision which questions the sanity of fact. It is a cartoon and comic-strip world—where a man's muscles can be "blown-up" like Popeye's arms after a taste of spinach—"a cartoon world, where the figures are flat and outlined in black, jerking through some kind of goofy story that might be real funny if it weren't for the cartoon figures being real guys." Not only is this a good image of Kesey's world, but it supplies the pattern for his character development. The movement from being a cartoon figure to becoming a painfully real guy is exemplified by Billy Bibbit. His name and his personality are reminiscent of comic-strip character Billy Batson, a little crippled kid, weak and helpless, who could say "Shazam" and turn into Captain Marvel. And just when Billy Bibbit stops being a little crippled kid, after the comic book fun of his tumble with Candy, just when his "whambam" Shazam should turn him into this big, powerful, unbeatable Captain Marvel, the Big Nurse turns him into a real guy—a judas, in fact, who proceeds from betrayal to slitting his very real throat. While Kesey attempts to employ the mode of black humor, and while he does see the value of laughter in coping with the waste land, one suspects that he is more pained and bittered by the "real guy" than a black humorist can afford to be. His humor often loses that fine edge between pain and laughter that we see in Elkin, Vonnegut, Barth, and Pynchon, while his "flat" portrayal of women and of Blacks is more stereotypic and uncomfortable than funny or fitting with his cartoon character pattern. It borders too much on the simplistic.

The romance elements also revolve around our new version of mystery. Though we may certainly be tempted to call it paranoia, it is definitely a part of the equipment of our times, and it is undoubtedly malevolent. The Big Nurse, The Combine, The Asylum—all three seem to symbolize that immense power that reduces us, and that seems to be mysteriously unlocatable. Kesey is one of those writers of the sixties who explore some mystery about Fact itself that portends mostly defeat for man. This sense of mystery adds complexity to the paradoxes of what is mad and sane, real and unreal, for it drives us to seek its heart in some huge force conspiring against us. Although it arises in connection with the image of the waste land, this mystery is the antipathy of Eliot's hoped-for God. It is only a further cause of divisive fear.

The mystery is best represented, to Kesey, by the asylum itself, but he leaves us with two possible locations of the mystery's source. It could be located somewhere external to us as Chief Bromden sees it, or as McMurphy tries to explain, maybe blaming it on a Combine is "just passing the buck." It may really be our own "deep-down hang-up that's causing the gripes." Perhaps there is some big bad wolf—and then perhaps there is only us. In the past the essential shock in American fictional experience has been a character's discovery that deep down he too is capable of evil; the shock in the sixties is the character's discovery that deep down he may be a source of unrelenting insanity. Down there, perhaps, that unknowable and seemingly immense power against us comes into being and then mounts to become a world gone mad. Against that or within that the writer, the prophet, sees new paradoxes of reason and irrationality, tact and mystery, and writes his novels no longer sure of what is fact or fiction and where malevolence lies—within or without. His only rationale can be the one stated by one of Kesey's characters: "These things don't happen. . . . These things are fantasies you lie awake at night dreaming up and then are afraid to tell your analyst. You're not *really* here. That wine isn't real; *none* of this exists. Now, let's go on from there."

BRUCE E. WALLIS

# Christ in the Cuckoo's Nest: or, the Gospel According to Ken Kesey

Considering the striking resemblances between the protagonist's actions in *One Flew over the Cuckoo's Nest* and Mr. Kesey's own subsequent activities as head of the Merry Pranksters—activities vividly recreated in Tom Wolfe's *The Electric Kool Aid Acid Test*—it is a profitable exercise to reinvestigate the fiction with an eye to determining its precise relationship to the fact. What such an examination reveals is a peculiarly Wildean instance of nature imitating art, for the author seems to have presented in his novel, a fictional program of action, which he thereafter attempted to translate into reality. To suggest, however, that the novelist's ensuing activities were prompted simply by afterthought about his artistic creation, is to understate the profound seriousness of the novel's original intentions, for despite its persistingly comic spirit, the novel is expressly formulated as nothing less than the bible for a twentieth-century religion of self-assertive action, with a message of salvation modulated to the needs of repressed individuals in a constrictively conformist society.

The novel is replete with specific comparisons of McMurphy to Christ, references designed to elevate the protagonist's martyrdom to a high level of significance. But the novel is also integrated by a sustained Biblical analogy, of which these comparisons are only a part, that begins as a series of unobstrusive allusions in the early chapters, intensifies in the novel's third section

From *Cithara* 12, (November 1972). © 1972 by St. Bonaventure University.

(the fishing trip), and completely dominates its conclusion. The analogy compares McMurphy to Christ not merely in terms of their martyrdoms, but more extensively in terms of some of the principal figures and events in the life of each. By doing so, it enables the novel to assume the configurations of a gospel, which, like the original Gospels, may serve as a source of inspiration for emulative and redemptive action.

The analogy is first struck in the third chapter, when McMurphy encounters the ward inmate Ellis, "nailed against the wall in the same condition they lifted him off the [shock shop] table for the last time, in the same shape, arms out, palms cupped." Ellis's cruciform figure recurs a few pages later, where, in attempting to move, he has "the nails pull his hands back to the wall." This repetition serves to establish the crucifixion metaphor as thematically significant, rather than merely incidental, and prepares the reader to follow its development as the novel continues.

The implications of the metaphor expand to touch most of the ward's other patients a few chapters later, when Harding explains to McMurphy the procedures of electro-shock therapy, the threat of which looms large in the life of each. "You are strapped to a table," he says, "shaped, ironically, like a cross, with a crown of electric sparks in place of thorns." Chief Broom has experienced such therapy, and explains how, in his fog of withdrawal, he would travel in mind to "the table shaped like a cross, with shadows of a thousand murdered men printed on it, silhouette wrists and ankles running under leather straps sweated green with use, a silhouette neck and head running up to a silver band goes across the forehead."

The epileptics alone are exempt from the threat of electric shock treatment, but only because they are spontaneously subject to shocks of their own, as we learn when Sefelt is discovered in an epileptic fit, "his hands . . . nailed out to each side with the palms up" just like men in the shock shop "strapped to the crossed table." Such use of the crucifixion image enables the novelist to render of the microcosm that is the hospital, a world full of men experiencing, or threatened to experience, symbolic death by crucifixion in punishment for their inability to adjust to the patterns of life in the macrocosm without. As well as enduring the threat of physical crucifixion by electric shock, however, they must also sustain continuing spiritual crucifixion in the form of the psychoses which render them effectively dead, and which remove them from the sources of life.

Into this world of death, like "a giant come out of the sky," steps R. P. McMurphy, another who cannot conform, yet a man in sufficient possession of his faculties to stand aloof from the threat of death. Indeed, with his red hair, his loud voice, his boisterous humor, and his "man smell of dust and dirt from the open fields, and sweat, and work," he is the personification of life.

All he need do is behave, and his release from the hospital is assured. But he is predestined not to do so, and from the moment of his entrance onto the ward until his selfless assault on Nurse Ratched, the novel is focused upon his developing recognition and acceptance of the inevitability and the necessity of his own crucifixion.

The conflict with Big Nurse that begins for McMurphy as a game, becomes, through the process of this recognition, a self-chosen mission in which, through the sacrifice of his own welfare, McMurphy attempts to effect the psychological salvation of his repressed fellows. He comes, in the course of this recognition, to understand not only the nature of the force to which he is opposed, the emasculating pressure of a conformist society towards the repression of self in the interests of social concord, but also his own unique power within the microcosm in which he has been placed to operate as a redemptive counterforce, exemplifying a masculine drive towards the assertion of self. He emerges, at the novel's conclusion, as a type of Christ, giving his own life by choice for the salvation of others, and his experiences in the novel are presented in terms that repeatedly echo events in the life of Christ.

His way has been prepared, for example, by a voice in the wilderness, that of the former inmate Taber, who attempted in the past many of the reforms McMurphy undertakes in the present, and who preceded McMurphy as the first case of frontal lobotomy (symbolic and effective beheading) to be used as an example to the rest of the ward. He is surrounded by his apostles, as we learn in one of the novel's few pointedly brief paragraphs, where the Chief tells us he has been describing what happened "As McMurphy led the twelve of us toward the ocean." And though the trip to the ocean begins with Ellis impossibly pulling "his hands down off the nails in the wall" and telling Billy Bibbit to "be a fisher of men," it is in fact McMurphy who is the master fisher of men, and who teaches the others by example to be fishers of men themselves.

Whether in conceiving the fishing trip the author intended allusion to the early acrostic ICHTHUS, composed of the first letters of the Greek words for "Jesus Christ, Son of God, Savior," and in its Greek form the word for "fish" which caused fish to become Christ symbols in early Christian art, only the author himself could know. But that the fishing trip effects the establishment of a church to continue McMurphy's ministry is certain. It is on this trip, by spurring the men to an independence of action of which they have not been capable for years, that McMurphy initiates them into the McMurphy-like way of life.

He has by example been teaching them the principles of this life all along. By repeated assertions of his masculine individuality against the sterile conformity of life in the ward—by brushing his teeth at the wrong hour, by wearing his whale-emblem briefs in front of the nurse, by singing loudly, by talking coarsely, by breaking windows, by throwing butter at the wall—he has consistently been demonstrating to them the possibility of self-assertion, and the helplessness of the establishment to resist it except by the most drastic measures. But it is on the fishing trip that he elicits at last their total commitment to the principles he has persistently exemplified. The trip is thus a modified mass baptism into the new religion of self-reliance (or self-assertion), and by its conclusion, McMurphy has largely prepared the disciples to carry on in his inevitable absence. As Chief Broom puts it, speaking as much for the others as for himself, "I was getting so's I could see some good in the life around me. McMurphy was teaching me."

The fishing trip offers as well the first unmistakable evidence that McMurphy has become a man of sorrows. He has been troubled since his arrival by the plight of his fellows, but only at this point is he approaching a full realization of his own identity as martyred redeemer. The Chief remarks that on the return to the hospital, "where the rest . . . looked red-cheeked and still full of excitement," McMurply appeared "beat and worn out," and goes on to say that he had "noticed McMurphy's exhaustion earlier, on the trip home." Shortly thereafter, we see McMurphy looking "dreadfully tired and strained and *frantic*, like there wasn't enough time left for something he had to do."

What McMurphy must do is complete the preparation of his disciples before he is overtaken by the fate he now sees as clearly unavoidable, and to which he yields with resignation. "Everybody could hear the helpless, cornered despair in McMurphy's voice," says Broom of the moment McMurphy stepped into the incident with the orderly Washington that triggered the chain of events leading to the end. The helplessness results not from McMurphy's own lack of power to resist his fate, but from the awareness that renders him unwilling to ignore the otherwise irremediable need of his fellows. As the Chief, emerging from his own psychosis because of McMurphy, comes to focus with clarity on the issues involved, he begins to wonder how McMurphy could ever have slept, "plagued by a hundred faces like that, or two hundred, or a thousand." By the time McMurphy effects his disasterous assault on the Big Nurse, the Chief is completely aware that "it was our need that was making him push himself slowly up from sitting. . . . It was us that had been making him go on for weeks." His thoughts only echo the earlier words of Harding, "It is us . . . Us."

In his awareness, which makes him increasingly grow to resemble his teacher, the Chief, son of a tribe of Indian fishermen from Oregon (Peter was a fisherman), is clearly the rock upon which McMurphy establishes his church. Coming out of a shock treatment in full control of himself for the first time, the Chief is greeted by Harding in terms that had formerly applied to McMurphy alone, and realizes suddenly "how McMurply must've felt all these months with these faces screaming up at him." And when McMurphy entertains transitory thoughts of escaping the ward, the Chief promises to stay on, because "somebody should stay here . . . to see that things don't start, sliding back." Of course, McMurphy could not in fact have rejected his own role, and even if he had gone, says the Chief, he "would have had to come back. . . . It was like he'd signed on for the whole game and there wasn't any way of him breaking his contract."

Prior to completing his contract, however, McMurphy arranges the hilarious midnight party in the ward, clearly a grotesque version (but fully consistent with the values of the new religion) of the Last Supper, which is shared by the disciple who, in his fear the next day, will turn Judas, Billy Bibbit. The betrayal leads to Billy's suicide (Judas's end), which in its turn leads to McMurphy's attack on the Big Nurse (symbolically a rape), his frontal lobotomy, and his ultimate death. In death, he leaves behind not only the disciples, but also the Spirit, "McMurphy's presence still tromping up and down the halls," that disenables the nurse from ever regaining her old power over the ward.

The analogy between the lives of McMurphy and Christ is thus fairly complete, and the elements composing it are too numerous and too sustained—especially in their repetition—to be accidental or incidental. The analogy functions to elevate the action of the novel to a high plane of significance, for it suggests that contemporary civilization is suffering from a spiritual illness so severe, that a redirection of spiritual focus such as that effected by the life and death of Christ is in order. The analogy makes of the novel, moreover, a bible for contemporary action, because by systematically comparing McMurphy to Christ, it implies that the life of this contemporary redemptive figure must, like the life of Christ, offer a pattern for active emulation. The analogy is culminated by the author's assignment of the narration to the particular "you" that the "giant come out of the sky" has the most dramatically saved from the Cuckoo's Nest. In narrating the life of the martyred McMurphy, Chief Broom has become an apostle in the fullest sense of the word.

That the gospel Chief Broom prepares is intended for serious adoption by its readers is evidenced by Mr. Kesey's ensuing endeavor to emulate R. P. McMurphy's experiences in his own life. The failure of that endeavor, the dropping away of his own disciples, and of the crowd of followers he initially collected, suggests that the doctrine he formulated in theory cannot be effected in practice. The cause of its practical failure is not hard to discover, for the religion he postulates, that of self-aggrandisement (call it by any contemporary term: "doing one's own thing," to the cost of the social fabric) fails to take into account original sin, the ineluctable depravity of man for which alone religion is necessary to atone.

It is no difficult task, within the configurations of a purely fictional action, to demonstrate the felicitous effects of independent and self-centered activity. One is bound to sympathize with a fictional hero who performs as an adult the pranks we all engaged in as children, but are inhibited from indulging in as adults ourselves, and to suppose that the people around him, moved by a like sympathy with his basic human desire to indulge the self, will feel a natural inclination to act the way he does. But one is not bound to make a logical extension of fiction into fact, and to suppose that such self-indulgence will have in reality the same meritorious outcome that it can be manipulated to achieve in art. One cannot gainsay the author's contention that the self-abnegation implicit in our conformity to social and ethical norms is dangerously frustrating. In theological, as well as psychological terms it is inevitably frustrating to attempt to contain the beast within. Yet life presents little evidence that the release from frustration attained by allowing a freer rein to that beast is more to be wished for than feared.

It is ironic, of course, that Mr. Kesey should compare directly to Christ, the paradigm of humility, a man whose life is intended to exemplify the value of pride. Rather than lose the self in order to save it, the gospel according to Ken Kesey suggests, one must assert the self in order to save it. In contradiction to the fundamentally Christian view of human depravity that considers the self one might assert as potentially a Kurtz in the jungle, Mr. Kesey has predicated his novel upon the romantic philosophy that man is naturally benevolent, and that his natural actions, undistorted by the pressures of social necessity, will invariably conduce to the greatest good. Mr. Kesey fails at any point in his novel to consider the possibility that the natural, self-assertive actions of his protagonists might be at least as often destructive as the presumably unnatural actions of his antagonists—that all human action will in fact be subject to the same human limitations.

The problem in Mr. Kesey's philosophy is not that the combine, his word for the establishment, is less evil than Mr. Kesey supposes (although it may possibly be so). It is rather that it is not the combine which generates the evil Mr. Kesey observes, but the evil which generates the combine, or at least makes of it what it is. The flaws in the system exist only because of anterior flaws in the men who created and maintain it. Attacking the system itself is attacking the symptom instead of the disease. That alternative systems will fall heir to the same human failings, Mr. Kesey discovered. His utopia collapsed as utopias have persisted in doing.

But Mr. Kesey's utopia was more foredoomed than most, since his prescription to combat the symptom, as we see in *One Flew over the Cuckoo's Nest*, was simply a larger dose of the disease. The most fundamental precept of the religion Mr. Kesey exploits for his literary analogy is the danger of pride, the original sin in the sense of that self-love or self-absorption that makes all other sins possible. Yet the cardinal virtue in what might be termed the "cuckoo philosophy," repeatedly exemplified by McMurphy despite his paradoxical (and improbable) self-immolation, is that very self-loving self-assertion, by virtue of throwing butter at walls, breaking in windows, stealing boats, and doing in general whatever comes naturally, that promises to render of the inmates carefree and vital individuals at last. A utopia composed of such self-centered children can spare itself the trouble of making any long range plans.

STEPHEN L. TANNER

# Salvation Through Laughter:
# Ken Kesey & the Cuckoo's Nest

K‍en Kesey's *One Flew over the Cuckoo's Nest* has been widely popular on college campuses. It is perhaps second only to Heller's *Catch-22* in frequency of selection as a text for contemporary literature courses or courses that require a sample of recent American fiction. There is a frankness and irreverence in the comedy of this novel which is appealing to current taste and which gives the novel an avant-garde flavor. But regardless of how experimental it might be in tone, in its basic structure and technique and pattern of action *One Flew over the Cuckoo's Nest* is really very conventional— not conventional in any pejorative sense, but conventional in the sense that Kesey has made very effective use of established methods of structure and imagery and of patterns of action which have archetypal significance. The real merit of this novel, and perhaps the real secret of its appeal, is to be found largely in its formal characteristics: its tight organization and its meaningfully consistent patterns of imagery.

The opposition of Nature and Machine is the primary conflict of the novel, and it is this opposition which constitutes the central nervous system for the patterns of imagery. The narrator, Bromden, whose father was an Indian, represents the man of nature. As a patient in a mental institution he is a victim of the Combine, the forces of technology and human manipulation whose avatar is Miss Ratched, the Big Nurse. Just when Bromden, over-

From *Southwest Review* 58, no. 2 (Spring 1973). © 1973 by Southern Methodist University.

come by feelings of fear and futility, is at the point of succumbing to the Combine, the boisterous McMurphy arrives as a kind of profane savior preaching the gospel of laughter. Upon examination the central struggle in this novel reveals itself as a bizarre version of the archetypal struggle between the forces of good and evil or freedom and bondage in which victory is achieved through the intervention of a savior or sacrificial hero. This remark on myth, however, is just made in passing as a framework for my interpretation. In the discussion which follows, my primary concern is with structure and imagery and not myth.

The novel is divided into four parts or cycles of action which are approximately parallel in structure. At the beginning of each cycle the Big Nurse is either ascendant or biding her time incubating a new strategy of attack, and at the end McMurphy or what he represents is ascendant. There is a progression in the movement from cycle to cycle, however, for despite setbacks McMurphy, by the end of each part, has brought Bromden closer to the freedom from fear which constitutes his salvation.

The first chapter of Part 1 introduces most of the major themes and images. The Combine is mentioned and Big Nurse and her minions are introduced through images of technology and machinery. The Big Nurse's name, Ratched, suggests "ratchet" (a mechanism consisting of a notched wheel, the teeth of which engage with a pawl, permitting motion of the wheel in one direction only). This name alone goes a long way in suggesting her impersonal singleness of purpose. From the viewpoint of the narrator, she has "equipment" and "machinery" inside; "she walks stiff"; her gestures are "precise" and "automatic"; each finger is like "the tip of a soldering iron"; she carries a wicker bag filled with "wheels and gears, cogs polished to a hard glitter"; when she is angry she blows up "big as a tractor"; her face is "smooth, calculated, and precision-made, like an expensive baby doll, skin like flesh-colored enamel." The only apparent mistake in her manufacture is her "big, womanly breasts." But these breasts, which would ordinarily represent natural warmth and maternal tenderness, she is bitter about and keeps tightly bound up within her stiff starched uniform. Her black orderlies also have "equipment" inside and their eyes glitter out of their black faces "like the hard glitter of radio tubes out of the back of an old radio." Bromden interprets their mumbling as the "hum of black machinery, humming hate and death."

After these images of mechanization and manipulation are introduced in the first chapter, they are used consistently in describing Miss Ratched and everything in her charge. She is a dedicated "adjuster" who wants her ward to run "like a smooth, accurate, precision-made machine." She sits in the center of a "web of wires like a watchful robot," tending her network with "mechanical insect skill," dreaming of a world of "precision efficiency and tidiness like a pocket watch with a glass back." The ward is a factory for the Combine, very similar in Bromden's mind to a cotton mill he had once visited. This factory fixes up mistakes made in the neighborhoods, schools, and churches, and Miss Ratched is pleased when a "completed product" goes back into society as "a functioning, adjusted component." The chronic patients are "the culls of the Combine's product"—"machines that can't be repaired." Sitting before her steel control panel, the Big Nurse controls and manipulates the patients, who are described variously as "arcade puppets," "mechanical puppets," and "shooting-gallery targets." Because of years of training, the three black orderlies are no longer controlled by direct wires; they are on the Big Nurse's frequency and are manipulated by remote control. If a patient is troublesome, he can be fixed by receiving a new "head installation." An obstreperous patient named Ruckly received this kind of overhaul and returned with eyes "all smoked up and gray and deserted inside like blown fuses"; after that he was "just another robot for the Combine."

It is noteworthy that the primary manipulators within the Combine or the realm of Machine are women. Kesey makes a point of identifying representatives of manipulating matriarchy with the forces of the Machine. As a complement to the character of the Big Nurse, her traits are echoed or doubled in the "old white-haired woman in an outfit so stiff and heavy it must be armor plate" who visited Bromden's village when he was a boy. This woman, whose speech reminds the narrator of the Big Nurse and whose eyes "spring up like the numbers in a cash register," has come with the intention of moving the Indians away from their salmon fishing village so that a hydro-electric dam can be built. Even Bromden's own mother serves as a component of the Combine. "Oh, the Combine's big—big," he says. My father "fought it a long time till my mother made him too little to fight any more and he gave up."

Thus, the first chapter establishes the pattern of imagery which is used consistently throughout the novel to describe the forces of the Machine, or Combine, as the narrator calls it. A set of images or motifs is also introduced in the first chapter which is consistently associated with Nature. Bromden's recollection of life in the Indian village on the Columbia River and of hunting is just the first of a number of references to or reminiscences of life in the outdoors which identify Bromden as a man of nature. His inordinate fear of machines which is revealed so emphatically in his fantasies accentuates the fact that he is a man whose natural element is the outdoors where life is simple and unrestrained. The supporting motifs for this characterization are the dog and the sense of smell. In the first chapter, the dog is "out there in the fog, running scared."

He sniffs in every direction but "picks up no scent but his own fear, fear burning down into him like steam." The parallels between Bromden and the dog are obvious: Bromden is intermittently engulfed in fog from "the fog machine" and his life is controlled by fear. He has a keen sense of smell which at first produces only fear as he smells the machinery inside the Big Nurse, but which later serves as a kind of barometer of his recovery as he begins again to register natural odors.

When the contrasting imagery of Machine and Nature is identified, the battle lines for the central conflict within the novel are readily apparent. The determining factor in that struggle is laughter, and this is the motif associated with Randle McMurphy. When McMurphy enters the Big Nurse's ward, he enters a world in which fear has driven out laughter, and without laughter the patients are defenseless and unable to cope with the manipulating forces of the Combine. McMurphy functions as a savior because, by teaching them to laugh, he enables the patients—Bromden in particular as the center of focus—to throw off fear or disengage themselves from Miss Ratched's Combine, his success in this endeavor not being complete until he has sacrificed himself. A brief survey of the action of the novel with special attention to imagery and motifs will demonstrate how this salvation is wrought.

At the beginning of Part 1 the Big Nurse is in full control. Bromden is mute (feigning deafness) and completely intimidated. The degree to which fear and a feeling of futility have loosened his grip on his manhood and sanity is revealed in his paranoiac fantasies of the fog and the terrifying, ubiquitous machinery. His sense of smell which links him to the world of nature registers only the odor of oil and heated machinery. And the other patients are in no better condition. When McMurphy arrives with "that big wide-open laugh of his," he is immediately a disruptive force: "Dials twitch in the control panel" and the Acutes "look spooked and uneasy when he laughs." There is no place for laughter in the Big Nurse's smooth-running machinery of manipulation, and the patients have been conditioned to the point where they are afraid of laughter. Harding, as a spokesman for the inmates, explains to McMurphy just what that brawling Irishman will be up against if he decides to fight Miss Ratched and her machinery. In the middle of his presentation, Harding attempts an ironic laugh, but "a sound comes out of his mouth like a nail being crowbarred out of a plank of green pine." His forced and grotesque "squeaking" is the nearest thing to real laughter that the patients are capable of producing. McMurphy, in an attempt to generate some resistance against Miss Ratched, calls attention to the patients' fear, telling them they "are even scared to open up and *laugh*." "You know," he says, that's the first thing that got me about this place, that there wasn't anybody laughing. I haven't heard a real laugh since I came through that door, do you know that? Man, when you lose your laugh you lose your *footing*. A man go around lettin' a woman whup him down till he can't laugh any more, and he loses one of the biggest edges he's got on his side.

Harding answers that he does not think laughter is an effective weapon against "the juggernaut of modern matriarchy" and challenges McMurphy to try his weapon of laughter against Miss Ratched. McMurphy accepts the challenge, after it has been made more attractive by the wager of five dollars from each of the other patients. Thus, he begins his calculated campaign to "bug" Miss Ratched "till she comes apart at those neat little seams, and shows, just one time, she ain't so unbeatable as you think."

McMurphy's campaign against Miss Ratched in Part 1 serves to awaken some hope within Bromden and he begins to establish control of himself again. This change within the narrator is marked by a renewed ability to smell natural odors, a reawakened recognition of the power of laughter, and finally an escape from the fog machine.

Just after McMurphy has momentarily staggered Miss Ratched by an impudent display of his flashy underwear, Bromden sweeps under McMurphy's bed and gets a smell of something that makes him realize for the first time since he has been in the hospital that though the dorm had been filled with many odors, not until McMurphy came was there "the man smell of dust and dirt from the open fields, and sweat, and work." Soon after this, again while sweeping, Bromden notices a picture of a mountain scene with a fisherman in it which he thinks was brought in when the "fog" had been too thick for him to see it. He imagines himself walking right into the picture and says, "I can smell the snow in the wind where it blows down off the peaks. I can see mole burrows humping along under the grass and buffalo weeds." This reawakened sensitivity to the world of nature, his natural element, is a positive sign that Bromden is developing a resistance to the machine world of the hospital.

After watching McMurphy humorously needling one of the black orderlies, Bromden feels good and remembers how his father once did much the same thing with some government men who were negotiating to buy off a treaty. His Papa had made the government men look ridiculous in the eyes of the Indians who had all "busted up laughing fit to kill." "It sure did get their goat," says Bromden, "they turned without saying a word and walked off toward the highway, red-necked, us laughing behind them. I forget sometimes what laughter can do." Bromden observes McMurphy closely and apprehends his strategy. McMurphy takes everything calmly and observes the humor in the behavior of the hospital personnel—"and when he sees how funny it is he goes to laughing, and this aggravates them to no end. He's safe as long as he can laugh, he thinks, and it works pretty fair."

The climax of the first part comes with the vote concerning TV time. It is when he raises his hand in that vote that Bromden takes the first action which commits him to fight back against the Combine. Even as he raises his hand he thinks, "I wouldn't do it on my own." McMurphy's influence is what causes him to act despite his fear. The drama of this incident is intensified by the motif of the fog machine. The fog, for Bromden, is a way of finding safety and comfort from the terrifying reality of life under the manipulative control of the Combine. "Nobody complains about all the fog," says Bromden. "I know why, now: as bad as it is, you can slip back in it and feel safe. That's what McMurphy can't understand, us wanting to be safe. He keeps trying to drag us out of the fog, out in the open where we'd be easy to get at." The tension mounts before Bromden raises his hand because he goes into one of his deepest fogs. He senses McMurphy trying to pull him out, but fear causes him to resist: "Why don't he leave me be?" "It's like . . . that big red hand of McMurphy's is reaching into the fog and dropping down and dragging the men up by their hands, dragging them blinking into the open." McMurphy succeeds in pulling Bromden out of the fog, for after the vote, "There's no more fog any place." Therefore, by the end of Part 1, though he still has a long way to go, Bromden, through McMurphy's help, has taken the first step toward recovering his autonomy and self-respect. This is made clear by the laughter motif which appears again on the last page of Part 1. Miss Ratched has lost her composure and Bromden, instead of being afraid, thinks it is funny: "I think how her voice sounds like it hit a nail, and this strikes me so funny I almost laugh." He *almost* laughs; this is all he is capable of at this point—his salvation will not be complete until he can laugh naturally and uninhibitedly.

At the beginning of Part 2 the results of McMurphy's initial victory are manifest: "All the machinery in the wall is quiet." But the narrator is beginning to comprehend "the full force of the dangers we let ourselves in for when we let McMurphy lure us out of the fog." Miss Ratched returns, "clearheaded," and begins to reassert her control. Her manipulative powers are confidently displayed in the staff meeting at which she persuades the doctor and other staff members that McMurphy should not be sent to the Disturbed ward. She will not agree that he is "some kind of extraordinary being" and wants him left in her ward so she can prove to the other patients he is not. She is afraid that the "redheaded hero" will be viewed as a martyr if he is taken away to Disturbed at this point.

But while Miss Ratched is initiating her new strategy to deal with the redheaded hero, it is made clear to us what effect McMurphy's first victory has had upon the narrator. "For the first time in years," he says, "I was seeing people with none of that black outline they used to have, and one night I was even able to see out the windows." Before he opens his eyes at that window, he smells the breeze. "It's fall," he thinks, "I can smell that sour-molasses smell of silage, clanging the air like a bell—smell somebody's been burning oak leaves, left them to smolder overnight because they're too green." When he opens his eyes he sees for the first time that the hospital is out in the country. Observing the moonlit pastureland reminds him of a night when he was off on a hunt with his father and uncles. All of this is the man of nature coming back to his true self, a reawakening which is emphasized once again by the dog motif. Looking out the window, he sees a gangly mongrel dog sniffing around at squirrel holes, "the breeze full of smells so wild makes a young dog drunk." This dog, who is thoroughly enjoying his freedom and the myriad smells in the night air, contrasts significantly with the bluetick hound of the first chapter, out in the fog, running scared, smelling only the scent of his own fear. The narrator and the dog hear and watch a flight of wild geese flying over. Then the dog lopes off, "steady and solemn like he had an appointment." The narrator holds his breath as he hears a car approaching and watches "the dog and the car making for the same spot of pavement." Before he can see what happens, however, a nurse and orderly put him back into bed. The symbolic significance of this incident is readily apparent: the dog (Nature) and the car (Machine) are on a collision course, but it is too soon at this point in the novel for us to see the outcome. On the last page of the novel, however, we will see Bromden escaping from the grounds of the hospital "in the same direction [he] remembered seeing the dog go."

One of Miss Ratched's most effective tools of intimidation is the threat of indefinite confinement which faces a patient who has been committed. After a conversation with the lifeguard at the pool, McMurphy realizes for the first time the full implications of that threat and becomes fully conscious of his vulnerability. Immediately thereafter he puts aside his rebelliousness and becomes pliable and cooperative. Bromden is quick to observe this change and is afraid: "The white tubes in the ceiling begin to pump their refrigerated light again . . . I can feel it, beams all the way into my stomach." With McMurphy ending his resistance Miss Ratched is in charge once again. "Whatever it was went haywire in the mechanism," remarks the narrator, "they've just about got it fixed again. The clean, calculated arcade movement is coming back . . . in the Nurses' Station I can see the white hands of the Big Nurse float over the controls." The clearest sign that McMurphy is retreating is the loss of his ability to laugh; this is the very danger he had warned the others against earlier. He is bewildered as he begins to realize that it is something more than the Big Nurse that is responsible for the trouble there. "I don't seem able to get it straight in my mind," he says. He does gradually get it straight in his mind, however, and comes to understand that it is not just the Big Nurse but also the Combine that he must fight. He understands also that although he has been committed, many of the other patients have not; therefore, while his struggle can only destroy himself, it may save others. He decides to fight.

The drama of his reversal, which comes in the last chapter of Part 2, makes use of a device similar to the fog machine in the last chapter of Part 1. Whereas at the end of Part 1 it was fog which built up in intensity and then disappeared, at the end of Part 2 it is the ringing sound in the narrator's head which builds up to a high pitch and then stops immediately after McMurphy defiantly smashes the window of the Nurses' Station.

The dog motif appears again at the end of Part 2, this time in connection with McMurphy. As McMurphy returns from the building where he has seen a patient entering shock treatment—the place of his mental struggling—the narrator says,

> I could see that there was some thought he was worrying over in his mind like a dog worries at a hole he don't know what's down, one voice saying, Dog, that hole is none of your affair—it's too big and too black and there's a spoor all over the place says bears or something else just as bad. And some other voice coming like a sharp whisper out of way back in his breed, not a smart voice, nothing cagey about it, saying. *Sic* 'im, dog *sic* 'im!

The temptation McMurphy faces in Part 2, made quite explicit in this passage concerning the two voices, manifestly parallels the temptation of Christ in the wilderness. Notice how McMurphy's temptation follows his baptismal swim at the pool. Such Christ parallels are not difficult to find throughout the novel; often they are perfectly overt: the table for the shock treatment is "shaped, ironically, like a cross, with a crown of electric sparks in place of thorns." One can be well aware of such parallels without taking them too seriously. Kesey uses them rather playfully, intending more to establish an archetypal pattern for the action of his story than to make McMurphy restrictively a Christ figure.

After passing through his temptation in Part 2, McMurphy begins his saving mission in earnest in Part 3. "The nurse was biding her time till another idea came to her that would put her on top again." Meanwhile, McMurphy organizes a fishing trip that becomes the climax of the novel. Laughter and outdoor nature are the dominant motifs in this climactic section.

The first convert to laughter in this part is the narrator himself. McMurphy discovers that Bromden has been chewing gum stuck to the bottom of the bed frames in the dorm. When McMurphy begins singing the old song, "Oh, does the Spearmint lose its flavor on the bedpost overnight?" Bromden's first impulse is to become angry, thinking that McMurphy is making fun of him. "But the more I thought about it," he says, "the funnier it seemed to me. I tried to stop it but I could feel I was about to laugh—not at McMurphy's singing, but at my own self. . . . I couldn't help but start to chuckle." At the end of Part 1 Bromden had almost laughed; now he does laugh, though it is a rather pitiful performance: "It didn't sound like much because my throat was rusty and my tongue creaked. He told me I sounded a little out of practice and laughed at that. I tried to laugh with him, but it was a squawking sound, like a pullet trying to crow. It sounded more like crying than laughing." This laughter (particularly once he is able to laugh at himself) is the key symptom of Bromden's recovery and is concomitant with the first words he utters since entering the hospital. In fact, it is not until he has laughed that he is able to speak.

One of the few references to machinery in this part is the description of the whore, whom McMurphy has invited on the fishing trip, entering the hospital. "I think apparatus burnt out all over the ward trying to adjust to her come busting in like she did," says the narrator—"took electronic readings on her and calculated they weren't built to handle something like this on the ward, and just burned out, like machines committing suicide." This is a delightful reversal because the machinery used to "adjust" the patients now must adjust itself and in so doing is destroyed.

It is "a fine woodsmoked autumn day" when they set out to go fishing. All of the patients but McMurphy are frightened and ill at ease with their freedom and are therefore pliable victims for the service station attendants who try to foist unneeded oil filters and windshield wipers on them when they stop to gas up. McMurphy's bravado saves that situation and inspirits the group with at least the appearance of self-confidence; but without the ability to laugh they have no real strength: "I think McMurphy knew better than we did that our tough looks were all show. Because he still wasn't able to get a real laugh out of anybody. Maybe he couldn't understand why we weren't able to laugh yet, but he knew you can't really be strong until you can see a funny side to things." The condition of the narrator and the other patients is objectified in the little boy from one of the "five thousand houses punched out identical by a machine and strung across the hills outside of town" whom they see always at the end of the game of crack-the-whip: "He'd always be so scuffed and bruised that he'd show up out of place wherever he went. He wasn't able to open up and laugh either. It's a hard thing to laugh if you can feel the pressure of those beams coming from every new car that passes, or every new house you pass."

The narrator's tension at passing through a region with so many signs of the Combine at work dissipates when he is aboard the fishing boat heading out to sea. "When we passed the last point of the jetty and the last black rock," he says, "I could feel a great calmness creep over me, a calmness that increased the farther we left land behind us." It is here at sea, away from the hospital, which is "the Combine's most powerful stronghold," that the process of salvation through laughter reaches its climax. McMurphy observes the group's uninhibited outdoor activity—the enthusiasm over fish caught, the tangled lines, the shouting and cussing—and begins to laugh:

> Rocking farther and farther backward against the cabin top, spreading his laugh out across the water—laughing at the girl, at the guys, at George, at me sucking my bleeding thumb, at the captain back at the pier and the bicycle rider and the service station guys and the five thousand houses and the Big Nurse and all of it. Because he knows you have to laugh at the things that hurt you just to keep yourself in balance, just to keep the world from running you plumb crazy.

McMurphy knows there is a painful side (this is something the narrator had doubted up until this moment), but he has a balanced view about it: "He won't let the pain blot out the humor no more'n he'll let the humor blot out the pain." The laughter becomes infectious and takes on cosmic proportions in this moment of epiphany:

> It started slow and pumped itself full, swelling the men bigger and bigger. I watched, part of them, laughing with them— and somehow not with them. I was off the boat, blown up off the water and skating the wind with those black birds, high above myself, and I could look down and see myself and the rest of the guys, see the boat rocking there in the middle of those diving birds, see McMurphy surrounded by his dozen people [his disciples], and watch them, us, swinging a laughter that rang out on the water in everwidening circles, farther and farther, until it crashed up on beaches all over the coast, on beaches all over all coasts, in wave after wave after wave.

After this moment of transformation, this Pentecost, the group radiates a new aura of self-assurance which is immediately apparent to the loafers on the dock: "They could sense the change that many of us were only suspecting; these weren't the same bunch of weak-knees from a nuthouse that they'd watched take their insults on the dock this morning."

Bromden, in particular, is greatly strengthened by this experience and restored to a sense of harmony with nature, from which the machines have separated him for so long. "I noticed vaguely that I was getting so's I could see some good in life around me. I was feeling better than I'd remembered feeling since I was a kid, when everything was good and the land was still singing kid's poetry to me." But this strength which Bromden and the others have acquired has been tapped from McMurphy, so at the same time Bromden remarks on the positive change within himself, he also remarks on the exhaustion apparent in McMurphy, whose face reveals him as "dreadfully tired and strained and *frantic*, like there wasn't enough time left for something he had to do." This is the sacrificial hero evidencing the cost of his sacrifice.

Part 4, of course, provides a resolution to the main themes and patterns of imagery. The narrator's salvation is complete enough to withstand the test of shock treatment: "It's fogging a little, but I won't slip off and hide in it. No . . . never again. . . . this time I had them beat." Harding also proves that he has found himself through McMurphy's example. It is made explicit that what McMurphy has done he has done for his fellow patients. Bromden thinks of him as "a giant come out of the sky to save us from the Combine." "It was us," he says, "that had been making him go on for weeks, keeping him standing long after his feet and legs had given out, weeks of making him wink and grin and laugh and go on with his act long after his humor had been parched dry between two electrodes." And his work as savior is consumated by the sacrifice of himself. There is another spectacular laughing scene when the girls and liquor are smuggled into the hospital itself. This laughing scene is a modulation of the one on the fishing boat and is necessary as a part of the falling action of the plot, in order to demonstrate that the patients are now able to laugh within the stronghold of the Combine as well as in the open freedom of nature. This laughter signifies the defeat of Miss Ratched: "every laugh was being forced right down her throat till it looked as if any minute she'd blow up like a bladder." As the laughter swirled around her, the "enamel-and-plastic face was caving in. She shut her eyes and strained to calm her trembling, concentrating. She knew this was it, her back to the wall." McMurphy's last defiant act of ripping open the Big Nurse's uniform and exposing her breasts, "bigger than anybody had ever even imagined, warm and pink in the light," is a final attempt to release the natural from the perverted restrictions of a regimented and mechanistic system. Miss Ratched returns in a new white uniform, but "in spite of its being smaller and tighter and more starched than her old uniforms, it could no longer conceal the fact that she was a woman." McMurphy himself is defeated, but his saving mission succeeds; even after he is gone his "presence" is "still tromping up and down the halls and laughing out loud in the meetings and singing in the latrines."

By skillfully drawing upon proven conventions within the literary tradition—a timeworn yet timeless pattern of myth, a conscious manipulation of images, a standard conflict-and-resolution plot—Kesey has created a novel which in terms of the social or cultural tradition is highly unconventional. His degree of formal skill is not common among recent writers and gives *One Flew over the Cuckoo's Nest* a significant place in recent fiction.

JOHN WILSON FOSTER

# *Hustling to Some Purpose:*
# *Kesey's* One Flew Over the Cuckoo's Nest

Homage to Buddha
*You don't leave much,*
*do you fat man?*
—poem by Ken Kesey

Wry tribute to the champion of enlightenment couched in the idiom of
Paul Newman's pool-room hustler: a convenient handle, I think, with which
to get a grip on Ken Kesey's first novel. *One Flew Over the Cuckoo's Nest* is
itself a combination of gamesmanship and inspired lyricism, innocent vision
and exploitive cunning. In the process of "conning" the reader with writing
that smacks of music-hall pathos, barroom anecdotage and comic-strip
vulgarity, Kesey achieves—for an apparently serious purpose—moments of
poetry not always alien to good hustling.

If an uneasy alliance between poetry and hustling is the novel's strategy,
it is also the novel's theme. Fundamental to the plot is the distinction
between two ways of interpreting and behaving in the world. One of these is
founded upon the spirit of fellowship and communion and leads, in its
profoundest moments, to the hierophanic vision we associate with Buddha,
Christ, mystics and many poets. The other is the way almost all of us practice and even believe in—the political way. To the political animal, and the
hustler is the saddest of examples, all things are secular, comprehensible and

From *Western American Literature* 9, no. 2 (August 1974). © 1974 by the Western Literature
Association.

exploitable. Kesey's nominal problem was to body forth these two attitudes and to forge some kind of synthesis out of their collision that would harmonize with the current realities of American society without permitting the apocalyptic among us to imagine that either total victory or total defeat is imminent. But I want to suggest here and in postscript that politics and hierophany are synthesized in the very conception of *Cuckoo's Nest* and that the novel can be regarded as either an elaborate game or the unravelling of a vision or both at once.

I

Reading *One Flew Over the Cuckoo's Nest* for the first time, one might be inclined, taking cue from the cover blurb perhaps, to see the novel as the story of a "boisterous, brawling, fun-loving rebel" who sabotages Big Nurse's repressive ward administration. Among other stereotypes, Randle Patrick McMurphy evokes the red-haired, Behanesque, Irish rebel of popular myth. This is a dangerous over-simplification. Even though the reader knows that Big Nurse's sly insinuations about McMurphy's egoism at the beginning of Part Four miss the gathering importance of the man (which we sense and Big Nurse does not), we have to admit that she has a point: everything that McMurphy has done for the men up to then has been to his financial advantage. For the largest part of the novel McMurphy is a con man, just as Big Nurse claims. In fact, the reason McMurphy provides such a challenge to Big Nurse is that he fights using her weapons and her ground-rules: from the beginning, McMurphy wants to beat Big Nurse "at her own game." Only superficially is he a rebel. Despite the difference between Big Nurse's officialese and McMurphy's homey Westernese, these two understand each other. And yet it is precisely *because* he stands in this relation to Big Nurse and her system that McMurphy is able to become a true rebel, someone who implicitly and totally rejects the whole thrust of the society that martyrs him.

His "man smell of dust and dirt from the open fields" to the contrary, it is not surprising that McMurphy belongs just as obviously to Big Nurse's world. School, the army, jail, prison camp, now the mental hospital: McMurphy has seen the inside of more institutions than most of us will ever see, and all of them called for a high capacity for survival. McMurphy has survived and even on occasions triumphed by learning the rules and seeing how to manipulate them. He is a product of the very system he combats. Big Nurse's world jealously penalizes the mercurial and the profit-seeking and so spawns the hustler who represents the principle of private enterprise driven underground.

Chief Bromden, on the other hand, though also a lifelong victim of the system, cannot use its methods to survive (the system after all is white and the Chief is red) and must instead develop his own. Despite being trained as an electrician's assistant by the army (the source of his machine-phobia), Bromden has long since stopped trying to communicate with the white man, and hauls his giant frame around as though it were invisible—which it is, except to McMurphy who, like most hustlers, has the dubious virtue of being non-discriminating when it comes to potential suckers. The Chief has vanished into the background the way society wants troublesome minorities to do, but paradoxically this is what saves him. Unable to become a hustler and infighter like McMurphy even if he wanted to (since the hustler must always be accepted at face value before plying his trade), Bromden adopts a different posture when confronted by institutionalism: he gets cagey.

There is all the difference in the world between McMurphy's gamesmanship and Bromden's caginess, and the Chief is at pains throughout the narrative to nail it down. "You got to understand," he says, "that as soon as a man goes to help somebody, he leaves himself wide open. He *has* to be cagey. . . ." When McMurphy learns that he is committed indefinitely and retires to re-think his tactics, "he's finally getting cagey, is all." Bromden then sees McMurphy in two minds, like a dog worrying "at a hole he don't know what's down, one voice saying, Dog, that hole is none of your affair . . . and some other voice coming like a sharp whisper out of way back in his breed, not a smart voice, nothing cagey about it, saying, *Sic* 'im, dog, *sic* 'im!" When Bromden helps McMurphy fight the black orderlies in the latrine, he does so "without thinking about being cagey or safe or what would happen" to him. To be cagey is to be restrained, unobtrusive, vigilant: in short, to think not of maximum profit, like the gamester, but of minimum loss.

Dogs occur time and again in the novel, always with reference to McMurphy. At one point, Bromden watches a mongrel in the moonlight and is to remember the direction it takes toward the highway as though, in anticipation of McMurphy, the dog is showing him the way out. And even before McMurphy enters the novel, Bromden's recollection of a hunting trip with his father when they used a pointer prefigures a distinction between McMurphy and the Chief. "All the village dogs are no-'count mongrels, Papa says, fish-gut eaters and no class a-tall; this here dog, he got *insteek!* I don't say anything, but I already see the bird up in a scrub cedar. . . ." The dog, like McMurphy, has instinct, but the Chief is somehow smarter, seeing the enemy before either of them. The dog's instinct for possible advantage is also an overweening curiosity and audacity that can get him hurt. And for all his daring, the dog can know fear, like the bluetick hound Bromden hears or hallucinates at the close of the first chapter (heralding McMurphy's entrance at the beginning of the second), like the mongrel in the moonlight, and like McMurphy himself toward the novel's end, white-faced and frantic. In its combination of strength and foolhardiness, solitariness and dependence, the dog is for Kesey an apt martyr-symbol.

It is true that McMurphy gets cagier upon learning of his indefinite committal, but he also continues to commit acts, such as putting a fist repeatedly through Big Nurse's window, or successfully proposing the salmon-fishing expedition, that fall short of being cagey and even break the first law of hustling by showing McMurphy's real speed. Why, instead of opting for Bromden's caginess or his old gamesmanship, does McMurphy choose to act in this audacious and self-defeating manner? At this point *Cuckoo's Nest* falters. Is it credible, for example, even within the novel's own universe, that McMurphy's pass for a weekend fishing-trip sponsored by "two sweet old aunts" would be granted in the light of his current behavior? And what is psychologically behind McMurphy's change? All we know is that McMurphy's new and foolhardy behavior accompanies his transformation from hustler to martyr. During his short-lived retirement from the conflict with Big Nurse, McMurphy seems to become conscious for the first time of the fear, pain and failure in others, notably in Sefelt, Frederickson, Harding, Billy Bibbit and the Chief. His subsequent self-sacrifice must be seen in the light of his growing involvement in the affairs of the weak men around him. What is at stake for the men, as Harding and later McMurphy are aware, is nothing short of their manhood and their humanity. To recover these, the men have to recover their privacy and individuality, their sense of genuine fellowship, their capacity for growth, their sexuality. It is the collective, hierarchical, static, asexual world of the ward that must be transcended. Above all, it is their present selves that must be transcended and, by dint of that, destroyed. Only through their own efforts can this be accomplished. On the fishing-trip, McMurphy purposely fades into the background and allows, even forces, the men to fend for themselves, like a father watching his children taking their first, hesitant steps outside the Big Nursery. When they come back to the ward ("like we'd brought the sea home with us"), the men have literally been sea-changed and thenceforth are rabbits no more.

McMurphy pays the price of their transformation. His audacity in the ward is also a desperation that grows into fatigue, from a "haggard, puzzled look of pressure" before the fishing-trip to total exhaustion after it. The sea voyage signifies a change in McMurphy even greater than that in the men, because once McMurphy ceases to be a hustler and becomes altruistic, his doom is sealed. And so because the trip marks the high point of McMurphy's altruism, it also marks the turning-point in his capacity for survival. Like a true martyr, he sacrifices his congeniality, volatility and sexuality to help others attain them. Unfortunately, because we do not see events from McMurphy's point of view, we cannot understand fully why he does so.

McMurphy's growing audacity, fatigue and altruism are in a word his humanization. For many fictional and mythic heroes, the championing of weaker men is concomitant with their own humanization, a transformation from hero to mere man and, through trial and sometimes death, to hero again. McMurphy becomes such a hero and even, as we shall see, a Christ "condescending" to become a man to redeem men by His suffering, but McMurphy's change on a less exalted level is merely that from hustler to half-willing victim. This too means his humanization: the hustler, by fraud or reputation, is other than he appears and as such is less than fully human. His victim, on the other hand, is only too vulnerably human. It is the hustler-turned-victim who makes the most effective hero-champion. McMurphy is only capable of making his sacrifice because he works from the inside, transmitting to the men the weaknesses and real motives of the Combine. His contamination by the system is what he for his part cannot escape and what he must expiate by his death. After the fashion of the tainted hero, "it was like he'd signed on for the whole game and there wasn't any way of him breaking his contract."

## II

If Chief Bromden is a six-foot-eight Vanishing American, as Harding claims, the novel's implication is that a great deal more than the Indians is vanishing. The recovery of their dignity and humanity is also the men's symbolic recovery of a large chunk of what is thought of as the American Way of Life. *Cuckoo's Nest*, in making this implication, barely conceals a number of allusions to the Manichean world of the cartoon and comic strip. There are also some American folk-motifs. Pitted against the machinery that bedevils Bromden's fevered brain is the muscled flesh of McMurphy and later of the Chief himself. This "John Henry" motif receives its symbolic fulfillment in the novel, not at the moment Bromden actually lifts the control panel, but when McMurphy loses blood in the attempt. For the motif conveys the ambiguously sad knowledge that "eventually we all got to lose" against the machine, and that the attempt to defeat it is itself humanity's victory and vindication. Closely related to this is the "Paul Bunyan" motif, established in Bromden's first description of McMurphy ("sailing fifty yards overhead, hollering at those below on the ground"), and continued throughout the novel in vivid portrayals of the man who, like Bunyan, is an outdoorsman and logger.

It is the frontier ethic that one aspect of McMurphy represents. Like Bromden, he is very different from the starchy hospital administrators and doctors who are products of the identical houses the city is now imposing on the land. And in good Western tradition, McMurphy often settles points of contention with his fists, is self-reliant, and tries never to stay in one place long enough to grow roots. On this level, McMurphy embodies the principles of independence and individualism upon which the United States was created and which were enshrined at their simplest in the old West, principles now being undermined by Eastern "civilization" and technology. The technocratic ward has apparently triumphed over free enterprise and human dignity while pretending to preserve those very things. Faced with McMurphy's disruptions, Big Nurse and her lackeys assert their concern for the welfare of the men, the need for civic responsibility, the necessity of law and order, the gratuitousness of dissent, and the progress which has taken place in mental hospitals. This is mere strategy. The concern for the patients' welfare is actually a patronizing (in this case, matronizing) interference in their affairs through a Big Brotherish refusal to grant them respite from administrative vigilance, as though they were children. Other aspects of authoritarian regimes echo. Big Nurse's repeated attempts to discredit McMurphy are close to an anti-personality cult designed to keep a tight rein on the hero's followers. We recognize, too, the doctrines of self-criticism and institutionalized squealing, not to speak of personality control and even thought control through EST and lobotomization. Behind the facade of benevolent government looms the specter of totalitarianism.

*Cuckoo's Nest* seems in part to be grim prediction, as though the ward ("the Combine's most powerful stronghold") is the shape of things to come. But the novel is also claiming surely that the Combine, however rudimentarily, is already in business, growing behind a fog of doublethink and technological gibberish. Further, it is arguable that the ward is the logical outcome when private enterprise is distorted, as it has been in America, by monopoly and political exploitation. It is in the land of the free that Big Nurse is able to hold autocratic sway, disguising her motives and power behind the camouflage of "progress" and "welfare." McMurphy must be destroyed, not because he is a total disbeliever in the system, but because he represents a one-man, smaller-scale, old-fashioned but still nonetheless dangerous version of the Big Nurse's own exploitation and oppression.

For it is untrue to say that McMurphy is a martyr for all that is good and vanishing in America. Like John Henry and Paul Bunyan, McMurphy has been an unwitting accomplice of the system (*is* in a way that system), deluded into believing himself capable of being free, deluded even into learning the system's own methods: fittingly, it was in the army that McMurphy learned how to play poker. "He has a healthy and honest attitude about his chicanery," says Harding with heavy irony, "and I'm all for him, just as I'm for the dear old capitalistic system of free individual enterprise, comrades, for him and his downright bullheaded gall and the American flag. . . ."

The games at which McMurphy hustles men, Monopoly, blackjack, poker, the World Series, are models of certain aspects of the free enterprise system. Indeed, that system has frequently been regarded in America as itself a kind of game. In once-popular myth, Americans, like players in a game, started equal but ended up, by dint of differing skill and luck, unequal. Life in the ward, itself a model of the free enterprise system now monopolized and the democratic process now technocratized, appropriately resembles a game. Big Nurse's wish to maintain the status quo and to prevent any change or development in the men (sending them home or to the Disturbance Ward very reluctantly), is her wish not to see the boundaries of her game transgressed. The players in Big Nurse's game do not, of course, start equal, for the game is rigged in favor of Big Nurse. It is one of McMurphy's functions in the novel to show the men just *how* the game is rigged, and here his experience as hustler and gamester is brought into play. Only such a man could see through the camouflage that makes Big Nurse's game appear as unalterable reality. Once the game is shown to be rigged, violation and not merely exploitation of its rules becomes not only morally justifiable but morally obligatory.

Because of its political implications, *Cuckoo's Nest* can be cautiously read as a revolutionary allegory. The notions of self-sacrifice and comradely succession are common to *Cuckoo's Nest* and revolutionary doctrine. The difference, perhaps, is Bromden's deep-rooted pessimism which would be frowned upon in revolutionary cadres: "All you could do was keep on whipping [the Combine], till you couldn't come out any more and somebody else had to take your place." McMurphy's death, too, is in the fashion of revolutionary myth, so that between the lines of Bromden's account of McMurphy's frontal-lobe castration, one can almost read Castro's reflection upon Che Guevara's murder: "they think that by eliminating a man physically they have eliminated his thinking—that by eliminating him physically they have eliminated his ideas, eliminated his virtues, eliminated his example." Nor is it surprising to discover a close correspondence between the presentation of McMurphy's death and that of the revolutionary leader in the film *Viva Zapata:* in each case the corpse of the slain hero is greeted by disbelief on the part of his followers for whom he has attained the stature of a god.

The fact that McMurphy begins as a hustler and manipulator does not clash with a revolutionary reading of the novel. The entrepreneur who is converted to the cause of the disfranchised is a firm part of revolutionary mythology. McMurphy's transformation from entrepreneur to revolutionary martyr is merely an extension of his transformation from hustler to victim.

## III

Is the cause which McMurphy mysteriously adopts and for which he dies vindicated? Are the treasurable aspects of American life, free from taint of profit, recoverable? On the credit side, there is at key points in the novel the kind of vision Big Nurse could not begin to understand or countenance. I am thinking of one scene in particular in which Kesey draws upon a love of Northwest wildlife. Chief Bromden is watching the mongrel in the moonlight out in the hospital grounds, when the dog freezes with one paw uplifted and the Chief hears from afar the humorous gabbling of southbound Canada geese. He sees the skein crossing the face of the moon—"a black, weaving necklace, drawn into a V by that lead goose. For an instant that lead goose was right in the center of that circle, bigger than the others, a black cross opening and closing, then he pulled his V out of sight into the sky once more." When we recall that McMurphy is the ward's "bull goose loony," we see how Kesey has wedded Bromden's moment of hierophany to a symbolic rendering of McMurphy's transient leadership of the men against the forces of darkness. There is added significance in the scene since the artificial light of the ward is tacitly contrasted throughout the novel with moonlight in which Bromden's crucial moments of insight or action take place.

It is fitting that Bromden is the one entrusted with the novel's visionary moments, as though as Indian he is in touch with the primal and ultimate forces of beauty and cosmic_energy. But on the debit side, Bromden's moments of vision are rare, and are mostly remembered rather than directly experienced. Moreover, that the Chief is only half-Indian and belongs to an almost defunct tribe seems to underscore both the contamination of Indian lifestyles by the white man and the tenuousness of our links today with the primal and ultimate forces. If the Indians are the last custodians of vision and ritual, then the ending of *Cuckoo's Nest*, with its picture of Indian scaffolding ramshackled over the hydroelectric dam, reads bleakly indeed. However, the fact that it is the corrupt white man McMurphy who makes Bromden's escape possible and who, having turned from hustler and entrepreneur into man, then turns from man into god, suggests that something less tangible, more subtle and vulnerable than an Indian lifestyle is kept flickeringly alive at novel's end. At this point a myth-reading of *Cuckoo's Nest* is necessary.

There are in the novel several allusions to the life and death of Christ. For instance, we recall the shape of the cross made by the lead goose against the moon. The table in the shock shop is shaped, "ironically, like a cross, with a crown of electric sparks in place of thorns." McMurphy, about to receive an electric charge, says, "Anointest my head with conductant. Do I get a crown of thorns?" Above all, there is the fishing-trip. The trip clearly has its origins in two incidents of New Testament lore: Christ's calming of the storm when on board a ship with his disciples (Mark 4, 36–40; Matthew 8, 23–28), and the miracle of the draught of fishes as a result of which Simon, James and John decide to follow Christ (Luke 5, 2–11). There are twelve on the fishing expedition, excluding McMurphy, as there are twelve disciples. Soon after embarkation, McMurphy disappears below deck with Candy, as though in ironic parallel to Christ's sleeping in the stern during the storm that frightened his disciples. Like the disciples, McMurphy's crew has little faith until they begin to catch fish (cf. Luke 5, 6–7) and consider themselves safe from the dangerous currents off the Oregon coast (cf. Mark 4, 39). Later, not long after his run of "miracles" has ended including his restoration of the Chief to full health—McMurphy is "crucified" and his power handed on to his apostolic successors.

Kesey's fish-symbolism has obvious and subtle aspects. The men catch fish, of course, as Simon, James and John did, but Kesey is not content with this. The fish the men catch seem to embody the strength McMurphy loses during the trip (in part, sexual potency), and thus become the agents through which that strength is transferred to the men. The fish are, in another sense, symbols of McMurphy himself. If this seems far-fetched, consider the scene in which the mongrel in the moonlight rolls around in the wet grass, remembering that the association of the dog with McMurphy has already been established: "He twisted and thrashed around like a fish, back bowed and belly up, and when he got to his feet and shook himself a spray came off him in the moon like silver scales." (It is interesting to note that the dog when it moves off is apparently going to collide with a car, as McMurphy is to die at the hands of technology.)

We must be careful not to oversimplify. For instance, it is not always McMurphy who is associated with Christ. Frederickson talks about Sefelt being crucified, while it is Ellis who is nailed against the wall, "arms out, palms cupped," and Ellis who tells Billy Bibbit to be "a fisher of men." Furthermore, McMurphy is to begin with an unChristly figure—a brash and physically-gifted womanizer, hustler and gambler. Nor does he become very much more Christlike later on, outside of becoming mysteriously altruistic. It is never clear whether his frantic posturing at novel's end is the result of extreme fatigue, a personality crisis, or a conscious desire to end it all and to do some good while about it. All along, the Christ-aspect is imposed upon McMurphy from without: by Bromden, for whom he is a savior come out of the sky, by Big Nurse who thinks McMurphy sees himself as a god, by Harding, and to some extent by all the men. After learning of his indefinite committal, McMurphy tumbles to why the men have been treating him as "some kind of saviour."

What we have in *Cuckoo's Nest*, then, seems closer to a parody than to a re-telling of Christ's career. In keeping with this, Kesey's Christ-symbolism fails on the face of it to answer my previous question: is McMurphy's cause vindicated? By which I now mean, is there redemption? Christ's death re-established God's kingdom on earth whereas, although McMurphy's "crucifixion" effects the men's escape from the ward and their apparent recovery of mental and bodily health, the larger war against the Combine is seemingly being lost. However, we must remember that in a sense Christ simply bore witness, aware as He was that wars, famine and false prophets would come after Him. He taught that it is not so much salvation that should concern the still-mortal flesh—since that is a posthumous regard—as the promise of salvation, a promise renewed each time someone follows His example. This spiritual renewal means also, if there is an unbroken succession of disciples, a physical renewal by which the mortality of the flesh is in a manner kept at bay. Kesey uses his Christ-symbolism to suggest the continuity and succession of ritual and vision rather than to suggest that McMurphy is a man of Christly motives whose "crucifixion" redeems the sinners around him.

In appreciating the seriousness of the novel concealed within the biblical parody, we can go farther afield than the story of Christ for the novel's mythic and ritual precedents. Consider this passage from Frazer:

> If the high gods, who dwell remote from the fret and fever of this earthly life, are yet believed to die at last, it is not to be expected that a god who lodges in a frail tabernacle of flesh should escape the same fate. The danger is a formidable one; for if the course of nature is dependent on the man-god's life, what catastrophes may not be expected from the gradual enfeeblement of his powers and their final extinction in death? There is only one way of averting these dangers. The man-god must be killed as soon as he shews symptoms that his powers are beginning to fail, and his soul must be transferred to a vigorous successor before it has been seriously impaired by the threatened decay.

I am suggesting the spirit rather than the letter of ritual allegory here. McMurphy does take on the aspect of a shaman-god who, having initiated his tribal children into manhood and imbued them with the life-giving forces of nature, tires soon after and must be succeeded. But although McMurphy's strength passes into all the men, it is Bromden who actually crushes the spark of life from his body and who therefore receives the bulk of that strength. Their relationship, at first a mutual pact (just as McMurphy helps Bromden, so Bromden in turn wins McMurphy a bet and is an ally in the latrine brawl), gradually becomes parasitic, the Chief growing stronger as McMurphy weakens. But it is parasitic in a good sense, and its intimacy should be emphasized. Bromden lies on top of the lobotomized McMurphy at the novel's end, as though in the embraces of love, but actually in a symbolic act of spiritual transfer. When the Chief tries on McMurphy's cap after the murder, it is too small and he casts it away. Nevertheless, the final gesture of succession has been made, two heads having successively worn what Frazer calls "the cap of sovereignty."

## IV

According to Kesey, we are losing the war against the urban, impersonal, technocratic, mentality of the Combine. If as of now the Combine cannot totally deny our humanity (as Big Nurse cannot quite conceal the breasts that tell us that even she is a woman and not a robot), it will no doubt continue to work on the problem. Nor is there much solace to be gained from Kesey's grim picture in the novel's coda of primal man creeping back on the sides of the hydroelectric dam in a defiant gesture of adaptation and survival. The government will surely knock down the wood scaffolding, defacing as it does Federal or State property. And Bromden's friends will likely have drunk themselves goofy as he fears.

Luckily, though, what can keep alive our awareness of the mystery and beauty of the world is less vulnerable to the Combine. Paradoxically, it is the re-discovery of the god within us (not however the arrogant god Big Nurse accuses McMurphy of aping) that best ensures the survival of our humanity. What is required is an unbroken succession of spiritual custodians, guarantors of an alternative bond with the universe and our fellow man to that offered by the technocrats of the Combine. *Cuckoo's Nest* charts this slow and painful transfer of visionary power from one custodian to another.

But those with vision, such as Bromden, will be deemed mad by the Combine. To safeguard such visionaries, men such as McMurphy, capable of translating vision into practicality, are periodically required. Practicality is the technique of revolution but it is also the working spirit of fellowship and communion without which Bromden would be lost. Indeed, though the Chief is a man of superior vision beside whom McMurphy is a philistine and mere activist, they are truly symbiotic characters in the end, perhaps even two aspects of the *same* character. It is significant that I began by comparing McMurphy with Big Nurse and have ended by comparing him with Chief Bromden. Corrupt white man and apathetic red man finally fuse against a common dehumanized enemy.

In terms of plot and character, Kesey achieves the synthesis I spoke of in my introductory section. But in a provocative sense, *Cuckoo's Nest* also enacts the synthesis. I have given a straight reading of the novel, but the work exists too, as I have hinted, on the plane of parody and caricature. Bits and pieces of myths and legends float through the narrative. The characters too are in part lifted from comic strips, cartoons and popular films. Because parody and caricature have in them a strong play element, *Cuckoo's Nest* can be seen as a kind of fictional game. In addition, an enduring irony of the novel is that we are forced to rely totally for our information upon the hallucinations of a patient in a mental hospital. The reader is locked within the closed-system of Bromden's paranoid point-of-view, as a player is locked within the rules of a game. Within the closed-system, what happens has its own verifiability. We might claim with McMurphy, for instance, that even though Bromden's is crazy talk, that does not mean it doesn't make sense. "If these things don't exist," asks the Chief anxiously, "how can a man see them?" And can't we consider the action of *Cuckoo's Nest* to be "the truth even if it didn't happen"?

Nonetheless: is the whole narrative Bromden's, or Kesey's, paranoid nightmare? Either we believe all of *Cuckoo's Nest*, Kesey is saying in the spirit of a man introducing the rules of a new game, or we believe none of it. But aren't visionaries equally uncompromising? For if a first-rate hustler like Minnesota Fats does not leave much, neither does a visionary like Buddha. Sometimes I have a disquieting hunch that the merry prankster who wrote *One Flew Over the Cuckoo's Nest* would see my efforts at a straight reading as the payoff to some successful hustling on his part. But I think that like McMurphy, Kesey through Chief Broom is hustling to some purpose.

BARRY H. LEEDS

# One Flew Over the Cuckoo's Nest:
## *"It's True Even If It Didn't Happen"*

Kesey's first novel, *One Flew Over the Cuckoo's Nest,* has been enormously popular at every level of academe for almost two decades. It is a book which holds the interest of the undergraduate who can say, "I'm not *into* reading." Yet its accessibility is deceptive; it is by no means a simple book. Close critical analysis illuminates the depth of Kesey's technical mastery of such aspects of novelistic form as symbolism and structure.

If these are essentially academic concerns, the success with which technique serves theme in this work is not. A careful reading of several central symbol patterns and an understanding of the narrative devices used to present them both enhance an appreciation of Kesey's art and show clearly that the central thematic thrust of this novel strikes even closer to the heart of the American experience now than it did in 1962.

Within a highly disciplined form, Kesey has dealt with issues which loom prominently in the minds of those whose primary criterion for any idea or pursuit is its "relevance." The questioning of a monolithic bureaucratic order, the rejection of stereotyped sexual roles, the simultaneous awareness that healthy sexuality and a clear sense of sexual identity are prerequisites for human emotional survival, the recognition and rejection of hypocrisy, the devotion to the expression of individual identity: all these leap into sharp focus through a study of Kesey's technique.

From *Ken Kesey.* © 1981 by Frederick Unger Publishing Co., Inc.

Randle Patrick McMurphy, the protagonist of *One Flew Over the Cuckoo's Nest*, is a man who has consistently resisted the strictures of society. Having decided that life on a psychiatric ward will be preferable to hard labor on the county work farm where he has been serving a sentence for assault and battery, McMurphy feigns insanity. This brings him into dramatic confrontation with "Big Nurse," a representative of the most repressive aspects of American society. Big Nurse is backed by the power of a mechanistic "Combine," a central agency for that society's suppression of individuality.

During his stay on her ward, McMurphy fights a constant guerrilla action against Big Nurse and her aides. He rallies the other patients behind him as he introduces gambling, laughter, and human vitality to the ward. He leads the patients on a therapeutically rejuvenating deep-sea fishing trip. In a penultimate rebellion, he smuggles whores and liquor onto the ward for a hilarious party.

Against this humorous backdrop, the struggle between McMurphy and Big Nurse continues to escalate. In the climactic final scenes, she is able to provoke him into outbursts of violence which provide the excuse to "treat" McMurphy with electro shock therapy (EST) and ultimately with a lobotomy. In the moving conclusion, McMurphy's friend Chief Bromden mercifully smothers him to death and makes his own escape. Although McMurphy is ultimately destroyed, he is not defeated. His courage and humor are never broken. Even after his death, his spirit pervades the ward; it is clear that he has beaten Big Nurse and damaged the Combine.

It is not only McMurphy's own struggle which is at issue in this novel. For one thing, McMurphy comes to represent the only hope for salvation open to his fellow inmates, a salvation which he brings about through the tutelage of example, making them aware of their own manhood in the dual senses of masculinity and humanity. Also, the novel's first-person narrator, Chief Bromden, assumes during the course of the novel a rebel role similar to that of McMurphy.

In a narrative structure analogous to that employed by F. Scott Fitzgerald in *The Great Gatsby*, Kesey places Chief Bromden in a pivotal position. In both novels, the narrator is a man closely associated with the protagonist and torn by ambivalent feelings of disapproval and admiration for him, who, during the course of the novel, learns and develops through the tutelary example of the protagonist's life and ultimate death, and who, in recounting the story of his friend's life, clarifies his own development to the point where he takes on both the strengths of the protagonist and an awareness of how to avoid a similar downfall and death. Bromden and Nick Carraway both become syntheses of their own latent strengths and abilities and the best aspects of McMurphy and Gatsby. This narrative structure provides the novelist with the advantages of both the first-person point of view (within which the narrator can be revealed in terms of his own internal cerebration) and a third-person (hence more credibly objective) view of the novel's central figure.

The progressive development of the characters of McMurphy and Bromden cannot be said to parallel one another; a more accurate geometric metaphor is that of two intersecting oblique lines: As McMurphy's strength wanes, Bromden moves toward the ascendant. But the two developments proceed simultaneously and are integral to one another, until the transfer of power from McMurphy to Bromden is complete.

Bromden is an American Indian, a 280-pound, 6 foot 8 inch former high school football player and combat veteran of World War II who has been robbed of identity and sanity by the combination of pressures brought to bear on him by twentieth-century American society. At the outset of the novel, he is literally cut off from even the most rudimentary communication. He is so fearful of the dangers of dealing with people that he has learned to feign total deafness and has maintained absolute silence for years. Considered incurable by the medical staff, he is forced to perform menial janitorial work by the orderlies, who ridicule him with the title "Chief Broom."

The nickname has an obvious significance: Defined by his menial function, Bromden is no more than an object to the staff, a tool. But even his legal name, "Bromden," represents a false identity that is imposed upon him by others. Ironically, Chief Broom really is the son of a tribal chief, a once-powerful leader whose Indian name meant "The-Pine-That-Stands-Tallest-on-the-Mountain." "Bromden" is the maiden name of his mother, a white woman; and the fact that his father allowed himself to be henpecked into adopting it is invested with great significance by Kesey. The loss of pride in the Indian heritage brought about by the pressure of white American society (especially its matriarchal element, as represented by Mrs. Bromden) lies at the heart of the twentieth-century problem of Bromden, his father, and their people. The plight of the American Indian comes to represent, for Kesey, that of the American individualist in highly distilled form. The artificial identities of "Mr. Bromden" and "Chief Broom" imposed upon Bromden by the matriarchal and mechanistic elements of society diminish him enormously. The first robs him of his masculine pride and his racial identity, the second of his very humanity. Kesey forces us to abstract from this extreme case the realization that our own identities as self-determining individuals have been considerably eroded and are further threatened by a computerized civilization.

The experiences which have undermined Bromden's strength and sanity are revealed later in the novel in brief flashbacks, each precipitated by McMurphy as he persists in forcing Bromden to leave his fortress of silence and forgetfulness and reenter by stages the external world. As McMurphy makes friendly overtures toward him, Bromden begins to remember and understand episodes from his own past. In persistently attempting communication with Bromden, McMurphy functions as a sort of combination lay psychiatrist and confessor, precipitating more and more painful and traumatic memories out of Bromden's mind until the Chief is able to face his own problems and begin the trip back to manhood.

These flashbacks help establish for the reader an acceptance of Bromden as a sympathetic and fully developed character of considerable potential so that his later resurgence of power is both credible and emotionally charged. In addition, these passages are thematically useful to the author, introducing graphic substantiation of his central indictment of the Combine-controlled American society and its capacity to crush individuality and communication. Chief Broom is the tangible representation of the human alienation produced by the system.

A good example of the use Kesey makes of Bromden's memories is the passage in which Bromden recounts his traumatic, dehumanizing experiences in combat on Anzio. The placement of Bromden's flashbacks is so effectively controlled that they become an example and a bulwark of the tight control of plot structure by which Kesey develops his theme. Kesey is able to observe a set of personal limitations similar to the classical unities, limiting his "onstage" action to a small immediate area and a relatively short time while substantiating character and theme by introducing each flashback at the most dramatically effective point in the narrative.

What is particularly impressive about *One Flew Over the Cuckoo's Nest* as a first novel is the highly credible integration of prose style and metaphorical patterns with the character of Bromden. Early in the book, Bromden's perceptions and the very rhythms of his speech are both informed and limited by his disturbed mental state. As he moves toward sanity and effective communication with others, Bromden perceives and articulates more clearly, and the prose style of the narrative reflects this development precisely. For example, fairly late in the novel, Bromden, who has been subject to frequent hallucination, takes the significant step of drawing a clear distinction between illusion and reality:

There was little brown birds occasionally on the fence; when a puff of leaves would hit the fence the birds would fly off with the wind. It looked at first like the leaves were hitting the fence and turning into birds and flying away.

Bromden's hallucinations during the earlier part of the novel serve to establish and support the central aesthetic of the book, based on a fascinating subjectivity within which Kesey masterfully commands a suspension of disbelief. This is brought about largely through absolute candor on Bromden's part. He admits his own subjectivity and the extent of his alienation from our societal "reality," but in a crucial statement which sums up precisely the relationship between the rich metaphorical structure of his hallucinations and the central truths they elucidate, Bromden tells us (referring to the entire McMurphy story): "It's true even if it didn't happen." It is the absence of this distinctive hallucinatory perspective that most weakens the movie version of *Cuckoo's Nest*.

Thus, the truths Bromden forces us to recognize are not dependent for their validity upon drawing a distinction between which of the events he recounts "really" happened and which proceed entirely out of his own labyrinthine imagination. When, for example, Bromden crushes a tranquilizer capsule and sees (in the split second before it self-destructs upon contact with the air and turns to white powder) that it is a miniature electronic element, intended by the Combine to control the man who swallows it, it is not necessary for the reader to determine what is illusion and what is "reality." The truth lies in the metaphor of the hallucination: The capsule, no matter what its ostensibly beneficial effect, is a device intended by society to control the inmates, to render them docile and bovine, and to rob them of any individual trait which might threaten the homogeneity and mediocrity of the established order.

Each of Bromden's hallucinations forms part of a complex system of recurrent symbols, and each is ultimately shown by Kesey to grow naturally out of Bromden's previous experiences. The transistor metaphor becomes part of a more comprehensive theory of Bromden's that the Combine exerts direct control over the citizenry through electronic devices; thus the reader is not surprised when Bromden later remarks in passing that he has studied electronics in the army and in his one year of college. When old Pete Bancini, a man so mentally retarded that the Combine has been unable to exercise control over him, physically resists the orderlies' efforts to subdue him, the hallucination Bromden creates of Pete's fist pumping up into the form of a huge steel ball ties into a recurrent series of references to hands as symbols of potency.

The psychological verisimilitude employed by Kesey in establishing these image patterns as natural outgrowths of Bromden's experience is so painstakingly precise that even the briefest metaphors used by Bromden can be traced to their source. For example, one morning Bromden is served a "canned peach on a piece of green, torn lettuce." Later, relating the story of how the orderlies forcibly administered medication to an inmate, Bromden describes the scene in the same terms: "One sits on his head and the other rips his pants open in back and peels the cloth until Taber's peach-colored rear is framed by the ragged lettuce-green."

Perhaps the most frightening product of Bromden's hallucinatory perception is the Combine itself. He defines it as a "huge organization that aims to adjust the Outside as well as the Big Nurse has the Inside." The Inside, as Bromden sees it, is different from the outside world only in the *degree* of control which must be exerted over its inhabitants. The Combine, committed as it is to the supremacy of technology over humanity, extends its influence by dehumanizing men and making them machines. But as the novel progresses, it becomes clear that Kesey envisions emasculation as a preliminary step in the dehumanization process. Ultimately, a pattern emerges: The Combine functions on two levels, mechanistic and matriarchal. The two are fused in the Big Nurse, Miss Ratched, who is a "high ranking official" of the Combine.

Big Nurse herself is conceived in mechanistic terms. Even her name, "Ratched," sounds like a kind of wrench or machine component, and the association with "rat" makes its very sound unpleasant. Bromden sees her as an expensive piece of precision-made machinery, marred in its functional design only by a pair of oversized breasts. Despite her annoyance at being forced to carry them, and despite Bromden's feeling that they mark an obvious flaw in an otherwise perfect piece of work, their presence is not inconsistent with the symbolic irony intended by Kesey. Miss Ratched's breasts are ironic reminders of the sexuality she has renounced. At the novel's end, they will be exposed by McMurphy as the palpable symbol of her vulnerability. Finally, they are her badge of membership in the Smothering Mother cadre of the Combine.

Nurse Ratched is frequently referred to, in varying degrees of admiration or irony, by the hospital's public relations man and by the inmates themselves as the "mother" of the men on her ward. As Kesey presents it, the role is an evil one. The problems of many of the men on the ward are largely sexual in origin, and in a number of cases an overbearing mother has contributed largely to the problem. Big Nurse, under the guise of compassion, perpetuates, through the role of solicitous mother, the debilitating environment which already has emasculated the inmates.

Upon McMurphy's arrival at the ward, he tells the inmates that "the court ruled that I'm a psychopath. . . . Now they tell me a psychopath's a guy that fights too much and fucks too much. . . ." Although Kesey renders McMurphy's character in such a way that his sanity never seems questionable to the reader, it is significant that his cunning but unschooled ruse is so readily acceptable both to prison authorities and to the medical staff of the hospital. The central issue seems to be that the two areas in which McMurphy's animal vitality manifests itself, rage and sexual energy, form a two-pronged threat to the dual repressive roles of the Combine: mechanistic order and matriarchal emasculation. Having classified brawling and promiscuous sexual activity as "antisocial" forms of behavior, the authorities make the easy assumption that a man who sees such behavior as a desirable and valid form of life must be insane.

McMurphy, for his part, recognizes Big Nurse's methods almost immediately:

> What she is is a ball-cutter. I've seen a thousand of 'em, old and young, men and women . . . people who try to make you weak so they can get you to . . . live like they want you to. . . . If you're up against a guy who wants to win by making you weaker instead of making himself stronger, then watch for his knee. . . . that's what that old buzzard is doing. . . .

This distinction between winning by making one's opponent weaker as opposed to making oneself stronger is central to McMurphy's ethic. A recurrent thematic concern of Kesey's, it prefigures the conflict between Lee and Hank Stamper in *Sometimes a Great Notion*.

The conflict which Bromden perceives between the individual and the Combine has in his experience never been a true contest. The Combine and, by extension, Big Nurse, appear monolithic and invincible to Bromden. Nurse Ratched's power derives largely from the apparatus of a society concerned with the maintenance of harmonious mediocrity: locked doors, psychiatric jargon, Seconal, EST. But it is also based in large part on human elements within her control. At her bidding, the patients spy on each other, ostensibly for therapeutic reasons. She has, over a period of years, created a constant turnover of doctors before finding Dr. Spivey, a man weak enough to be manipulated. In much the same way, she has gone through an enormous number of black orderlies on a trial basis, dismissing scores of them before finding those who are so full of hatred that they will zealously fulfill the task of subduing and humiliating the inmates. Foremost among their methods is the habit of brutal homosexual rape. The hatred and violence by which the act is characterized serve both to dehumanize the aides themselves and to underscore the emasculation of the inmates, removing the last vestige of their pride and reducing them to *objects* of humiliation.

The fact that the process of selection for both aides and doctors has taken some years makes it clear that Kesey is not making simplistic judgments against particular racial or occupational groups. In conjunction with the plight of Chief Bromden, the black aides' rage against white people is shown to be a *result* of racism, and thus Kesey makes an indictment against racial prejudice as a self-perpetuating process. In addition, the novel is strewn with sympathetic exceptions to these characters. Mr. Turkle, the black night orderly, is an attractive character, who abets and participates in the patients' clandestine party. The Japanese nurse in charge of the Disturbed Ward repudiates Nurse Ratched's methods. Dr. Spivey, by the novel's conclusion, begins to assert himself. Even the use of EST as a punitive measure is carefully shown to be atypical, peculiar to Big Nurse's ward.

From the outset, McMurphy pays more attention to Bromden than anyone has in years: Where others have belittled the Chief, McMurphy marvels at his size and recognizes the latent strength it represents. Almost immediately, McMurphy begins to establish contact with Bromden, although it is at first superficial and unarticulated. In a passage which significantly pre-figures the central thematic process of the book, the transfusion of power from McMurphy to Bromden, McMurphy offers to shake hands with Bromden, who, unwilling to relinquish the protection of his feigned deafness, remains passive and stares dumbly at the outstretched hand. McMurphy picks up Bromden's limp hand, with the result that "my hand commenced to feel peculiar and went to swelling up out there on my stick of an arm, like he was transmitting his own blood into it. It rang with blood and power. It blowed up near as big as his, I remember." The pumping up of Bromden's hand is an erectile image, parallel to that of Old Pete in the steel ball hallucination, which progresses to an explicit genital reference later in the book, when Bromden experiences his first erection in years. The pattern is repeated throughout the novel, with hands as a symbol of male potency introducing the more crucial issue of emasculation.

McMurphy's hands are of primary importance. Immediately before McMurphy shakes Bromden's hand, the Chief is impressed enough to give the reader a lengthy description of McMurphy's offered hand. It is a record of his tough, nomadic life, with various scars, tattoos, and stains detailing the occupations, struggles, and general life-style of the man. Bromden concludes, "The palm was callused, and the calluses were cracked, and dirt was worked in the cracks. A road map of his travels up and down the West." Not only is this hand a map of the land which Bromden will later find his way back to; it quite literally carries in its cracks some of the earth from that land.

The experience and power which repose in McMurphy's hands are emphasized repeatedly. Later, during the fishing trip, he is able to intimidate two surly service station attendants without striking a blow by showing them his calluses and scars.

The symbolic value of hands is important in other characters as well, notably Dale Harding, a slender, sensitive, almost effeminate man who has retreated behind a shield of intellectual irony because he feels unable to cope with his big-breasted, sexually demanding wife. Harding's hands are an index of his character: "hands so long and white and dainty I think they carved each other out of soap . . . it bothers him that he's got pretty hands." Harding's feeling of shame at his "pretty" hands is reinforced when his wife, on her visit to the hospital, derides the male friends who have visited their home in his absence for their "limp wrists." More obviously and crucially, when the World Series vote approaches, McMurphy prods Harding by asking,

> "You afraid if you raise your hand that old Buzzard'll cut it off."
> Harding lifts one thin eyebrow. "Perhaps I am; perhaps I *am* afraid she'll cut it off if I raise it."

Harding is too intelligent a man not to be aware of the dual significance of his own statement; and the admitted fear of symbolic castration ties into another obvious manifestation of the theme of sexual identity. All the men have been to one degree or another emasculated; but the horror of the situation is dramatically underlined by a literal castration, when an inmate commits suicide by amputation: "Old Rawler. Cut both nuts off and bled to death, sitting right on the can in the latrine. . . ."

It should be made clear that the polarity established between the externally effeminate hands of Harding and the more obviously masculine hands of McMurphy is not a simplistic one. Although Harding's "pretty" hands are a symbolic manifestation of his confused sexual identity, it is Harding himself who sees them as shameful, not McMurphy or Bromden. The brand of manhood admired by Kesey and represented by McMurphy is not limited exclusively to brawny men with scarred hands, as is shown by the fact that Harding grows to manhood by the novel's end under McMurphy's tutelage without changing his physical appearance and by Bromden's revelation that McMurphy is no stereotyped beer advertisement he-man:

> I'd see him do things that didn't fit with his face or hands, things like painting a picture at OT with real paints on a blank paper with no lines or numbers . . . or like writing letters to someone in a beautiful flowing hand. . . . He hadn't let what he looked like run his life. . . .

Being a man is more than being physically strong or even courageous. It entails sensitivity and a commitment to other people, because manhood, as Kesey sees it, is not merely the quality of being male but of being human. What McMurphy teaches the inmates is not merely how to be aware and proud of their sexual identity but how to be human beings as well, responsible for one another. In the process, he himself develops greater maturity and responsibility, progressing from good-natured selfishness to a selfless commitment to his fellows.

As McMurphy's determination and influence increase, the threat posed by his sexual vitality is so clear that even the most superficial accoutrements

which attach to him—the sound of laughter and song, the smell of sweat—
are condemned by Big Nurse as disruptive and "dirty." Ultimately, the issue
is that McMurphy is opposed to sterility in both its medical and symbolic
implications. What makes this opposition particularly effective is that he is
not susceptible to the Combine's most insidious weapon, guilt. When Miss
Ratched assigns McMurphy the job of cleaning toilet bowls, he turns the
menial task into a humiliation for her rather than for himself, writing an
obscene word backward inside the rim of one bowl so that when she inspects
it with a hand mirror she is startled. She tells McMurphy that his job is to
make the place cleaner, not dirtier. The humor of the incident does not
detract from the serious thematic implication, the polarity between the
mechanical sterility of Big Nurse and the fertile animality of McMurphy.

The barrier between the two is a tangible as well as a symbolic one: the
glass shield which surrounds the nurses' station, separating Big Nurse from
the men but allowing her to spy on them. McMurphy calls the enclosed
office a "Hothouse," an intuitive metaphor which strikes at the heart of the
issue, for the office is the center of a sterile environment which makes the
inmates dependent and thus unable to survive in the outside world. One of
the crucial events of the book is McMurphy's breaking of this barrier by
deliberately running his *hand* through it. The breaking of the protective
barrier, Big Nurse's horror, the presence of blood, and the recurrence of the
hand as symbol emphasize the sexual implications of the act as well as the
movement from sterility to fertility represented throughout by McMurphy.

Big Nurse has a number of allies and subordinate satellites, notably the
supervisor of the hospital, another old army nurse who is a lifelong friend of
Miss Ratched. A second friend and ally is the hospital receptionist, mother
of Billy Bibbit. Billy is a particularly sympathetic character who, under the
double load of two mothers, his own and Miss Ratched, is ultimately broken.
On the other extreme of the female hierarchy is Candy, a whore friend of
McMurphy who is feminine in a most attractive way. She likes men, enjoys
sex, and ultimately holds out the only hope Billy Bibbit has ever had of
becoming a man. Associated with Candy are several similar women,
including her companion Sandy and the sexually open women who come
alive in McMurphy's tales of his past.

The clearest example of the American woman caught indecisively in
the untenable position between these two extremes is Vera Harding, Dale's
wife. Like Nurse Ratched, she is big-breasted and garishly disguised by
cosmetics; and like Ratched, she has subtly contributed to the erosion of her
husband's masculinity. Nonetheless, Vera Harding still possesses the potential to move toward the camp of Candy, as Kesey shows in a scene in which
she meets and flirts with McMurphy. Although Vera uses her sexuality as a

weapon of subjugation, she is at least aware and proud of it. In her conversation with McMurphy, Vera reveals herself as a person who moves instinctively in search of a viable heterosexual relationship; despite her dubious methods and her own lack of perception about her plight, her harsh qualities are mitigated somewhat. Although Vera has damaged her husband's sense of sexual identity, he has failed her in similar fashion by abdicating too readily the responsibilities of the male role. It is one measure of the qualified hope Kesey offers for future male-female relations in America that by the novel's end Dale Harding is able to accept some of this responsibility and sign himself out of the hospital to try again, armed with a new honesty derived from his contact with McMurphy.

Those inmates who are totally irreclaimable by society for use as tools are, significantly, termed "vegetables." But there are intermediate steps in the dehumanizing process; and in their regressive development toward their ultimate roles as machines or vegetables, the patients, brutalized by Big Nurse and her orderlies, are pointedly and repeatedly compared by Kesey to various animals: a dog, a bug, a gorilla, a mare, a moose, and a mustang, among others.

In addition, several extended patterns of animal imagery are employed by Kesey. Early in the book, Harding expresses to McMurphy his own metaphor for the situation in the ward. He sees himself and his fellow inmates as rabbits incapable of surviving without the repressive supervision of a wolf such as Miss Ratched. He suggests that McMurphy too may be a wolf. Although McMurphy rejects Harding's metaphor, annoyed that the patients can consider themselves anything but men, he has already ventured an analogy of his own, describing the first group therapy meeting he attends as a "bunch of chickens at a peckin' party."

Other bird images occur as well. When Bromden first attempts to laugh, he sounds "like a pullet trying to crow." Miss Ratched is often compared to a buzzard. The novel's title makes use of a slang connotation of "cuckoo." But the image pattern which is set in direct opposition to the pejorative connotations of the chicken simile is that which attaches to the wild goose. Although early references to the goose are humorous and deprecating (McMurphy and Harding argue over the dubious honor of who is to be the "bull goose loony," and later Harding evaluates McMurphy's sensitivity as no more than that of a goose), this bird comes to represent the pride and self-determination to which men should aspire. When, on his way to recovery, Bromden looks out of the dormitory window at night, viewing the outside world clearly for the first time in many years, he sees a young dog excitedly exploring for new experiences. Then, both Bromden and the dog are entranced by the majestic passage of a flock of Canada honkers:

> I heard a high, laughing gabble. . . . Then they crossed the
> moon—a black, weaving necklace, drawn into a V by that lead
> goose. For an instant that lead goose was right in the center of
> that circle, bigger than the others, a black cross opening and
> closing. . . .

This passage suggests an interpretation of the novel's title. McMurphy,
"bigger than the others," wild and free and migratory, is like the lead goose,
pulling his followers in the direction he has chosen. Never truly trapped
and grounded by the ward's restrictions, McMurphy does fly over the
"cuckoo's nest." In fact, upon his first admission to the ward, McMurphy
"sounds like he's . . . sailing fifty yards overhead, hollering at those below
on the ground. He sounds big." In addition, the "laughing" sound of the
geese's gabble and the metaphor of the cross echo patterns which attach to
McMurphy, as does the fact that in the center of the moon's circle the lead
goose wears a sort of halo.

If at this point the goose symbolism attaches primarily to McMurphy,
the young dog is associated with Bromden. In the episode quoted above,
both Bromden and the dog experience the awakening of new sensations.
During his escape, Bromden runs "in the direction I remember seeing the
dog go." The symbol cluster of goose and dog is, however, a complex one, in
which Bromden is ultimately associated with the goose and McMurphy with
the dog. Insofar as he grows "bigger," takes over McMurphy's leadership
role, and ultimately flies from the "cuckoo's nest"—"I felt like I was flying.
Free."—Bromden assumes the strengths of the Canada honker. His ultimate
destination is Canada.

Perhaps the most poignant aspect of this pattern is the foreshadowing
of McMurphy's fate by that of the dog. The last glimpse Bromden has of the
dog, before he is pulled from the window by the night nurse, Miss Pilbow,
shows the animal heading toward the highway, "loping steady and solemn like
he had an appointment." A car comes out of a turn, and Bromden sees the
"dog and the car making for the same spot of pavement." Later, when
McMurphy is about to make the difficult decision to escalate his rebellion
against Big Nurse, he is compared to a dog overcoming his fear of a
dangerous adversary; and just before McMurphy announces his decision by
breaking the window of the nurses' station, Bromden hears a sound in his
head "like tires speeding down a pavement." The implicit parallel is clear:
McMurphy and the dog, vital and vulnerable, move inexorably toward their
head-on collisions with massive machines—the Combine and the car.

The credibility of McMurphy's character stems largely from the fact
that several times in the escalating struggle with Big Nurse he falters,
backing off before taking the painful step to the next plateau of courage and

commitment. Bromden's growing personal involvement in McMurphy's battle is emphasized by the fact that his narration is clearly influenced in tone and content by McMurphy's behavior. When McMurphy succeeds in a particularly absurd practical joke at Big Nurse's expense, Bromden recalls similar situations perpetrated upon white bureaucrats by his father and other tribesmen, in the happier time before Pine-That-Stands-Tallest-on-the-Mountain was beaten by Mrs. Bromden and the Combine. During periods of victory by McMurphy, Bromden's perceptions become clearer, and he recognizes the therapeutic effect of laughter and sheer animal vitality.

The most obvious indication of Bromden's reaction to McMurphy's successes is the temporary shutting down of the fog machine, a nonexistent device, palpably real to Bromden, which grows out of his experience with real fog machines at an English airfield in World War II. Kesey uses it as a recurrent metaphor which serves to elucidate Bromden's ambivalent attitude toward his own madness. The fog machine provides Bromden an excuse to remain camouflaged in a docile role which, because it presents no threat to the Combine, allows him some measure of security. McMurphy's function, which Bromden resists at first, is to draw the Chief out of that refuge into open resistance to the Combine.

When McMurphy does falter momentarily, the possibility that he is little different from the other inmates is seized upon by Bromden with ostensible relief. The word he uses most often to describe McMurphy's behavior during such quiescent periods is "cagey." Bromden sees "caginess" as a necessary and perhaps even admirable trait, the capacity to survive through cunning. He is correct to a limited extent, and it will be his Indian "caginess" which, combined with the physical courage transmitted to him by McMurphy, will enable him to survive. But the word as applied by Bromden in the earlier stages of the book to the total abandonment of struggle against Big Nurse's rule is no more than a euphemism for cowardice. Bromden affects relief at McMurphy's first setbacks and resultant caution because any success on McMurphy's part exposes Bromden to the painful awareness that struggle against the Combine is possible and to the heavy responsibility of trying to be a man. More introspective than ever, Bromden has, under McMurphy's influence, begun a painfully honest reappraisal of his own identity problem:

> . . . I'd take a look at my own self in the mirror and wonder how it was possible that anybody could manage such an enormous thing as being what he was. . . . It don't seem like I ever have been me. How can McMurphy be what he is?

By accepting society's evaluation of him, Bromden has abdicated the frightening responsibility of defining himself. Forced by McMurphy's example to face this responsibility, he is understandably ready to grasp at any rationalization which will once again free him from it. Seeing McMurphy acting cagey provides such a rationalization. But no matter how much Bromden insists upon his admiration for caginess, he betrays his disappointment subconsciously by an immediate retrogression from his progress toward rehabilitation each time McMurphy seems beaten or stalemated. His memories of the tribe become unpleasant, and he remembers how his father, under pressure from society and his wife, slipped from bold resistance to caginess to alcoholic defeat: "My Papa was full Chief. . . . He was real big when I was a kid. My mother got twice his size. . . . He fought [the Combine] a long time till my mother made him too little to fight any more and he gave up."

The metaphor of physical size is one which grows naturally out of the erectile imagery introduced in the first McMurphy-Bromden meeting. In his hallucinatory understanding of his father's downfall, Bromden remembers him shrinking in size; and although he himself is still a physical giant, he perceives himself as small and weak. In an irony so painful that it loses all humor, Bromden stands on the floor of the swimming pool while McMurphy treads water next to him and blithely tells the reader that McMurphy "must of been standing in a hole." Again, Bromden tells McMurphy later, "You're . . . lot bigger . . . 'n I am." It is McMurphy's stated task to make Bromden "big" again by making him aware of his own identity.

The swimming pool episode has more far-reaching ramifications. In conversation with the life-guard, McMurphy learns for the first time that he, unlike most of the other inmates, is committed and that his release from the hospital can be withheld indefinitely. A major faltering point for McMurphy follows, with the result that Cheswick, an inmate who had begun to develop resistance to the Combine in emulation of McMurphy, loses all hope and commits suicide by drowning on the next swimming day. This marks the second in a group of three progressively more significant suicides. The first was the self-executed castration of Rawler; the third will be that of Billy Bibbit.

McMurphy's reaction to Cheswick's death and to the concomitant loss of hope by the other patients is not long in coming. After a period of unprecedented personal anguish, he makes the clear moral choice to abandon self-interest and fight the Combine once again. For a time, McMurphy is again in the ascendant. The patients begin to gain confidence, and Big Nurse returns to her frighteningly patient biding of time. It is during this period that McMurphy conceives of the fishing trip.

The patients' fishing trip is a hilarious sequence that is significant in the further development of the central characters. Its humor intensifies the tragedy to follow, and the primary symbol which informs it, that of McMurphy as Christ figure, lends substance to the progressive series of moral steps still to be taken by McMurphy. The parallel is drawn most explicitly and with a wry awareness of its overt quality in a conversation between Harding and McMurphy, during which the former explains the procedure of electro shock therapy: "A device that might be said to do the work of the sleeping pill, the electric chair, *and* the torture rack. . . . You are strapped to a table, shaped, iron- ically, like a cross, with a crown of electric sparks in place of thorns." Toward the book's conclusion, when McMurphy has brought EST upon himself, he echoes the comparison:

> Climbs on the table without any help and spreads his arms out.
> . . . A switch snaps the clasps on his wrists, ankles, clamping
> him. . . . They put graphite salve on his temples. "What is it?"
> he says. "Conductant," the technician says. "Anointest my head
> with conductant. Do I get a crown of thorns?. . . ." Put on those
> things like headphones, crown of silver thorns. . . .

These are by no means isolated instances of the Christ metaphor. Before the fishing trip, which is attended by twelve followers of McMurphy, including Candy, who is decidedly Magdalene-like in her sweet, generous compassion, Billy Bibbit is advised by his fellow inmate Ellis to "be a fisher of men."

The more significant aspects of McMurphy's role as savior lie not in such simple symbolic leads but in the moral circumstances of his situation. He is, to begin with, fated. Bromden has shown us that no man can meet the Combine head on and escape retribution. Yet McMurphy, a cunning man who prides himself on playing the percentages and on gambling boldly only for personal gain, chooses again and again to fight Big Nurse in increasingly overt ways until his doom is sealed and his victory assured. Kesey takes pains to show us that McMurphy becomes fully aware at an early stage of the conflict that he is dooming himself, an awareness which is echoed (in a humorously melodramatic flamboyance) by one of the tattoos on McMurphy's arm: aces and eights, the "dead man's hand." Finally, given an easy opportunity to escape from the hospital near the end of the novel, he refuses by making a transparent excuse of fatigue and allowing himself to be trapped by oversleeping. Even when offered a chance to escape further shock treatments and lobotomy by admitting that his actions (and hence his teach- ings and morality) are wrong, McMurphy refuses.

The significance of McMurphy's hands looms still larger when it begins to coincide with the Christ imagery. McMurphy's hands, already scarred by experience, are cut repeatedly in the course of his hospital stay. One such instance is that of the glass shield. Another, the attempt to lift the control panel, is particularly worthy of note because it is a pivotal episode in the development of the men's loyalty to McMurphy.

At a point when the men are still unwilling to take the risk of voting with McMurphy for the privilege of watching the World Series on television, he maneuvers them into a discussion of possible escape methods and then into a bet on whether he is capable of lifting a massive, obsolete control panel, formerly used to regulate water therapy and resembling a torture device. It is four hundred pounds of steel and concrete, no longer of any use to the Combine; but during McMurphy's attempt to lift it (and finally in Bromden's successful use of it as a battering ram in his escape), it comes to represent the monolithic weight of the Combine, a machinery which claims to be invulnerable to the efforts of any single man to move it.

The men, all of whom have lost money to McMurphy gambling, seize gleefully on the sure bet he offers them. As at the end of the book, McMurphy fails physically but wins a clear moral victory.

> His whole body shakes with the strain as he tries to lift something he *knows* he can't lift, something *everybody* knows he can't lift. . . . Then his breath explodes out of him, and he falls back limp. . . . There's blood on the levers where he tore his hands . . . he fishes in his pockets for all the IOU's he won the last few days at poker. . . . "But I tried, though," he says.

The attempt provides an insight into McMurphy's character for the inmates as well as the reader. The lesson that one must strive to be and do more than one thinks he can is one of the more important aspects of the legacy McMurphy will leave them. Furthermore, he has given the lie to his often-proclaimed policy of shrewd self-interest and at the same time given the others a taste of victory by letting them win back their money. The immediate result is that those present do vote for the World Series proposal, including Bromden, for whom it is a daring step back into the world.

Bromden has said only a giant could lift the control panel. Later he sees McMurphy as a "giant come out of the sky to save us." By the conclusion of the novel, Bromden has come to realize that this is a false evaluation and a false hope. Despite his size and strength, his courage and colossal vitality, the flamboyant mannerisms which make him resemble a comic-book hero, McMurphy is not a giant but a man; and Bromden's salvation will come from within.

Bromden has idealized McMurphy, but Nurse Ratched makes an equally great error in underestimating him. In a meeting with the medical staff (whom she dominates), she defines McMurphy pejoratively in terms of his humanity: "I don't agree that he is some kind of extraordinary being—

some kind of 'super' psychopath. . . . He is simply a man and no more, and is subject to all the fears and all the cowardice and all the timidity that any other man is subject to." McMurphy is most certainly subject to human fears and weaknesses. The difference between him and the "rabbits" who have hitherto constituted Big Nurse's experience with inmates is that he refuses to be governed and debilitated by these limitations. Despite McMurphy's recognition of his own vulnerability and mortality, he sets himself to a constant testing of the limits of the human condition. Although he is not superhuman, he does show himself to be extraordinary.

Big Nurse has smugly dismissed McMurphy as "simply a man and no more," but by the climax of their confrontation he will have shown her that being a man, rising to the heights of human potential, is enough. In addition, he will demonstrate that she is no invincible machine but simply a woman, a human being with all the attendant human vulnerability and fallibility.

At one point, during McMurphy's temporary absence from the ward, Big Nurse asks the patients whether they consider him "a martyr or a saint." They agree that he is neither, and in pressing her point (the essential self-interest which she feels is McMurphy's constant motivation), she reiterates these terms several times. The consummate irony, of course, is that McMurphy, for all his pretensions to the role of cunning con man, is to rise to heights of selfless sacrifice bordering on the saintly, while Big Nurse, smugly confident of her own moral superiority, reaches the nadir of her function as agent of repression. By underestimating the commitment and courage of which her adversary is capable, she undertakes a struggle which is to end in a true martyrdom for him and in her own irrevocable defeat.

Other references to Christ and Christianity which seem at first to bear no consistent relationship to the pattern which attaches to McMurphy emerge finally as part of a sophisticated statement on organized religion. One of these is provided by the inmate Ellis who, his sensibilities bludgeoned by repeated EST treatments, stands perpetually in the attitude of crucifixion. One of the Combine's most bizarre failures, Ellis is a clearly symbolic example of the atrocities it commits in the name of society.

Still more revealing of Kesey's intent is the treatment of another peripheral character, the anxiety-ridden Nurse Pilbow. A devout Catholic, she has a morbid fear of sex and a hatred of her patients, especially McMurphy, whom she considers a sex maniac. The tangible representation of Miss Pilbow's repressed sexuality is her hideous purple birthmark, which is itself the subject of one of Bromden's hallucinatory perceptions of truth. Pilbow persists in the attempt to externalize evil. Her denial of her sexual instincts has resulted in hatred and fear rather than love and acceptance. Her rigidly prescriptive morality, when held in ludicrous juxtaposition to

McMurphy's guiltless, relaxed, and fertile pleasure in life, suggests that the organized church has failed to bring the essential Christian message of love to the people. And in perpetrating the kind of rigid morality which has scarred not only Pilbow but most of the inmates, organized religion has become an arm of the Combine.

McMurphy, in opposing this, is performing a function similar to that of Christ: attacking an outmoded morality and sweeping away its hypocrisies while assimilating and perpetuating its positive aspects in a new moral code. Thus, although McMurphy espouses an apparently amoral sexuality, he infuses his followers with a brotherly love which is distinctly Christian and which a mechanistic society has forgotten.

From the outset, McMurphy has been aware that guerrilla action is the method by which Big Nurse may be harassed safely. But as Miss Ratched, after losing a few hands, calmly continues to raise the stakes from behind her mechanical poker face, McMurphy is forced to choose between backing off and calling her bluff.

What keeps the contest from becoming either morbidly dull or unbearably terrifying to the reader is Kesey's capacity to render absurd humor. Toward the end of the book, Harding says of the farewell party for McMurphy, "It isn't happening. It's all a collaboration of Kafka and Mark Twain. . . ." and one gets the idea that Kesey extends this judgment to the entire world of the Combine.

It is in this spirit of easygoing humor that McMurphy begins to break through Bromden's defenses and draw him back into the world. Although the central improvement in Bromden is psychological, its outward manifestations are tied to the metaphor of physical size and potency. When the partially reclaimed Bromden lies awake, anxious to go on the fishing trip, McMurphy talks to him and offers to make him "big" again. After listening to McMurphy describe the two whores who are coming on the trip, Bromden experiences his first erection in many years; and McMurphy, pulling back the blankets, bawdily puns, "look there, Chief. . . . You growed a half a foot already." The pun is significantly close to literal truth, for sexual potency is shown as both a symptom and a function of masculine identity; Bromden's new self-awareness will result in a fearsome potency which thwarts the Combine and its agents, combined with a commitment to his fellow inmates which spells hope for all men.

After the fishing trip, events proceed rapidly and inexorably to a conclusion. Although the trip is a great success for the men, who return to an awareness of a more primitive, active, fertile world and bring that awareness back to contaminate and erode the sterility of the hospital, McMurphy pays a high personal price. Pushing and carrying them back to life drains his stores of vitality. During the drive back to the hospital, he entertains the men with tales of his exploits: "[he] doled out his life for us to live . . . full of . . . loving women and barroom battles over meager honors. . . ." But the lights of a passing car reveal to Bromden that McMurphy's face looks "dreadfully tired and strained and *frantic*, like there wasn't enough time left for something he had to do. . . ." McMurphy is clearly aware that the men are feeding vicariously off his energies and is even more acutely aware of the greater sacrifice to come. But, as Bromden later points out, McMurphy could never have avoided the final battle because, as is shown by his memory of "barroom battles over *meager* honors," he knows that in life the fight itself is what matters.

The battle lines are drawn by the agents of the Combine; but instead of demoralizing the men, this pulls them closer together. In defense of another inmate, and with resignation rather than anger, McMurphy allows an orderly to goad him into a fistfight which he knows will provide Big Nurse the excuse she needs to bring more formidable weapons into play. Perhaps more significant is the fact that Bromden, accepting responsibility for his fellow man, steps in to help McMurphy when he is outnumbered.

From this point on, Bromden is his own man, growing in strength as McMurphy declines. The two go together to the EST room. For Bromden, this shock treatment, his last ever, is a turning point. With McMurphy as an example, he fights his panic, takes his treatment, and then works his way back out of the fog, never to hide in it again. Bromden returns to the ward to be greeted as a hero by the other men, largely assuming McMurphy's former position, while McMurphy, the focus of Big Nurse's vengeance, undergoes repeated shock treatments.

With no end to the treatments in sight and Big Nurse considering more drastic methods, it is decided that McMurphy's escape from the hospital must be engineered. McMurphy agrees but insists on postponing his departure until after a secret midnight visit from Candy and her friend Sandy, which turns into a farewell party, fueled by cocktails made of codeine-based cough syrup and a few friendly tokes of marijuana with Mr. Turkle.

The party is a success on every level. Billy Bibbit loses his virginity to Candy in the seclusion room, the men draw closer together and begin to entertain hopes of overcoming the control of the Combine, and McMurphy's escape before dawn, using Turkle's key to unlock a window, is assured. Bromden articulates the full significance of the rebellion: "I had to keep reminding myself that it had *truly* happened, that we had made it happen. . . . Maybe the Combine wasn't all-powerful." But although they have in the past overestimated the strength of the Combine and Big Nurse, this time Bromden and the others have underestimated it. It is only McMurphy who still recognizes the extent of the control held over the men and understands the fact that his own complete sacrifice is necessary to effect their freedom. He decides to take a nap before leaving, "accidentally" oversleeps, and is discovered by the morning staff.

In retrospect, Bromden is able to understand McMurphy's motives and the inevitability of the events to follow:

> . . . it was bound to be and would have happened in one way or another . . . even if Mr. Turkle had got McMurphy . . . off the ward like was planned. . . . McMurphy would have . . . come back . . . he could [not] have . . . let the Big Nurse have the last move . . . It was like he'd signed on for the whole game. . . .

When Billy Bibbit is discovered asleep in Candy's arms (a scene notable for its childlike innocence), Big Nurse proceeds to barrage him with recriminations until the old habit patterns of guilt and dependence are reawakened. Moments later, Billy commits suicide by cutting his throat.

Nurse Ratched's reaction is typical of her smug confidence in the infallibility of her own Combine-sanctioned values. She lays the blame immediately at McMurphy's feet. Bromden watches him

> . . . in his chair in the corner, resting a second before he came out for the next round. . . . The thing he was fighting, you couldn't whip it for good. All you could do was keep on whipping it, till you couldn't come out any more and somebody else had to take your place.

Bromden is the man who will take McMurphy's place, and because of this he understands what McMurphy must do. He is acting as an agent for all the men, and as Bromden realizes, "We couldn't stop him because we were the ones making him do it." In his final, physical attack on Nurse Ratched, McMurphy rips her starched uniform off, tearing down her insulation as he did with the glass wall, exposing her large, fleshy breasts, and making it clear that she is a vulnerable woman rather than an invincible machine. She will never again command absolute power over the inmates.

The aftermath is the complete disintegration of Miss Ratched's rule. Most of the men sign themselves out, but Bromden postpones his departure because he suspects that Big Nurse may make one last play. He is correct: One day, McMurphy, now a vegetable after undergoing a lobotomy (perhaps the ultimate castration), is wheeled back into the ward. In a scene characterized by an intense intimacy, Bromden performs a merciful service for McMurphy, smothering him to death. The transfer of power is complete. Bromden picks up McMurphy's hat, tries it on, and finds it too small. He feels "ashamed" at trying to wear it because he knows that McMurphy has taught him that one must find one's own identity. Then he picks up the control panel, smashes it through a window, and makes his escape.

Bromden is McMurphy's most successful disciple. It is not until the very end of the novel, however, that it becomes clear that Bromden has surpassed his teacher in the capacity to survive in American society and to maintain personal identity in spite of the Combine. It must be remembered that Bromden is a half-breed and that this mixed heritage has been a major contributing factor to his severe alienation and identity problems. But Bromden shows that his half-breed status also represents a capacity to combine the strengths of both the Indian and the white man. From his father he inherited a functional cunning, a patient caution which in its original form was conducive to both survival and pride. Although this quality has been perverted into the fearful "caginess" he once practiced and professed to admire, it is, in a less extreme form, a valuable attribute.

From the first page, it is clear that Bromden has long practiced the tactic of evasion against the onslaughts of the Combine. The price he has paid in loss of pride and identity obscures for a time the undeniable fact that he is the only man who has *fooled* the Combine successfully: Big Nurse and her staff believe that Bromden is a deaf-mute, and he is able to eavesdrop safely on their most private dealings. McMurphy, because he fights the Combine head-on, dies; but Bromden, who learns to practice a fusion of evasive cunning and sheer courage, survives as the hope for the future.

It is clear that one need not have the physical prowess of a McMurphy or a Bromden to renounce rabbithood and become a man. Kesey suggests that someone like Dale Harding has a very real chance to thwart the Combine, and even Billy Bibbit is able to go part of the way. Despite Billy's failure, Kesey's feeling is clear: It is better to be destroyed in the attempt to fight the Combine than to accept the role of rabbit for life.

Randle Patrick McMurphy is a compelling figure. Into the sterility of Bromden's world and the stifling American society it represents, he brings a breath, a breeze, a wind of change. In the wasteland of the ward, his sexual vitality makes him loom as a figure of mythic proportions. Yet the most important part of the legacy he has left Bromden and his fellows is that he was just a man. And that, finally, is enough.

M. GILBERT PORTER

# The Plucky Love Song of Chief "Broom" Bromden: Poetry from Fragments

*A song of love is a sad song,*
*Hi-lili, hi-lily, hi-lo . . .*
—Helen Deutsch and
Bronislaw Kaper

*Hey Jude, don't make it bad*
*Take a sad song and make it better.*
—The Beatles

## The Big Picture

*O*ne *Flew Over the Cuckoo's Nest* examines the disturbing effects of dehumanization in modern society. People have become things. Men have become chronics, acutes, and vegetables. Women have become either confused puppets of a security-obsessed system or misguided "terrible mother" figures who perpetuate dependency relationships. Big Brother has given way to Big Nurse. Society has become an intimidating force for consumerism and conformity called a "Combine." The Combine and Big Nurse are presented as the ostensible enemies in the novel, but they prove at last to be only manifestations of the problem, not the cause of it—as a water moccasin in the well is the occasion for horror, not the source of it. The real

From *The Art of Grit: Ken Kesey's Fiction.* © 1982 by University of Missouri Press.

enemy in Kesey's view is the failure of self-reliance growing out of fear. Bird-like, the men have submitted to the snake-eyed hypnosis of social and institutional forces, acquiescing in their own victimization.

McMurphy discovers that most of the men in the cuckoo's nest are there voluntarily. Facing their individual incapacities and the complexity of the world, they have consigned themselves to passive escape. They cower in their wards, as Harding says, "like rabbits." Fearing disorder, Big Nurse has devoted herself zealously to control for its own sake, becoming a servant of the system and a tyrant over the men on the ward, both a victim and a victimizer. All of them, however, have submitted out of fear to the mindless machinery of a collective will that operates at the expense of the individual.

A free spirit and fearless individual, McMurphy can perceive the problem because he stands apart from the conformity-stricken world that the cuckoo's nest reflects, like a funhouse mirror, in all of its grotesque distortions. To their weakness and fear he brings strength and courage born of mythical American rebellion, from the wayward human charm of Huck Finn to the fierce superhuman protectiveness of the Lone Ranger. McMurphy pits his will to live against their will to die (implied in everyone's passivity, pathetically enacted by Cheswick and Billy Bibbit). Ironically, their lives are granted only in exchange for his death, a messianic bargain that McMurphy heroically agrees to in the name of values larger than his individual life, but all of them subsumed under the banner of Love and attended by tragicomic Christian symbolism.

The strategy of the novel places McMurphy between the power represented by the Big Nurse and the weakness represented by the men. The impact of the novel inheres in the transformation McMurphy effects in the ward to strengthen the weak against the powerful, particularly in the case of Bromden. That a man of Bromden's potential strength could be reduced to a phony deaf and dumb broom-wielder lost in a defensive fog of his own creation testifies to the power and real danger of the Combine and Big Nurse—as do the problems of the men on the ward and the eventual deaths of Cheswick, Bibbit, and McMurphy himself. The change of Bromden into a courageous, self-reliant, strong defender of other weak souls testifies to the humanistic power of McMurphy, the salvific nature of love, and the validity of heroism. Imbued with the spirit of McMurphy, Bromden moves from one battleground to another, from passiveness on the mental ward to active conflict in the tribal village by the site of the government's new hydroelectric dam, to do for others what was done for him, to change fearful drunks into resistant men, to inspire each self to achieve its own true stature, to make things back into people. That is the message of the novel.

Kesey has embodied this vision artistically in a number of effective ways, employing humor, allusion, contrasting image patterns, caricature, and the Christian symbolism, but his most important devices are a poetic first-person point of view and a prose use of synecdoche. As synecdochist, Kesey seeks to make a whole from scattered parts. In the novel the task assumes the form of McMurphy's evolved mission to restore to wholeness the fragments of men in the ward (spare parts for whom Bromden imagines to be in the Big Nurse's wicker bag). Thus Kesey uses motifs of significant parts: laughs, hands, faces. Each motif is fully developed and tightly integrated into the novel's central design, and Bromden as narrator is the most important device in Kesey's use of synecdoche. The most broken of all the fragmented lives in the story, Bromden's is the most dramatically restored at the end. His developing mental health is a paradigm writ large for the similar development of the others. The presentation of the story through the tortured consciousness of a sick man who becomes well enables the reader to move with Bromden from the stultifying fog of fear to the sunlit sky of human freedom and possibility. Bromden, then, is Kesey's poet and synecdochist. He is a fragmented man viewing fragmented men from a psychic distance that distorts wholes yet clarifies parts. Under McMurphy's provocative influence, though, he moves to the control of his faculties and the ability to see the world steadily and whole. His progress toward final integrated vision is the integrating principle in the novel and thus the focus of critical attention here.

## Bromden: Poetic Sensibility in the Fog

Like the stereotypical invisibility of Ellison's Invisible Man, the initial deafness and dumbness of Chief Broom is a condition he discovers, not one he creates. Breaking his silence of many years, he reveals to McMurphy one night on the ward that "it wasn't me that started acting deaf; it was people that first started acting like I was too dumb to hear or see or say anything at all." He remembers painfully that at ten years old he was ignored by the government purchasing agents who came to buy the tribal lands; this early sense of insignificance was intensified as he witnessed the Combine's reduction of his father, Tee Ah Millatoona (The-Pine-That-Stands-Tallest-on-the-Mountain), to a miniature of his former manhood. To his surrogate father, McMurphy, Bromden describes the final image he has of his real father: "And the last I see him he's blind in the cedars from drinking and every time I see him put the bottle to his mouth he don't suck out of it, it sucks out of him . . . and we had to cart him out of the cedars, in a pickup, to a place in Portland, to die." The demonstrated power of the Combine and

Bromden's growing sense of his own insignificance lead him to cultivate his deafness and dumbness as a psychological defense.

Although Bromden discovers and then exploits his role as deaf-mute, he creates from actual experience the fantasy-fog that enables him to withdraw even farther from a confusing world. Bromden first encountered fog machines in the military service overseas, where they were used to camouflage airfields and protect troops from enemy fire. In that surreal, artificial cloud, men groped for direction, fearing danger from without and confronting startling revelations from within: "And then some guy wandering as lost as you would all of a sudden be right before your eyes, his face bigger and clearer than you ever saw a man's face before in your life. Your eyes were working so hard to see in that fog that when something did come in sight every detail was ten times as clear as usual." Significantly, one found his way out of this military fog "by following a . . . horn, sounded like a goose honking." Since Bromden is the only one who ever comments on the "fog machine" in the ward, he is clearly imagining its presence there, but he is willfully producing its effect to protect himself from danger. Whenever things get troublesome, Bromden escapes into his mental fog. That he is reconciled to such escape is a measure of his sickness. "Being lost," he says, "isn't so bad." That he reports the fog accurately—or slips into it in the form of a blank page—is a measure of his reliability as a narrator despite his feigned malady and fragmented vision.

For there are really two Bromdens in the novel. One is the narrator-participant, who opens the novel in the ward with the scared comment, "They're out there," and who relives his experiences through an unconventionally recreated historical present. This Bromden thinks of himself as "little," fears everything, escapes into his fog, touchingly enters the pastoral painting on the wall to distance himself from ridicule, and reports his distorted but detached perceptions with a sharpness alive with pain. To him the Big Nurse in anger is a thundering eighteen wheeler, the sexual shame of the Roman Catholic nurse leads her to attack her birthmark with a wire brush, the death of the old vegetable Blastic is a descent into the demonic machinery of the hospital's underworld, and time is a metaphysical commodity controlled arbitrarily—and sometimes packaged in plastic—from the glass-enclosed nurse's station. His subjective distortions carry the weight of impressionistic truth.

The other Bromden is the narrator-observer, who is both aware of his role as narrator and sensitive to the issue of the reliability of his report as a recent inmate of a mental institution. His time is an analytical Now, connected to but distinguishable from the historical present, like the stable rope that secures the twisting tire swing. This Bromden frequently detaches himself from the action to comment on himself and the others. He does so amid the celebrative laughter of the fishing scene, for example: "I watched, part of them, laughing with them—and somehow not with them. I was off the boat, blown up off the water and skating the wind with those black birds, high above myself, and I could look down and see myself and the rest of the guys." At other times he reflects deliberately on the turns his tale takes: "I've given what happened next a good lot of thought, and I've come around to thinking that it was bound to be and would have happened in one way or another . . . even if Mr. Turkle had got McMurphy and the two girls up and off the ward like was planned." And it is this narrator-observer who at the outset calls attention to the retrospective/re-creative complexity of his narration and to the complicated nature of its reliability:

> It's gonna burn me . . . finally telling about all this, about the hospital, and her, and the guys—and about McMurphy. I been silent so long now it's gonna roar out of me like floodwaters and you think the guy telling this is ranting and raving my *God*; you think this is too horrible to have really happened, this is too awful to be the truth! But, please. It's still hard for me to have a clear mind thinking on it. But it's the truth even if it didn't happen.

Although this statement ends the first chapter, it fits chronologically after Bromden's admission at the end, "I been away a long time." Having just emerged, battered, from his long subjection to the stings and sorrows of outrageous therapeutics, he looks back on his experiences, relives them, and reports them exactly as he recalls them in an exercise of psychic ordering. To articulate his experience is to possess it and control it. His observation that "it's the truth even if it didn't happen" is not an admission that his narrative is the raving of a madman, but the acknowledgment that he cannot always sort out in the "floodwaters" of memory and impression the actual from the hallucinatory, the real from the surreal. Both were true to his experience, and he wishes to report them as he lived them in his movement from fragmentation to wholeness, from chronic to man.

Bromden's narrative achieves the universal validity that Aristotle claimed for imaginative, mimetic literature. It transcends the limitations of both historical fact and philosophic abstraction. It emerges as an "impossible probability," convincing in its consistency, appropriateness to character, and ultimate wholeness. For whatever else Bromden may be at any stage of his development—Vanishing American, coward, schizoid, rebel, heroic reformer—he is always a poet. Whether we are talking about Bromden-participant in the historical present or Bromden-observer in the analytical

Now—and these distinctions are occasionally blurred as he moves toward clarity—his hypersensitive perceptions are those of the seer, and his vivid descriptions are those of the sayer. He "translates the unseen into the seen, the abstract into the concrete, giving the Nurse's hatred or the patients' frustrations palpable, visible form."

Bromden's images, metaphors, and analogies are consistent with his character and appropriate to the figures or events he describes. He remembers his father, the full-blooded Columbia Indian chief, as "hard and shiny as a gunstock," whereas McMurphy, his new hero and father-surrogate, is "hard in a different kind of way from Papa, kind of the way a baseball is hard under the scuffed leather." He sees his fellow chronics as society's battered wrecks, moving toward demolition and often found "bleeding rust in some vacant lot." A young dog joyously sniffing digger squirrel holes in the wet grass and the moonlight appears to Bromden to be thrashing around "like a fish," then shakes off a spray "in the moon like silver scales." Empathetically reporting one of Sefelt's epileptic seizures, Bromden describes Sefelt's head hitting "the tile with a crack like rocks under water." The seizure over, Sefelt "melts limp all over the floor in a gray puddle." On the way to the coast in temporary though uneasy freedom, Bromden views birds as emblematic of the condition of the inmates worrying over their fetters and their flight to freedom: "the pigeons fretted up and down the sidewalk with their hands folded behind their backs," and "there was little brown birds occasionally on the fence; when a puff of leaves would hit the fence the birds would fly off with the wind. It looked at first like the leaves were hitting the fence and turning into birds and flying away." Bromden's machine images (gears, cogs, wheels, tubes, wires, the Combine) contrast throughout the novel with his images of nature (birds, animals, landscapes, water), but occasionally the images integrate nature and the machine in evidence of technological encroachment. He describes a commuter train, for example, "stopping at a station and laying a string of full-grown men in mirrored suits and machined hats, laying them like a hatch of identical insects . . . then hooting its electric whistle and moving on down the spoiled land to deposit another hatch." But whatever the image patterns, and even when the metaphors are mixed, Bromden employs imagery extensively, like a poet working his way to understanding. His concretions mark the path to clarity and poetic truth.

Bromden's movement to mental health is of a piece with the renewal of his senses and his poetic sensibilities. He reveals to McMurphy first that he can hear, then that he can speak. Under the health-giving influence of McMurphy, Bromden experiences the sharpening of his senses and the heightening of his perceptions. He begins to move out of the fog and into life. "For the first time in years," he admits, "I was seeing people with none of that black outline they used to have." Looking out the ward window one memorable night at the stars and the young, frolicking dog, Bromden feels the coldness of the window, smells the breeze, hears the popping of the window shade, tastes the "sour-molasses smell of silage," and, with all his senses at attention, witnesses the dog follow the lead of the honking geese through the moonlight away from the cuckoo's nest, an event that harks back to his past and prefigures his future. It is a poetic scene and an objective correlative of his own eventual liberation, for it carries the same ambivalence. The dog heads toward the highway and a set of headlights. Bromden will set out for the tribal falls on the new hydroelectric dam and further conflicts with the Combine. The point is clear: Life involves risks. Bromden indicates his willingness to take the risks in the image with which he couples his resolution to abandon the protective fog forever. Although after his last electroshock treatment he imagines himself inside dice showing snake-eyes—the throw in a dice game that eliminates one seeking to make his point—he is not intimidated by the odds. "I thought the room was a dice. The number one, the snake eye up there, the circle, the white *light* in the ceiling . . . in this little square room . . . means it's after dark. How many hours have I been out? It's fogging a little, but I won't slip off and hide in it. No . . . never again. . . ." The poet presents an image suggesting both the loaded dice of Fortune and the serpentine Christian symbol for Evil, but the man is not frightened by either. This time he knows he "has them beat." McMurphy's model probably serves Bromden here, too: The swaggering gambler plays life's game without caution despite the "aces and eights"—the deadman's hand—he has tattooed on his arm.

### Bromden as Rhymer

Another remarkable manifestation of Bromden's poetic faculty is his use of rhyme. The novel's title comes from a rhyming game Bromden learned from his grandmother (capitalization and versification added):

> Tingle, tingle, tremble toes
> She's a good fisherman,
> Catches hens,
> Puts 'em inna pens . . .
> Wire blier, limber lock,
> Three geese inna flock . . .
> One flew east, one flew west,
> One flew over the cuckoo's nest.

Bromden remembers that he disliked Mrs. Tangle Toes, who imprisoned free creatures, but he liked the game and he liked his grandmother. During his last electroshock treatment Bromden recalls, also in rhyme, a hunt with his father (capitalization and versification again added):

> Hit at a lope,
> Running already down the slope.
> Can't get back, can't go ahead,
> Look down the barrel an' you dead dead dead.

Rhyming, then, has long been a part of Bromden's consciousness and his subconscious word selection. The impulse to rhyme—an impulse to order—culminates in the afterglow of the restorative fishing trip. Here Bromden savors his feelings and reflects on the changes taking place within him as a result of his exposure to McMurphy and his gusto for life. "McMurphy was teaching me. I was feeling better than I'd remembered feeling since I was a kid, when everything was good and the land was still singing kids' poetry to me." Following this observation, Bromden gives an account of part of the day and a significant bit of McMurphy's personal history. The two-page passage is arranged as conventional prose, but it contains a striking number of rhyme words. Arranged as "poetry," the passage reads as follows:

### The Land Was Still Singing Kids' Poetry To Me

> We'd drove back inland instead of the coast,
> To go through this town McMurphy'd lived in the most
> He'd ever lived in one place.
> Down the face
> Of the Cascade Hill,
> Thinking we were lost till . . .
> We came to a town
> Covered a space
> About twice the size of the hospital ground.
> A gritty wind had blown out the sun
> On the street where he stopped.
> He parked in some reeds
> And pointed across the road.
> "There. That's the one.
> Looks like it's propped up outta the weeds—
> My misspent youth's humble abode."

Out along the dim six-o'clock street,
I saw leafless trees standing,
Striking the sidewalk there like wooden lightning,
Concrete split apart where they hit,
All in a fenced-in ring.
An iron line of pickets stuck out of the ground
Along the front of a tangleweed yard,
And on back was a big frame house
With a porch, leaning a rickety shoulder hard
Into the wind so's not to be sent tumbling away a couple of
    blocks
Like an empty cardboard grocery box.
The wind was blowing a few drops of rain,
And I saw the house had its eyes clenched shut and locks at
    the door banged on a chain.
And on the porch, hanging, was one of those things
The Japs make out of glass and hang on strings—
Rings and clangs in the least little blow—
With only four pieces of glass left to go.
These four swung and whipped
And rung little chips
Off on the wooden porch floor.

McMurphy put the car back in gear.
"Once, I been here—
Since way the hell gone back in the year
We were all gettin' home from that Korea mess.
For a visit.
My old man and old lady were still alive.
It was a good home."
He let out the clutch and started to drive,
Then stopped instead.
"My God," he said,
"Look over there, see
A dress?" He pointed out back.
"In the branch of that tree?
A rag, yellow and black?"
I was able to see
A thing like a flag,
Flapping high in the branches over a shed.

"The first girl ever drug me to bed
Wore that very same dress.
I was about ten and she was probably less,
And at the time a lay seemed like such a big deal
I asked her if didn't she think, *feel*,
We oughta *announce* it some way?
Like, say, tell our folks, 'Mom,
Judy and me got engaged today.'
And I meant what I said,
I was that big a fool;
I thought if you made it, man, you were legally wed,
Right there on the spot,
Whether it was something you wanted or not,
And that there wasn't any breaking the rule.
But this little whore—
At the most eight or nine—
Reached down and got her dress off the floor
And said it was mine,
Said, 'You can hang this up someplace,
I'll go home in my drawers,
Announce it that way—
They'll get the idea.'
Jesus, nine years old,"
He said, reached over and pinched Candy's nose,
"And knew a lot more than a good many pros."
She bit his hand, laughing,
And he studied the mark.
"So, anyhow, after she went home in her pants
I waited till dark when I had the chance
To throw that damned dress out in the night—
But you feel that wind? Caught the dress like a kite
And whipped it around the house outa sight
And the next morning, by God, it was hung up in that tree
For the whole town, was how I figured then, to turn out and
    see,"
He sucked his hand, so woebegone
That Candy laughed and gave it a kiss.
"So my colors were flown, and from that day to this
It seemed I might as well live up to my name—
Dedicated lover—and it's the God's truth:

> That little nine-year-old kid out of my youth's
> The one who's to blame."
> The house drifted past.
> He yawned and winked.
> "Taught me to love,
> Bless her sweet ass."

End rhymes provide the principle of line division here, and the stanzas are divided according to thought units. What emerges is a primitive poetry. Most lines are tetrameter with dominant iambic or anapestic feet, though there are many dimeter lines and hypermetric lines. No consistent rhyme scheme is developed, but enough couplets, triplets, internal and alternating rhymes occur to provide an aural pattern and, with the metrics, to justify the claim that Bromden's rhapsodic feelings, his phrasing of McMurphy's observations, and his own memories of the scene assume the jubilant form of exactly what Bromden designates them—kids' poetry. The poem showcases two major points: that McMurphy has long defined himself as a "dedicated lover," a role that sets up his messianic self-sacrifice, and that Bromden as the poet of the novel displays rhyme on his way to reason, celebrating the lover and the love that is a giving to others.

Whether distorted or detached, Bromden's observations are essentially poetic. He has both the special vision that characterizes the seer and the power of description that characterizes the sayer. His sentences are vivid with image, metaphor, simile, and analogy, rhythmical with meter, sometimes roughly harmonized with rhyme, and expansive with symbol. He also employs synecdoche as a central poetic element, and here Bromden, who is not conscious of his poetic devices, serves as Kesey's intimate functionary in the perception, articulation, and embodiment of the thematic progress from fragmentation to wholeness. Focusing with his fragmented vision on laughs, hands, faces, Bromden as partial man and synecdochist works his way toward completeness of character and vision and thus validation of Kesey's thesis that broken men—however frightened, beleaguered, splintered, and dehumanized—can be restored to manhood and wholeness. Though Bromden reports much of the story out of his personal fog, he has testified that in his fog, parts are especially revealing, because "your eyes were working so hard to see in that fog that when something did come in sight every detail was ten times as clear as usual." The clarity of parts leads Bromden—and the novel—eventually to the clarification of wholes.

## Bromden as Synecdochist

Bromden is very sensitive to the sound and significance of laughter, for example, or to its absence. For twenty years he has been confined in a ward where "the air is pressed in by the walls, too tight for laughing. There's something strange about a place where the men won't let themselves loose and laugh." Even the impulse to laugh is stifled: "They tell jokes to each other and snicker in their fists (nobody ever dares let loose and laugh . . . )." McMurphy, though, enters the ward and Bromden's consciousness laughing, with a laugh that "spreads in rings bigger and bigger till it's lapping against the walls all over the ward." Calling it "real" and the first laugh he has "heard in years," Bromden identifies the sound with the character: "Even when he isn't laughing, that laughing sound hovers around him, the way the sound hovers around a big bell just quit ringing." Such laughter is free, natural, healthy, honest, and celebrative.

Bromden encounters other laughter, however, of a much different stripe. The black aides belittle Bromden—"Big enough to eat apples off my head an' he mine me like a baby"—and laugh hatefully: "They laugh and then I hear them mumbling behind me . . . humming hate and death and other hospital secrets." Public Relation laughs constantly and mindlessly: "Public Relation's shirt collar is so tight it bloats his face up when he laughs, and he's laughing most of the time I don't ever know what at, laughing high and fast like he wishes he could stop but can't do it." His laughter is hysterical, a result of the stark discrepancy between the appearances he sells and the reality that belies them. The attendants at the service station near the hospital mock them when Dr. Spivey euphemistically calls them a "work crew": "Both of the guys laughed. I could tell by the laugh that they'd decided to sell us the gas—probably it would be weak and dirty and watered down and cost twice the usual price—but it didn't make me feel any better." Bromden's sense of worthlessness is intensified by the derisive laughter he and the other inmates hear at the docks, where a "bunch of loafers" were "making comments and sniggering and goosing one another in the ribs." Slipping into the pathetic fallacy in his misery, Bromden imagines even nonhuman elements ridiculing them: "The wind was blowing the boats at their moorings, nuzzling them up against the wet rubber tires along the dock so they made a sound like they were laughing at us. The water was giggling under the boards." Unhealthy laughter is a weapon, cutting sensitive spirits like Bromden to the quick.

Such intimidation imposes on the vulnerable a deathly silence, the clutch of the Combine on the throat. Bromden is a deaf-mute embodiment of the ultimate force of the intimidation, and he imagines how it begins in others in his poignant scenario of the little boy in the schoolyard who is forever cracked off the end of the whip into the fence in a symbolic game of crack-the-whip. All the other five thousand kids are a part of the whip and thus unidentifiable and interchangeable in the identical five thousand homes. The cracked-off kid is identifiable by his bruises and lacerations and thus does not fit in anywhere: "He wasn't able to open up and laugh either. It's a hard thing to laugh if you can feel the pressure of those beams coming from every new car that passes, or every new house you pass." The problem is the same in the ward, where Bromden sees a kind of "cartoon world . . . that might be real funny if it weren't for the cartoon figures being real guys. . . ."

The inability to laugh, then, is both a gauge of the Combine's pressure and, ironically, a tipped scale of psychic imbalance. "Man, when you lose your laugh," says McMurphy, "you lose your *footing*." In the cuckoo's nest he finds a ward full of men who have lost their footing and who are controlled by the humorless Big Nurse, whose mechanical "doll smile" cannot disguise her "little white knot of tight-smiled fury" or her Combine-inspired commitment to a world that runs "like a smooth, accurate, precision-made machine." "She has the ability to turn her smile into whatever expression she wants to use on somebody, but the look she turns it into is no different, just a calculated and mechanical expression to serve her purpose." Her therapy induces fear and silence. McMurphy's countertherapy leads to liberating laughter. Bromden perceives McMurphy's aims, but cannot, out of long habit, respond any faster than the rest of the inmates. During McMurphy's second day on the ward, Bromden observes the newcomer "being the clown working at getting some of the guys to laugh. It bothers him that the best they can do is grin weakly and snigger sometimes." Later he reports that McMurphy would "whack his leg and throw back his head and laugh and laugh, digging his thumb into the ribs of whoever was sitting next to him, trying to get him to laugh too." Though Bromden is slow to laugh, he is engaged by McMurphy and compares his laughter to the defensive laughter Tee Ah Millatoona used to turn against the white man, remarking, "I forget sometimes what laughter can do."

McMurphy's therapy and the laughter motif culminate in the fishing scene. Here the men, escaping all derision and pressure, finally achieve the liberating laughter McMurphy has labored so hard to teach them, and thus he, as a laughing Christ, becomes the "fisher of men" Ellis, a chronic, had called for. McMurphy's healing laughter that initially was "lapping against the walls all over the ward" has now been multiplied by twelve disciples and cast on the waters:

I could look down and see myself and the rest of the guys, see
the boat rocking there in the middle of those diving birds, see
McMurphy surrounded by his dozen people, and watch them,
us, swinging a laughter that rang out on the water in ever-
widening circles, farther and farther, until it crashed up on
beaches all over the coast, on beaches all over all coasts, in wave
after wave after wave.

It is the dramatic climax of the novel, and as usual Bromden reports it in
hyperbole, but unlike most of his other exaggerations, this hyperbole is affirmative and celebrative. Amid the sound of newly created and now unified
laughter, Bromden experiences an inspiring power and visualizes the tidal
force of freedom, fellowship, and love washing incessantly against the
universal shores of absurdity. Yet despite his hyperbole, he keeps his balance
and retains the explicit moral of McMurphy's lesson: "you have to laugh at
the things that hurt you just to keep yourself in balance, just to keep the
world from running you plumb crazy." From this point until his death,
McMurphy maintains his laughter with increasing difficulty, but his persis-
tence stamps on the growing awareness of Bromden the existential nature of
heroic resistance: "The thing he was fighting, you couldn't whip it for good.
All you could do was keep on whipping it, till you couldn't come out any
more and somebody else had to take your place." The boxing metaphor that
Bromden uses here implies that he will be the new contender and emphasizes
the importance of hands, another synecdoche Bromden is sensitive to in his
movement toward wholeness.

Like the laughter motif, the hands motif is introduced with
McMurphy. Greeting silence with laughter, he meets weak hands with
strong ones.

Bromden records faithfully the afflictions in the ward conveyed by
hands. Big George paranoiacally keeps his hands to himself, fearing the
polluting touch of others. Harding has expressive hands, "free as two white
birds," but he is ashamed of what he has been taught is a feminine trait and
thus "traps them between his knees; it bothers him that he's got pretty
hands." Like Prufrock, Ellis has been "pinned . . . wriggling on the wall" by
the formulations of the Combine. Incapable of leaving his place of self-cruci-
fixion, he cannot even move to the latrine "before the nails pull his hands
back to the wall." A guilt-ridden Pilate figure on the Disturbed ward wants
to "wash [his] hands of the whole deal," thus mindlessly but pointedly under-
lining McMurphy's messianic function. Old Pete Bancini, forever tired,
manages once in anger to pump his useless hand into what Bromden sees as
"a big rusty iron ball at the end of a chain"; he accompanies this transforma-

tion with a poignant speech about the difficulties of the handicapped, and then "his iron ball shrank back to a hand." Thereafter he is useless, like most of his fellow inmates. Bromden compares him to "an old clock that won't tell time but won't stop neither, with the hands bent out of shape and the face bare of numbers and the alarm bell rusted silent, an old, worthless clock that just keeps ticking and cuckooing without meaning nothing." To these needy ones McMurphy offers the helping hand of friendship to counteract the debilitating influence of Big Nurse, whose hand affects most of them as it affects Mr. Taber: "the Big Nurse . . . locked her hand on his arm, paralyzes him all the way to the shoulder."

The hand that McMurphy offers is thrust into Bromden's fog with the impact of an illuminated painting:

> I remember real clear the way that hand looked: there was carbon under the fingernails where he'd worked once in a garage; there was an anchor tattooed back from the knuckles; there was a dirty Band-Aid on the middle knuckle, peeling up at the edge. All the rest of the knuckles were covered with scars and cuts, old and new. I remember the palm was smooth and hard as bone from hefting the wooden handles of axes and hoes, not the hand you'd think could deal cards. The palm was callused, and the calluses were cracked, and dirt was worked in the cracks. A road map of his travels up and down the West.

This is the hand that intimidates the black aide in the corridor over the toothpaste issue, threatens the bullying service-station attendant on the fishing trip—"He put his hands up in the guy's face, real close, turning them over slowly, palm and knuckle"—and defeats Washington, the sadistic black aide, in the battle over human dignity. And this is the hand McMurphy offers in greeting and encouragement to the residents of the cuckoo's nest: "He shakes the hands of Wheelers and Walkers and Vegetables, shakes hands that he has to pick up out of laps like picking up dead birds, mechanical birds, wonders of tiny bones and wires that have run down and fallen." The effect of McMurphy's handshake contrasts sharply with the paralyzing touch of Big Nurse's hand. Bromden remembers his "fingers were thick and strong closing over mine, and my hand commenced to feel peculiar and went to swelling up out there on my stick of an arm, like he was transmitting his own blood into it. It rang with blood and power." Inspired by McMurphy's audacious challenge to Big Nurse, the men begin to emulate him: "'You're *betting* on this?' Cheswick is hopping from foot to foot and rubbing his hands together like McMurphy rubs his." Significantly, Big Nurse calls McMurphy a "manipulator," which he is, but his manipulations lead other patients to manhood.

The hands motif culminates in the television vote, when McMurphy calls on the men to show some semblance of manhood: "I want to see the hands," he says. "I want to see the hands that don't go up, too." Retreating to the safety of his fog, Bromden reports the first hand signals of manhood's timorous entry into the ward:

> The first hand that comes up, I can tell, is McMurphy's. . . .
> And then off down the slope I see them, other hands coming up
> out of the fog. It's like . . . that big red hand of McMurphy's is
> reaching into the fog and dropping down and dragging the men up
> by their hands, dragging them blinking into the open. First one,
> then another, then the next. Right on down the line of Acutes,
> dragging them out of the fog till there they stand, all twenty of
> them, raising not just for watching TV, but against the Big Nurse,
> against her trying to send McMurphy to Disturbed, against the
> way she's talked and acted and beat them down for years.

Finally, Bromden, too, lifts his hand: "McMurphy's got hidden wires hooked to it, lifting it slow just to get me out of the fog. . . . He's doing it, wires . . . No. That's not the truth. I lifted it myself." The chief's vote makes twenty-one, "a majority," significant here as the legal age of manhood and the winning hand in blackjack. Typically, however, Big Nurse disallows the vote on a technicality. Undaunted and led again by McMurphy, the men defy the Big Nurse and watch TV at the appointed time anyway, leaving her unchar-acteristically out of control, "ranting and screaming . . . about discipline and order and recriminations." Seeds of manhood are sown here with this show of hands and strength. They fructify, with laughter, in the climactic fishing scene, when the men seek McMurphy's helping hand but discover after he demurs the resourcefulness of their own hands instead.

Beyond the laughter and the hands, Bromden as Kesey's synecdochist is compelled by the significance of faces, and a survey of his perceptions provides a study of the evolution of McMurphy's heroism and its shift to Bromden. In the ward Bromden examines the faces of victims. Framed by his fog, these faces reveal their pain to Bromden starkly, as though, he claims, he were looking through "one of those microscopes:"

> I see a Chronic float into sight a little below me. It's old
> Colonel Matterson, reading from the wrinkled scripture of that
> long yellow hand. . . . His face is enormous, almost more than I

can bear. . . . The face is sixty years of southwest Army camps, rutted by iron-rimmed caisson wheels, worn to the bone by thousands of feet on two-day marches. . . .

There's old Pete, face like a searchlight. . . . He tells me once about how tired he is, and just his saying it makes me see his whole life on the railroad . . . doing his absolute damnedest to keep up with a job that comes so easy to the others. . . .

Here comes Billy Bibbit. . . . His face is out to me like the face of a beggar, needing so much more'n anybody can give. . . .

Put your face away, Billy.

They keep filing past.

It's like each face was a sign like one of those "I'm Blind" signs the dago accordion players in Portland hung around their necks, only these signs say "I'm tired" or "I'm scared" or "I'm dying of a bum liver" or "I'm all bound up with machinery and people *pushing* me alla time." I can read all the signs, it don't make any difference how little the print gets. . . . The faces blow past in the fog like confetti.

Bromden can read the signs—and does so with poetic intensity—but he cannot help. In weakness and despair he admits, "None of us can. You got to understand that as soon as a man goes to help somebody, he leaves himself wide open." McMurphy comes to prove Bromden only half right: Commitment to others does leave one vulnerable, but help is possible; something can be done. McMurphy learns this lesson in the process of teaching it when he rises to the challenges presented by these human faces crying out for understanding and help and by the nonhuman face of Big Nurse, "smooth, calculated, and precision-made" proclaiming the formidable power of the Combine. Public Relation documents that power in another way: "He never, never looks at the men's faces. . . ."

Bromden studies McMurphy's face in its responses to other faces and learns the nature of heroism. Fresh from the Pendleton Work Farm, McMurphy first appears to Bromden as a swaggering free spirit; he has a "wide grinning mouth" and "his face and neck and arms are the color of oxblood leather from working long in the fields." He has no heroic intentions in the beginning but only "to bring . . . fun and entertainment around the gamin' table." What starts as a lark becomes quickly serious, though, as McMurphy witnesses the faces of affliction in the clutch of the Combine. Battered by Group Discussion, Harding's "face is tilted oddly, edged, jagged purple and gray, a busted wine bottle"; Pete's face is tired, Ruckly's burnt out; Billy Bibbit and Cheswick have rabbit features—"faces all round . . . trapped screaming behind the mirrors." Such entrapment is a challenge to a man who holds a "Distinguished Service Cross . . . for leading an escape from a Communist prison camp," and that history of commitment to freedom leads McMurphy to challenge "old frozen face" to please the men: "He looks at the faces a minute, then shrugs and stands up from his chair." A momentary hesitation to proceed with the challenge to Big Nurse's control makes him look "away from the bunch of faces hung out there around him"; then, however, he rises to the occasion in response to the faces and makes what turns out to be the biggest wager of his life. The novel's exposition is thus completed with the engagement of the central conflict between the repressive power of Big Nurse and the liberating force of McMurphy.

The stages of McMurphy's developing heroism are captured in the faces. Letting the men win at games of chance, McMurphy encourages them to participate in the game of life, until "there . . . isn't a man raking his pile of cigarettes . . . that doesn't have a smirk on his face like he's the toughest gambler on the whole Mississippi." McMurphy's face almost explodes with the effort "to lift something he *knows* he can't lift, something *everybody* knows he can't lift," but when he looks up from the massive control panel, his eyes meet the faces around them, challenging the men to match his effort: "He opens his eyes and looks around us. One by one he looks at the guys." This effort produces the triumphant faces of the second TV vote and the subsequent defiant faces that undo the Big Nurse for the first time. Bromden is inspired by the courage of McMurphy and the complexity beneath the bravado: "I was seeing more to him than just big hands and red sideburns and a broken-nosed grin. I'd see him do things that didn't fit with his face or hands. . . . How could a man who looked like him paint pictures or write letters to people or be upset and worried?" Wondering how McMurphy can have the courage to "be what he is," Bromden compares his own face in the mirror: "That ain't me," he says, "that ain't my face. It wasn't even me when I was trying to be that face." Bromden learns, though, that McMurphy's courage, despite the affected swagger, is human courage after all, and thus subject to faltering.

When McMurphy learns from the symbolic lifeguard that Big Nurse controls his sentence in the hospital, he withdraws from heroics for his own survival and thus refuses to back up Cheswick over the cigarette issue. The men follow his lead, exposing Cheswick's weakness: "He looked at McMurphy and got no look back, and went down the line of Acutes looking for help. Each time a man looked away . . . the panic on his face doubled." The effect of McMurphy's defection is a "canceled row of faces." McMurphy returns to the fray only after Cheswick's suicide, Sefelt's seizure, and the startling discovery that most of the men, unlike himself as a committed inmate, remain in the cuckoo's nest voluntarily. The impact of these events and discovery, true anagnorisis, can be traced in McMurphy's face. Like the face of seizure-torn Sefelt, McMurphy's "face has commenced to take on that same haggard, puzzled look of pressure that the face on the floor has." He has dreams in which he is plagued by "Nothing but faces . . . just faces." He cannot see the faces of the victims in straps that Martini hallucinates, but Martini tells him, "Hold it a minute. They need you to see thum." He can see Billy's "face boiling tears" as he joins the others in admitting the fear that makes him voluntary. Transfixed at the news, McMurphy "stands there a minute with the row of eyes aimed at him like a row of rivets." Bromden first uses this image to describe the door to the EST room, the major source of dehumanization in the hospital. Here the image underlines the choice McMurphy has either to protect himself and abandon these weaklings or endanger himself to rescue them. Studying his face, Bromden imagines his *agon* over the choice in a hunting analogy: "I could see that there was some thought he was worrying over in his mind like a dog worries at a hole he don't know what's down, one voice saying, Dog, that hole is none of your affair. . . . And some other voice coming like a sharp whisper out of way back in his breed, not a smart voice, . . . saying, *Sic* 'im, dog, *sic* 'im!" His "breed" here is, of course, hero, and because he has the courage to "be what he is," McMurphy becomes again the champion of the weak, driving his fist through the glass of the nurse's station to defy the cigarette restriction and leaving the Big Nurse "with her face shifting and jerking."

From this point on Bromden notices the increasing contrast between the two faces of McMurphy, between the fearless face of hero he presents to inspire the men and the exhausted face of overextended man he tries to keep hidden from them as he pays the price of superhuman heroism. The laughing face of the triumphant fisher of men in the novel's climactic scene is balanced by the fatigued face of the "dedicated lover" bringing home his "catch": "Then . . . a set of tail-lights going past lit up McMurphy's face, and the windshield reflected an expression that was allowed only because he figured it'd be too dark for anybody in the car to see, dreadfully tired and strained and *frantic*, like there wasn't enough time left for something he had to do. . . ." McMurphy's sense of messianic urgency is kept alive daily because "that circle of faces waits and watches." Repeated shock treatments do not alter his resistance nor reduce his defiance: "aware that every one of those faces on Disturbed had turned toward him and was waiting . . . he'd tell the nurse he regretted he had but one life to give for his country and she could kiss his rosy red ass before he'd give up the goddam ship. *Yeh!* Then stand up and take a couple of bows to those guys grinning at him." Yet behind McMurphy's theatrics Bromden sees after each shock treatment "his whole face drained of color, looking thin and scared—the face . . . seen reflected in the windshield on the trip back from the coast." The faces of victims—"us," as Harding tells him—drive McMurphy "down that road" to "craziness," to existential heroism in the face of absurdity. Finally, Billy Bibbit's death, his face bloodied by his own hand, compels McMurphy to attack Big Nurse and thus to receive a lobotomy. Having "doled out his life" for others to live, he has emptied his own. Over McMurphy's lobotomized husk, Bromden pronounces the depletion: "'There's nothin' in the face.'"

But Bromden is now ready to carry on where McMurphy has left off. When he returns to the ward from Disturbed with tales of McMurphy, he finds himself a hero by association, and he feels for the first time the pressure that the weak can apply to the strong: "Everybody's face turned up to me with a different look than they'd ever given me before. Their faces lighted up as if they were looking into the glare of a sideshow platform. . . . I grinned back at them, realizing how McMurphy must've felt these months with these faces screaming up at him." Bromden's first act of courage has been to assist McMurphy in the shower fight, his second to abandon his insular fog, and his third—the ultimate test—to assume the responsibility for killing his friend and heroic model, an act that he performs lovingly, though in an anguish of spirit. At last "big" and whole again, he liberates himself with the symbolic control panel, and amid a "baptizing" of splintered glass heads in the direction set earlier by the dog and the geese, "flying free," regenerated by RPM, with the courageous, salvific impulse to go to his home grounds "to see if there's any of the guys . . . back in the village who haven't drunk themselves goofy." As a fragmented man grown whole in McMurphy's image, Bromden is now strong enough to leave the microcosm of the ward for the macrocosm outside, seeking out and ministering to the faces of need, extending the range of heroism. Bromden's final act of courage is to relive his experience honestly and tell it truthfully despite the pain it causes, "burning" him to tell "about all this, about the hospital, and her, and the guys—and about McMurphy."

The reality of the pain and the surreality of the experience come alive and are convincing despite Kesey's extensive use of caricature because the narrator achieves his stature in the telling of his tale. Bromden's documented growth from fog to clarity, from chronic to man, from Vanishing American to resistant hero embodies and thus validates the novel's theme that what is good in man, properly nourished, can overcome what is evil in him. To witness Bromden's transformation through the influence of McMurphy is to believe in the principle that transforms him and the vehicle that reveals the change.

The principle is love. As a "dedicated lover" from the age of ten, McMurphy is driven by love of freedom, friendship, and life to lay down his life for his friends—and "greater love hath no man than this." Doing so, he transcends caricature, moving from con man to savior, from self love to brotherly love. He comes alive through his compassion and his death. Bromden is directed by the same spirit of love and goes out into the world to help others overcome their fears and troubles and become fully human. Kesey has made such salvation seem possible because he has shown its effects dramatically in the evolution of McMurphy and the transformation of Bromden. Though moving and sad, the death of McMurphy is necessary to document at once the forces of oppression and fear and the power of love and courage to overcome such forces. The novel ends not on the tragic loss of McMurphy's life but on the reclamation through McMurphy's sacrifice of the lives of others, especially Bromden's. The tonal focus is finally elegiac and celebrative, fully affirmative in both moods.

The affirmation is earned in the psychical distance Bromden travels from sickness to health and in the verisimilitude of the narrative vehicle that records the journey. Though Bromden as narrator never claims to be a poet, his perceptions reflect the intensity of a poetic sensibility and are embodied in concretions organically related to character and theme. His chosen role as deaf-mute observer removes him from active life, but it makes him an attentive and reliable witness, and thus lends vividness to his images appropriate to the seer. His early attraction to rhyme expresses itself occasionally as a rhyming rhapsody on the way to reason. His hyperbole, impressionism, and surrealism document both his paranoia and the distortion of values and people in the world he perceives. His movement from fragmented patient to whole man is captured in his splintered yet almost systematic examination of those isolated parts of other men that reflect his own fragmentation: laughs, hands, faces. This synecdoche is a most important part of his progression to wholeness, as is his exchange of the microcosmic ward for the macrocosmic outside world. His spiritual renascence, verbal resourcefulness, and heroic resolve at the end evoke a poetic response to the possibilities of life. Such affirmation is difficult to deny when the affirmer is a fully realized American Indian who moves his six-foot-eight-inch, two-hundred-and-seventy-pound body in a joyous gallop across a land "singing kids' poetry to him" in order to celebrate his freedom and rescue others from the formidable forces of fear and oppression. In the overall iconography of the novel it is a powerful image (like Bellow's Henderson the Rain King dancing around the plane in symbolic Newfoundland), created here by the narrator's words and actions and emblematic of the lesson he learned from McMurphy and is carrying faithfully and bravely to others: "Maybe the Combine wasn't all-powerful."

STEPHEN L. TANNER

# One Flew Over the Cuckoo's Nest

## Breadth of Appeal

*One Flew Over the Cuckoo's Nest* has had a broad appeal. Its language and situations offend some, particularly among parents and schoolboards. Others are offended by its treatment of women and blacks. Some find it simplistic in philosophy; and some find its plot, setting, and characters too carefully contrived. But it continues to appeal to a wide audience, including literarily sophisticated readers. It is one of few works to achieve acclaim in three forms: novel, play, and film. The play, written by Dale Wasserman, appeared on Broadway starring Kirk Douglas in 1963 and was revived in 1971. Although it was unsuccessful there, it has enjoyed continued success on college campuses. The film version in 1975, directed by Milos Forman and starring Jack Nicholson, was a box-office hit and won six Academy Awards.

This success as play and movie as well as novel suggests that the story's themes are fascinating and congenial to a contemporary audience. When the novel appeared in 1962, it supplied a critique of an American society that was portrayed in the serious media of the 1950s as consisting of a lonely crowd of organization men, offered affluence only if willing to pay the price of strict conformity. That critique continued to suit the mood of the 1960s and 1970s because larger themes were involved: the modern world as technologized and consequently divorced from nature; contemporary society as repres-

From *Ken Kesey*. © 1983 by G. K. Hall & Company.

sive; authority as mechanical and destructive; contemporary man as victim of rational but loveless forces beyond his control; and contemporary man as weak, frightened, and sexless. The novel's apparent message that people need to get back in touch with their world, to open doors of perception, to enjoy spontaneous sensuous experience and resist the manipulative forces of a technological society was particularly appealing to the young, but not just to them. An admiration for self-reliant action runs deep in the American psyche. Ruth Sullivan, in a psychological analysis of the novel's appeal, suggests that it gives the reader an opportunity to feel the self-pity of being unjustly persecuted. Americans feel oppressed by Big Goverment and the novel provides them justification. And the self-pity is enhanced by the anti-establishment tone. The novel "richly gratifies latent or conscious hostile impulses against authority," and also satisfies the tendency to depend upon strong, heroic figures and "to feel unjustly treated (masochistic and moral-righteousness pleasures)."

Besides embodying engaging themes, the novel for most readers is a pleasure to read. It is filled with comic language and incidents. Randle Patrick McMurphy is a vivid, unforgettable character; Big Nurse is an eminently hatable villain; and the perennial conflict of Good and Evil is reenacted with sufficient suspense to generate lively interest.

Another reason for the novel's appeal is that it treats or touches upon a wide variety of subjects, issues, and disciplines. *Lex et Scientia*, the official organ of the International Academy of Law and Science, devoted an entire 100-page double issue to essays on *Cuckoo's Nest*, which the editor describes as "a cornucopia of source material from disciplines so numerous and varied as to challenge the mind and imagination." It reaches, he says, into such areas as psychology, psychiatry, medicine, literature, human relations, drama, art, cosmology, and law and even carries overtones of religion, American culture, and folk-culture. And it does this with a mixture of tragedy, pathos, and humor. It is not surprising that the novel has been used as a text for courses in a variety of subjects and disciplines. Sociologists, for example, are interested in it because, as Doctor Spivey within the novel points out, Big Nurse's ward is "a little world Inside that is a made-to-scale prototype of the big world Outside." An essay by sociologists explaining how it can be used in a sociology course lists these topics for discussion: the phenomenon of power; the reality of the social; patterns of integration; personal organization; social organization; patterns of differentiation; social/cultural change; and societal institutions. Psychology, English, and American Studies departments have found it equally rich in thought-provoking topics.

The variety of interests it has attracted is of course paralleled by the variety of responses it has evoked. Here is a partial list of phrases and topics that show up in treatments of *Cuckoo's Nest:* the patterns of romance, the patterns of comedy, the patterns of tragedy, black humor, the absurd, the hero in modern dress, the comic Christ, folk and western heroes, the fool as mentor, the Grail Knight, attitudes toward sex, abdication of masculinity, the politics of laughter, mechanistic and totemistic symbolization, the comic strip, ritualistic father-figure, the psychopathic savior. The list could easily be extended. Although the novel has elements of comic-strip exaggeration and oversimplification, it touches upon root motives and conflicts that have many branches. Readers will continue to focus on the branch or branches attracting their immediate interest.

### Inspired by the Tragic Longing of Real Men

Much of the inspiration for *Cuckoo's Nest* came from Kesey's experiences at the Veterans' Hospital in Menlo Park. He went there first as a paid volunteer for government experiments with "psychomimetic" drugs. He was given drugs and asked to record exactly how they affected him. Kesey was well suited in several ways to be a subject for such experiments. He had a natural and lively curiosity about what the human mind is capable of; and he was particularly interested in the visions, inspirations, and creative consciousness that might lie just beyond ordinary thinking and dreaming. For the sake of his own personal research, as it were, he was probably more interested in the experiments than were those conducting them. Along with this willingness, he possessed an unusual ability to register impressions and express them; he had a highly developed imagination and considerable verbal skill. At times, however, his talent for writing down his impressions was wasted because of the effects of the drug. After sitting in a room for an hour or so rapidly recording what he considered to be remarkable impressions and insights, he would later discover that what he had written was gibberish. But when the particular drug or dosage allowed him to be reasonably coherent, he had the verbal power to convey vividly the flux of impressions exploding in his mind. When he later turned from writing novels to concentrate on achieving heightened consciousness and perception through psychedelic drugs, he used a technique similar to that used in these first volunteer experiments. Many of the tapes in the Kesey Collection are of him recording, as they occur, his impressions under drugs. They display singular skill in vivid spontaneous description. Similes, so necessary in conveying an unusual, dreamlike experience to others, come fluently and are often strikingly evocative. It is likely that the fantasies or hallucinations described by Chief Bromden, the narrator of the novel, are modeled after ones Kesey had experienced in the hospital experiments.

After the experiments concluded, Kesey continued at the hospital as a psychiatric aide. He has said that McMurphy was "inspired by the tragic longing of the real men I worked with on the ward." His midnight-to-eight shift allowed him periods of five or six hours, five days a week, during which he had nothing to do but a little mopping, buffing, and checking the wards with flashlight. He used this time for writing his novel. The taped conversations with friends in which he describes his work at the hospital reveal how much of his own experience went into the novel, transformed to one degree or another. He had unpleasant encounters with rigid and demanding nurses; he scuffled once with a black aide; he attended patients with a variety of peculiar behavior patterns; and he observed generally how a psychiatric ward functions. A letter to Babbs, written when Kesey was completing four weeks of training as an aide, describes several patients he worked with. The exact characteristics and phrases of some of these patients appear in the novel. According to Wolfe, he arranged for someone to give him, clandestinely, a sample of shock therapy so he could describe it firsthand.

Kesey says some of the novel was written while he was under the influence of drugs. The most notable instance is the first few pages, in which he created the narrator. "I was flying on peyote, really strung out there, when this Indian came to me. I knew nothing about Indians, had no Indians on my mind, had nothing that an Indian could even grab onto, yet this Indian came to me. It was the peyote, then, couldn't be anything else. The Indian came straight out from the drug." This example is of special importance because his decision to have Bromden tell the story was perhaps the most significant one he made in writing the novel. Most critics agree that his treatment of point of view is a masterstroke.

There is something disingenuous, however, about Kesey's claim of drug-generated inspiration. Maybe the phrase concerning knowing about Indians requires qualification; there are many degrees of knowing. As a matter of fact, Kesey did know a good deal about Indians and had thought and written about them. For an assignment in his radio and television writing class at Oregon he had written "Sunset at Celilo," a script about an Indian who returns from the Korean Conflict at a time when the dam was being built at The Dalles and his tribe was being forced to leave their village. An interviewer reports Kesey's telling of "an Indian in a logger's camp suddenly crazed with the recollection of his blood and racing headlong from the mountain side to attack with his knife the grillwork of a diesel hurtling down the highway paved through his grandfather's land, dying out there bravely and badly, living again in the idea for Chief Broom Bromden, the narrator of *One Flew Over the Cuckoo's Nest.* . . ." On tape he tells about playing football on the same team with a large Indian, about an Indian who had worked for them, and about an Indian he had once seen with lipstick all over his face, his cowboy shirt spattered with blood. And mention has already been made of the unpublished story "The Avocados," which sympathetically treats two displaced Indians. It may be that Kesey was looking so anxiously for evidence that drugs could expand consciousness, partly as a justification of his drug experimenting and proselytizing, that he attributed too much to the peyote.

Wherever the inspiration for Bromden came from, it was a fortunate one and Kesey did remarkable things with it. The point of view in the novel is an unusual achievement. On the one hand, Bromden fantasizes. This gives the reader a singularly vivid impression of the emotional and psychological state of the patients. The novel is about rescue or salvation, and Bromden's inner condition gives us a clear idea of what the patients need rescue from; and the exaggeration in his fantasies also spotlights and emphasizes the matters important to theme. For example, the phantom machines Bromden describes in the walls and in people are part of a significant pattern of imagery used to develop the central theme concerning technological manipulation. But at the same time Bromden is an unreliable witness he is also an extremely reliable one. We feel he tells us the truth about McMurphy; in fact, he tells it with such penetration and insight that it has a consistent and coherent shape and meaning for us. The combination of hallucination and truth in the narration is a notable stylistic accomplishment. Fact and fantasy alternate, but the reader has no difficulty distinguishing one from the other, and thus they successfully complement each other.

Kesey began working on the novel using a more conventional first-person narrator. In a letter to Babbs, he mentions, "I tried working on the novel you have now [*Cuckoo's Nest*] from the PV of an aide, me, and realized how much the narrative sounded like other promisingyoungwriter narrative." He did not want this. He was aiming at a narrator—he lists Holden Caulfield, Benjy Compson, Gulley Jimson (of Joyce Carey's *The Horse's Mouth*) and Humbert Humbert as examples—who leaves the ground and lives and breathes in print.

In a letter to Kirk Douglas, he explains that Bromden's point of view is necessary

> to make the characters *big enough* to be equal to their job. McMurphy, as viewed from the low-angle point of view of the Chief, is a giant, a god, he's every movie show cowboy that ever walked down a mainstreet toward the OK corral, he's every patriot that ever died for his countrymen on a scaffold in history books. The Big Nurse is seen more clearly by the Indian than by anyone else, as that age-old ogre of tyranny and fear simply

dressed in nice neat white. Of course, McMurphy and the nurse are also people, in a human situation, but in the distorted world inside the Indian's mind these people are exalted into a kind of immortality. To do this you need fantasy. You need to jar the reader from his comfortable seat inside convention. You need to take the reader's mind places where it has never been before to convince him that this crazy Indian's world is *his* as well.

Thus the distortion or exaggeration in the novel is deliberate, and is created by manipulation of point of view.

Kesey's choice of Bromden as narrator allows for a hero of event and a hero of consciousness; McMurphy is the former and Bromden the latter. When these two are juxtaposed, each is better delineated. John W. Hunt has pointed out that "Kesey's use of the single narrator who is telling a story deeply important to his own understanding of himself forces the reader to follow a double story line, one centering upon the tale told and the other upon the teller and the telling." In this regard the novel resembles other American novels that raise the question "whose story is this?"—*Moby-Dick, The Great Gatsby, Absalom, Absalom!* As Bromden tells McMurphy's story, he comes to understand himself better and eventually regains control of himself and acquires sufficient strength to flee the institution and face the world once again. Hunt explains that an examination of the two stories reveals an exchange of visions, "a clash between the originally tragic view of Bromden, to which hope has been added, and the hopeful view of McMurphy, which became completely qualified by tragedy from the day he signed on for the whole game." By using Bromden, Kesey not only has a vehicle for telling McMurphy's story, he has a center of consciousness for interpreting and judging it and a specific example of the significance of it.

An unpublished story written after Kesey began work at the hospital reveals a transitional stage between "Zoo" and *Cuckoo's Nest*. The main character of "The Kicking Party" is a jazz musician, a North Beach type with goatee and a drug habit. He is a mental patient who one of his fellow patients says is "plotting to undermine the whole system with his evil laugh and sinful stories." The head nurse watches him "through her protective glass shield from her sterilized isolation booth." He tells "heightened, hilarious stories of jazz days or junk days or juice days." The undermining of the system, the laughter and stories, and the head nurse suggest *Cuckoo's Nest*; but at this point Kesey is still caught up with Beat life. The Beat response to an uncongenial conformist society was withdrawal by such means as wine, pot, jazz, and Zen. Kesey's temperament was not suited for withdrawal. He grew up admiring strength and responding to competition. It was natural that his background and inclinations would eventually bring his creative energies to focus on an active and self-reliant character like McMurphy rather than on a jazz musician like the one described in "The Kicking Party." Moreover, the point of view in the story is conventional; he had yet to discover a narrative key like Bromden. In the story the laugher and the mental patient are a single person. The turning point would come when he separated them as hero of event and hero of consciousness.

## "He Sounds Big"

*Cuckoo's Nest* is dedicated to Vic Lovell, "who told me dragons did not exist, then led me to their lairs." In explaining to Gordon Lish what he meant by this, Kesey said that Lovell had "argued against the existence of spiritual dragons," or in other words, against a spiritual realm of experience, one transcending ordinary life and rational explanation. But, ironically, it was Lovell who arranged for him to participate in the drug experiments, which he believed introduced him to a new realm of experience. The dedication is a reflection of his persistent fascination with the transcendent, his impatience with the attitude that dreams are *only* dreams and imaginative experiences are *just* fictions. His introduction to drugs was a major phase in the search that began in childhood with his interest in magic.

*Cuckoo's Nest* appears more experimental and unconventional than it actually is. The tone is irreverent and antiestablishment, and the psychotic Indian narrator is original; but for the most part Kesey has made skillful use of well-established techniques and patterns. He draws upon the most familiar of myth patterns—the savior and sacrificial hero, death and rebirth, and the search for the father. He also alludes frequently to popular types from American folk tradition and popular culture. His patterns of imagery are unmistakably explicit and developed in conventional ways, and the structure of the novel is clear and symmetrical. The novel's success results from a skillful application of established literary methods to an apparently iconoclastic theme. The iconoclasm is more apparent than real because the Establishment is largely caricatured and the values asserted are basically those at the heart of Western American culture.

The opposition of Nature and Machine is the primary conflict of the novel, and this opposition constitutes the central nervous system for the patterns of imagery. The narrator, Bromden, who is really only half Indian, represents the man of nature. As a patient in a mental institution, he is a victim of the Combine, the forces of technology and human manipulation whose avatar is Miss Ratched, the Big Nurse. Just when Bromden, overcome by feelings of fear and futility, is at the point of succumbing to the Combine, the boisterous McMurphy arrives as a kind of profane savior preaching the gospel of laughter, the first principle of which is self-reliant strength. The central conflict is a singular version of the archetypal struggle between the forces of good and evil or freedom and bondage in which victory is achieved through the intervention of a savior or sacrificial hero.

The novel is divided into four parts of cycles of action that are approximately parallel in structure. At the beginning of each cycle the Big Nurse is either ascendant or biding her time incubating a new strategy of attack, and at the end McMurphy or what he represents is ascendant. There is a progression in the movement from cycle to cycle, however, for despite setbacks, McMurphy by the end of each part has brought Bromden closer to the freedom from fear that constitutes his salvation. The climax comes in Part 3, and Part 4 is falling action or denouement.

The first section of Part 1 introduces most of the major themes and images. The Combine is mentioned and Big Nurse and her minions are introduced through images of technology and machinery. The Big Nurse's name, Ratched, suggests "rachet" (a mechanism consisting of a notched wheel, the teeth of which engage with a pawl, permitting motion of the wheel in one direction only). This name alone goes a long way in suggesting her impersonal singleness of purpose. From the viewpoint of the narrator, who drifts in and out of hallucinatory states, she has "equipment" and "machinery" inside; "she walks stiff"; her gestures are "precise" and "automatic"; each finger is like "the tip of a soldering iron"; she carries a wicker bag filled with "wheels and gears; cogs polished to a hard glitter"; when she is angry she blows up "big as a tractor"; her face is "smooth, calculated, and precision-made, like an expensive baby doll, skin like flesh-colored enamel." The only apparent mistake in her manufacture is her "big, womanly breasts." But these breasts, which would ordinarily represent natural warmth and maternal tenderness, she is bitter about and keeps tightly bound up within her stiff starched uniform. Her black orderlies also have "equipment" inside and their eyes glitter out of their black faces "like the hard glitter of radio tubes out of the back of an old radio." Bromden interprets their mumblings as the "hum of black machinery, humming hate and death."

After these images of mechanization and manipulation are introduced in the first section, they are used consistently in describing Miss Ratched and everything in her charge. She is a dedicated "adjuster" who wants her ward to run "like a smooth, accurate, precision-made machine." She sits in the center of a "web of wires like a watchful robot," tending her network with "mechanical insect skill," dreaming of a world of "precision efficiency and tidiness like a pocket watch with a glass back." The ward is a factory for the

Combine, very similar in Bromden's mind to a cotton mill he had once visited. This factory fixes up mistakes made in the neighborhoods, schools, and churches, and Miss Ratched is pleased when a "completed product" goes back into society as "a functioning, adjusted component." The chronic patients are "the culls of the Combine's product"—"machines that can't be repaired." Sitting before her steel control panel, the Big Nurse controls and manipulates the patients, who are described variously as "arcade puppets," "mechanical puppets," and "shooting-gallery targets." Because of years of training, the three black aides are no longer controlled by direct wires; they are on the Big Nurse's frequency and manipulated by remote control. If a patient is troublesome, he can be fixed by receiving a new "head installation." An obstreperous patient named Ruckly received this kind of overhaul and returned with eyes "all smoked up and gray and deserted inside like blown fuses"; after that he was "just another robot for the Combine."

These images are the product of the narrator's fear-distorted imagination. They are abundant in the first section because at this point his fear is intense. Kesey wants to establish clearly in the beginning what victimization by the Combine means—fear, paranoia, weakness, and disorientation from nature. Bromden mentions a fog machine. When he loses touch with reality and his hold upon his individual personality and spiritual strength weakens, the fog increases. Throughout the novel the fog serves as a barometer of his emotional and psychological state and thickens and dissipates according to the fluctuations of his mental and spiritual health.

Just as the first section establishes the pattern of imagery consistently associated with the forces of the Machine or Combine, it also introduces a set of images or motifs linked with nature. In an attempt to control his fear, Bromden tries to remember things about his village on the Columbia River and about hunting with his father. These recollections are the first of a number of references to or reminiscences of life in the outdoors that identify him as a man of nature. His inordinate fear of machines, revealed so emphatically in his fantasies, accentuates his being a man whose natural element is the outdoors, where life is simple and unrestrained. The supporting motifs for this characterization are the dog and the sense of smell. In the first section, the dog is "out there in the fog, running scared." He sniffs in every direction but "picks up no scent but his own fear, fear burning down into him like steam." The parallels between Bromden and the dog are obvious. He has a keen sense of smell, which at first produces only fear as he smells the machinery inside the Big Nurse, but which later begins to register natural odors as he recovers.

According to Ronald Billingsley, the images function in six major ways: "they make of the narrative a concrete presentation; they serve as a device of foreshadowing; they give the language the feel and effect of poetry; they give a reflexive power to the flashback sequences; they serve to more accurately define character; finally, they help to objectify theme."

When the contrasting imagery of Machine and Nature is identified, the battle lines for the central conflict are readily apparent. "The determining force in that struggle is Randle Patrick McMurphy, who is introduced in the second section. His initials (R.P.M.—revolutions per minute) suggest the motion and energy characteristic of his personality. He is thirty-five, has never been married, and is a wanderer up and down the West. He has worked as a logger and as a carnival wheel man. Mostly he has been in and out of jail for brawling, disturbing the peace, and repeated gambling. He has been committed by the state from the Pendleton Correction Farm. He looks upon the change as relief from hoeing peas and an opportunity for finding new suckers to fleece. When he is introduced, and repeatedly throughout the novel, he is likened to an auctioneer or carnival pitchman. He is brassy, vulgar, and fast-talking. A significant item in his description is that he received the "Distinguished Service Cross in Korea, for leading an escape from a Communist prison camp." But, characteristically, he afterward received a dishonorable discharge for insubordination. He will prove insubordinate in the mental ward and in essence lead an escape. On two occasions he will liken the Big Nurse's ward to a Chinese Communist prison and her methods to those used there. In a letter to Babbs, written while Kesey was at work at the hospital, he mentions he has just been called upstairs to listen to a tape about the brainwashing of Korean War prisoners. "It was most enlightening, especially in terms of the book I'm writing. It had a lot to do with the 'Code of Conduct.' Remember it? we used to ridicule it upstairs in the ROTC office at Stanford? Well, I'm becoming very square or something—but I'm beginning to believe the code has a lot to it, a lot about strength. Strength is the key. We need strong men." In both of his novels, the main theme is this need for strong men.

Bromden realizes immediately that the new man is no ordinary Admission. He does not "slide scared down the wall" or submit meekly to the aides. "He sounds like he's way above them, talking down, like he's sailing fifty yards overhead, hollering at those below on the ground. He sounds big." Throughout the story Bromden uses size as a metaphor for emotional strength. Later, he refers to McMurphy as "a giant come down out of the sky to save us from the Combine. . . ." And when through McMurphy's "special body-buildin' course" Bromden has grown, one of McMurphy's female friends describes him as "A Goliath—fee, fi, fo, fum."

The characteristic of McMurphy that is emphasized when he is introduced and that takes on increasing significance as the story unfolds is his laughter. His laughter "is free and loud and it comes out of his wide grinning mouth and spreads in rings bigger and bigger till it's lapping against the walls of the ward." Bromden suddenly realizes it is the first real laugh he has heard in years. Everyone in the ward, patients and staff, is stunned by it; and "even when he isn't laughing, the laughing sound hovers around him, the way the sound hovers around a big bell just quit ringing—it's in his eyes, in the way he smiles and swaggers, in the way he talks."

McMurphy's hands are also given prominent and frequent mention. He makes a point of shaking everybody's hand when he arrives. This human touching contrasts with the cold and sterile treatment the patients receive from Big Nurse, but there is more to it than this. Along with his laughter, his hand symbolizes his strength and represents his power to save. It becomes a helping hand indeed. Bromden says at a climactic point near the end of Part 1, "It is like . . . that big red hand of McMurphy's is reaching into the fog and dropping down and dragging the men up by their hands, dragging them blinking into the open." When McMurphy leads the patients out of the hospital on a fishing trip and they are intimidated by a service station attendant, "He put his hands up in the guy's face, real close, turning them over slowly, palm and knuckle. 'You ever see a man get his poor old meat-hooks so pitiful chewed up from just throwing the *bull?* Did you, Hank?'" Those hands represent action and assertion, just the qualities the patients lack. The effeminate hands of Harding are played off against those of McMurphy. Until he benefits from McMurphy's example, Harding is embarrassed about his hands (described as doves) and keeps them hidden in his lap. After he has found strength and the courage to take the initiative, he uses his hands forcefully and unselfconsciously to shape and emphasize what he says.

Another thing that should be noted about McMurphy's introduction into the novel is that Bromden links him with his father—"He talks a little the way Papa used to. . . ." His father was chief of the tribe and at one time an object of his son's admiration. He was "big" in his eyes. But the Combine made him small and weak. Part of the reason Bromden is in the hospital is the debilitating disillusionment he experienced observing what happened to his father: "But when I saw my Papa start getting scared of things, I got scared too. . . ." The frequent connection between McMurphy and his father suggests Bromden's need for a strong father figure, someone who can demonstrate that fighting against the Combine is not futile. This will restore him to the way of life he knew while his father was strong, a life close to nature.

At the beginning of Part 1, Big Nurse is in full control. Bromden is mute (feigning deafness) and completely intimidated. The degree to which fear and a feeling of futility have loosened his grip on his manhood and sanity is revealed in his paranoid fantasies of the fog and the terrifying, ubiquitous machinery. His sense of smell, which links him to the world of nature, registers only the odor of oil and heated machinery. And the other patients are in no better condition. When McMurphy arrives with "that big wide-open laugh of his," he is immediately a disruptive force: "Dials twitch in the control panel" and the Acutes "look spooked and uneasy when he laughs." There is no place for laughter in the Big Nurse's smooth-running machinery of manipulation, and the patients have been conditioned to the point where they are afraid of laughter. Harding, as a spokesman for the inmates, explains to McMurphy just what that brawling Irishman will be up against if he decides to fight Miss Ratched and her machinery. In the middle of his presentation, Harding attempts an ironic laugh, but "a sound comes out of his mouth like a nail being crowbarred out of a plank of green pine." His forced and grotesque "squeaking" is the nearest thing to real laughter that the patients are capable of producing. McMurphy, in an attempt to generate some resistance against Miss Ratched, calls attention to the patients' fear, telling them they "are even scared to open up and *laugh*. You know that's the first thing that got me about this place, that there wasn't anybody laughing. I haven't heard a real laugh since I came through that door, do you know that? Man, when you lose your laugh you lose your *footing*. A man go around lettin' a woman whup him down till he can't laugh any more, and he loses one of the biggest edges he's got on his side." Harding answers that he does not think laughter is an effective weapon against "the juggernaut of modern matriarchy" and challenges McMurphy to try his weapon of laughter against Miss Ratched. McMurphy accepts the challenge, after it has been made more attractive by the wager of five dollars from each of the other patients, and begins his calculated campaign to "bug" Miss Ratched "till she comes apart at those neat little seams, and shows, just one time, she ain't so unbeatable as you think."

McMurphy's campaign against Miss Ratched in Part 1 awakens some hope within Bromden, and he begins to establish control of himself again. This change is marked by a renewed ability to smell natural odors, a reawakened recognition of the power of laughter, and finally an escape from the fog machine.

Just after McMurphy has momentarily staggered Miss Ratched by an impudent display of his flashy underwear (black satin shorts with big white whales on them—a gift from a female literature major who said he was a symbol), Bromden sweeps under McMurphy's bed and gets a smell of something that makes him realize for the first time since he has been in the hospital that although the dorm had been filled with many odors, not until McMurphy came was there "the man smell of dust and dirt from the open fields, and sweat, and work." Soon after this, again while sweeping, Bromden notices a picture of a fisherman on a mountain stream that he thinks must have been brought in when the "fog" had been too thick for him to see it. He imagines himself walking right into the picture and says, "I can smell the snow in the wind where it blows down off the peaks. I can see mole burrows humping along under the grass and buffalo weeds." This reawakened sensitivity to the world of nature, his home environment, is a positive sign that Bromden is developing a resistance to the machine world of the hospital.

After watching McMurphy humorously needling one of the black aides, Bromden feels good and remembers how his father once did much the same thing with some government men who were negotiating to buy off a treaty. His Papa had made them look ridiculous in the eyes of the Indians who had all "busted up laughing fit to kill." "It sure did get their goat; they turned without saying a word and walked off toward the highway, red-necked, us laughing behind them. I forget sometimes what laughter can do." Bromden observes McMurphy closely and apprehends his strategy. McMurphy takes everything calmly and observes the humor in the behavior of the hospital personnel—"and when he sees how funny it is he goes to laughing, and this aggravates them to no end. He's safe as long as he can laugh, he thinks, and it works pretty fair."

The climax of the first part comes with the vote concerning television time. When he raises his hand in that vote, Bromden takes the first action that commits him to fight back against the Combine. Even as he raises his hand he thinks, "I wouldn't do it on my own." He thinks McMurphy put "some kind of hex on it with his hand" when they shook hands the first day. McMurphy's healing influence and touch cause him to act despite his fear. The drama of this incident is intensified by the motif of the fog machine. The fog is a way for Bromden to find safety and comfort from the terrifying reality of life under the manipulative control of the Combine. "Nobody complains about all the fog," he says. "I know why, now: as bad as it is, you can slip back in it and feel safe. That's what McMurphy can't understand, us wanting to be safe. He keeps trying to drag us out of the fog, out in the open where we'd be easy to get at." The tension mounts before Bromden raises his hand because he goes into one of his deepest fogs: "I feel I'm going to float off someplace for good this time." This is a crisis fog because McMurphy's influence has brought him to face clearly once again the hurt that led him to his disturbed condition. In a flush of sympathy, he understands the pain in the life of one of his fellow patients: "I can see all that, and be hurt by it, the way I was hurt by seeing things in the Army, in the war. The way I was hurt by seeing what happened to Papa and the tribe. I thought I'd got over seeing those things and fretting over them. There's no sense in it. There's nothing to be done." But Bromden cannot resist McMurphy's "big red Hand," which pulls him out of the fog. After the vote, he remarks, "there's no more fog anyplace." Therefore, by the end of Part 1, although he still has a long way to go, Bromden, through McMurphy's help, has taken the first step toward recovering his autonomy and self-respect. This is made clear by the laughter motif, which appears again on the last page of Part 1. Miss Ratched has lost her composure and Bromden, instead of being afraid, thinks it is funny: "I think how his voice sounds like it hit a nail, and this strikes me so funny I almost laugh." He *almost* laughs; this is all he is capable of at this point. His salvation will not be complete until he can laugh naturally and uninhibitedly.

McMurphy's first major victory, the television vote, results from his unsuccessful attempt to lift a control panel. Bromden notes, "yesterday, before he tried lifting that panel, there wasn't but four or five men might of voted." Why did his attempt make such a difference? The answer lies in the example it provided. "His whole body shakes with the strain as he tries to lift something he *knows* he can't lift, something *everybody* knows he can't lift." To the patients—"rabbits" Harding calls them—this manifestation of all-out exertion in an attempt that obviously appears futile is inspiring. It causes them to reexamine their commitment to passive weakness and generates a flicker of hope that asserting themselves might not be futile. And of course the control panel has a symbolic dimension, for although it is not presently in operation, it is a *control* machine and representative of the Combine. Later, McMurphy tells Bromden he will make him strong again so he can lift the panel. He does and Bromden lifts it, and eventually he throws it through the window to obtain his escape. This is an ironic touch since a control panel is used to destroy control, the moral being that dehumanizing technological control is impossible when man remains strong and refuses to submit. The first control panel incident also fore-shadows that McMurphy will be able to provide the example but unable to save himself.

There is other careful foreshadowing in Part 1. The case of Ruckly is presented early to suggest what could happen to McMurphy. Because he was "being a holy nuisance all over the place," Ruckly was taken away for treatment and brought back two weeks later, his eyes "all smoked up and gray and deserted inside like blown fuses." McMurphy eventually pays a similar price for making himself a nuisance and is brought back to the ward, his eyes "like smudged fuses in a fuse box." And the case of a Mr. Taber is referred to several times as a foreshadowing parallel to McMurphy. On the whole, Part 1 effectively introduces and sets in motion all the significant elements of plot, theme, and imagery.

"Keep An Eye Out for Old Number One"

At the beginning of Part 2, the results of McMurphy's initial victory are manifest: "all the machinery in the wall is quiet." But the narrator is beginning to comprehend "the full force of the dangers we let ourselves in for when we let McMurphy lure us out of the fog." Miss Ratched returns, "clearheaded," and begins to reassert her control. Her manipulative powers are confidently displayed in the staff meeting at which she persuades the doctor and other staff members that McMurphy should not be sent to the Disturbed ward. She will not agree that he is "some kind of extraordinary being" and wants him left in her ward so she can prove to the other patients he is not. She is afraid the "redheaded hero" will he viewed as a martyr if he is taken away to Disturbed at this point.

But while Miss Ratched is initiating her new strategy to deal with the redheaded hero, it is made clear to us what effect McMurphy's first triumph has had upon the narrator. "For the first time in years," he says, "I was seeing people with none of that black outline they used to have, and one night I was even able to see out the windows." Before he opens his eyes at that window, he smells the breeze. "It's fall," he thinks, "I can smell that sour-molasses smell of silage, clanging in the air like a bell—smell somebody's been burning oak leaves, left them to smolder overnight because they're too green." When he opens his eyes he sees for the first time that the hospital is out in the country. Observing the moonlit pastureland reminds him of a night when he was off on a hunt with his father and uncles. All of this is the man of nature coming back to his true self, a reawakening that is emphasized once again by the dog motif. Looking out the window, he sees a gangly mongrel dog sniffing around at squirrel holes, "the breeze full of smells so wild makes a young dog drunk." This dog, who is thoroughly enjoying his freedom and the myriad smells in the night air, contrasts significantly with the bluetick hound of the first section of Part 1, out in the fog, running scared, smelling only the scent of his own fear. The narrator and the dog hear and watch a flight of wild geese overhead. Then the dog lopes off, "steady and solemn like he had an appointment." The narrator holds his breath as he hears a car approaching and watches "the dog and the car making for the same spot of pavement." Before he can see what happens, however, a nurse and orderly put him back into bed. The symbolic significance of this incident is readily apparent: the dog (Nature) and the car (Machine) are on a collision course, but it is too soon at this point in the novel for us to see the outcome. On the last page of the novel, however, we will see Bromden escaping from the grounds of the hospital "in the same direction [he] remembered seeing the dog go."

One of Miss Ratched's most effective tools of intimidation is the threat of indefinite confinement that faces a patient who has been committed. After a conversation with the lifeguard at the pool, McMurphy realizes for the first time the full implications of that threat and becomes fully conscious of his vulnerability. Immediately thereafter he puts aside his rebelliousness and becomes pliable and cooperative. Bromden is quick to observe this change and is afraid: "The white tubes in the ceilings begin to pump their refrigerated light again . . . I can feel it, beams all the way into my stomach." With McMurphy ending his resistance, Miss Ratched is in charge once again. "Whatever it was went haywire in the mechanism," remarks Bromden, "they've just about got it fixed again. The clean, calculated arcade movement is coming back . . . in the Nurses' Station I can see the white hands of the Big Nurse float over the controls." The clearest sign that McMurphy is retreating is the loss of his ability to laugh; this is the very danger he had warned the others against earlier. It is appropriate that this reversal is linked with the control panel where he had previously displayed his determined strength. Now, playing cards near the control panel, he loses his self-control when Martini kids him, "and the cards splash everywhere like the deck exploded between his two trembling hands." These hands are of course what the other patients depend on.

He is bewildered as he begins to realize that it is something more than the Big Nurse that is responsible for the trouble there. "I don't seem able to get it straight in my mind," he says. He does gradually get it straight in his mind, however, and comes to understand that it is not just the Big Nurse but also the Combine that he must fight. He eventually understands also that although he has been committed, many of the other patients have not; therefore, while his struggle can only destroy himself, it may save others. He ultimately decides to fight.

But before he decides to fight he undergoes a period of temptation, beginning with his talk with the lifeguard at the swimming pool. Some see a parallel between his test and that of Christ in the wilderness following his baptism. This may be far-fetched but suggests itself because of the more explicit Christ images in the novel. Harding describes the table in the Shock Shop as "shaped, ironically, like a cross" and the patient receives "a crown of electric sparks in place of thorns." Fredrickson accused Miss Ratched of wanting to "crucify" his friend Sefelt, who is described as being pinned to the wall, his hands "nailed out to each side with the palms up." As the group leaves for fishing, Ellis tells Billy to be "a fisher of men." When taken for the shock treatment, McMurphy says, "Anointest my head with conductant. Do I get a crown of thorns?" On McMurphy's way there a patient looks at him and says, "I wash my hands of the whole deal"; and another says, "It's my cross, thank you Lord." After Bromden suffocates McMurphy, Scanlon asks, "Is it finished?" McMurphy's healing hands, his leading twelve people to the sea to fish, his sacrifice of himself—these and other things according to one's interpretive ingenuity can be considered Christ images. But one can be well aware of such parallels without taking them too seriously. It is a mistake to do so. Kesey uses them playfully, intending more to excite archetypal reverberations for the action of the story than to make McMurphy restrictively a Christ figure.

His talk with the lifeguard makes him aware of what being committed means. His reaction is to think only of himself. In leaving the pool, he refuses to help a man with hydrocephalus out of the footbath, where he is blowing bubbles in the milky-looking water. Later the same day, he fails to support Cheswick when the latter challenges one of the Big Nurse's policies. The other patients sense immediately that he is no longer standing up for them. Bromden thinks he is finally "getting cagey" like the rest of them: "The way Papa finally did when he came to realize that he couldn't beat that group from town who wanted the government to put in the dam because of the money and the work it would bring, and because it would get rid of the village. . . ." The advantage of being cagey is that "It's safe. Like hiding." But when Cheswick drowns himself after McMurphy's failure to back him up, McMurphy begins to realize that his actions have generated obligations. He has pulled the men out of the fog and increased their vulnerability. A sense of responsibility begins to dawn in his essentially self-centered nature. When Scanlon says, "Hell of a life. Damned if you do and damned if you don't," McMurphy knows what he means. If he continues his campaign against Miss Ratched, the others benefit but he sacrifices his freedom and possibly destroys himself. If he "keeps an eye out for old Number One," he benefits but his fellow patients are lost.

The dog motif appears again at the end of Part 2, this time in connection with McMurphy. As he returns from the building where shock treatments are given, having just heard the treatment described, and consequently knowing the full consequences of continued resistance, Bromden says of him, "I could see that there was some thought he was worrying over in his mind like a dog worries at a hole he don't know what's down, one voice saying, Dog, that hole is none of your affair—it's too big and too black and there's a spoor all over the place says bears or something else just as bad. And some other voice coming like a sharp whisper out of way back in his breed, not a smart voice, nothing cagey about it, saying, *Sic* 'im, dog, *sic* 'im!" The two voices here make explicit the temptation McMurphy is undergoing. In Part 1 his behavior was self-centered showing off. In Part 2 he is brought to realize the obligation the strong incur toward the weak, and he becomes soberly aware of the risk he runs by resistance to what he now understands is more than simply control by a single Big Nurse.

The drama of his reversal, which comes in the last section of Part 2, makes use of a device similar to the fog machine at the end of Part 1. Whereas at the end of Part 1 it was fog that built up in intensity and then disappeared, at the end of Part 2 it is the ringing sound in the narrator's head that builds up to a high pitch and then stops immediately after McMurphy defiantly smashes the window of the Nurses' Station. This action signals that McMurphy has weighed the situation carefully and has chosen to save his fellow patients regardless of the peril to himself.

## "McMurphy Led the Twelve of Us to the Ocean"

After passing through his temptation in Part 2, McMurphy begins his saving mission in earnest in Part 3. "The nurse was biding her time till another idea came to her that would put her on top again." Meanwhile, McMurphy organizes a fishing trip that becomes the climax of the novel. Laughter and outdoor nature are the dominant elements in that climactic section.

The first convert to laughter in this part is the narrator himself. McMurphy discovers that Bromden has been chewing gum stuck to the bottom of the bed frames in the dorm. When he begins singing the old song, "Oh, does the Spearmint lose its flavor on the bedpost overnight?" Bromden's first impulse is to become angry, thinking that McMurphy is making fun of him. "But the more I thought about it," he says, "the funnier it seemed to me. I tried to stop it but I could feel I was about to laugh—not at McMurphy's singing, but at my own self. . . . I couldn't help but start to chuckle." At the end of Part 1 he had *almost* laughed; now he does laugh, although it is a rather pitiful performance; "I didn't sound like much because my throat was rusty and my tongue creaked. He told me I sounded a little out of practice and laughed at that. I tried to laugh with him, but it was a squawking sound, like a pullet trying to crow. It sounded more like crying than laughing." This laughter (particularly once he is able to laugh at himself) is the key indicator of Bromden's recovery and is concomitant with the first words he utters since entering the hospital. In fact, it is not until he has laughed that he is able to speak.

In this part we learn why Bromden has been feigning deafness. He recalls that "it wasn't me that started acting deaf; it was people that first started acting like I was too dumb to hear or see or say anything at all." He had first noticed this when he was a boy and three people came to the village to talk to his father, their purpose being to persuade the Indians to leave so the dam could be built. The leader of this trio was "an old white-haired woman in an outfit so stiff and heavy it must be armor plate." This description and other of her characteristics link her with Big Nurse; in fact, Bromden says she spoke in "a way that reminds me of the Big Nurse." And like Miss Ratched she knows how to get her way through cold manipulation, in this instance by using Bromden's mother for leverage in obtaining his father's cooperation. Bromden is amazed that he can remember this incident: "It was the first time in what seemed to me centuries that I'd been able to remember much about my childhood. It fascinated me to discover I could still do it." This reawakening to his past is a sign of health, of course; the only way he will recover mental and emotional stability is by facing such recollections. A contrasting parallel situation from McMurphy's childhood is provided a few pages later. As the only child in a group of bean pickers, he was ignored and therefore gave up talking for four weeks. But finally he opened up and, in characteristic fashion, told them all off, lost the job, but felt it was worth it.

One of the few references to machinery in this part is the description of what happens when the prostitute whom McMurphy has invited on the fishing trip enters the hospital. "I think apparatus burned out all over the ward trying to adjust to her come busting in like she did—took electronic readings on her and calculated they weren't built to handle something like this on the ward, and just burned out, like machines committing suicide." This is a delightful reversal because the machinery used to "adjust" the patients now must adjust itself and in so doing is destroyed. Machinery is shunted into the background in this part of the novel because nature has the principal role.

It is "a fine woodsmoked autumn day" when they set out to go fishing. All of the patients but McMurphy are frightened and ill at ease with their freedom and are therefore pliable victims for the service-station attendants who try to foist unneeded oil filters and windshield wipers on them when they stop to gas up. The doctor is with them. Because he is dominated by Miss Ratched, he needs McMurphy's cure as much as the patients do. McMurphy's bravado saves the situation at the service station and inspires the group with at least the appearance of self-confidence; but without the ability to laugh they have no real strength: "I think McMurphy knew better than we did that our tough looks were all show, because he still wasn't able to get a real laugh out of anybody. Maybe he couldn't understand why we weren't able to laugh yet, but he knew you can't really be strong until you can see a funny side to things." The condition of the narrator and the other patients is objectified in the description of the little boy from one of the "five thousand houses punched out identical by a machine and strung across the hills outside of town" whom they see always at the end of the game of crack-the-whip: "He'd always be so scuffed and bruised that he'd show up out of place wherever he went. He wasn't able to open up and laugh either. It's a hard thing to laugh if you can feel the pressure of those beams coming from every new car that passes, or every new house you pass."

Bromden's tension at passing through a region with so many signs of the Combine at work dissipates when he is aboard the fishing boat and heading out to sea. "When we passed the last point of the jetty and the last black rock, I could feel a great calmness creep over me, a calmness that increased the farther we left land behind us." It is here at sea, away from the hospital, which is "the Combine's most powerful stronghold," that the process of salvation through laughter reaches its climax. McMurphy observes the group's uninhibited outdoor activity—the enthusiasm over fish caught, the tangled lines, the shouting and cursing—and begins to laugh: "Rocking farther and farther backward against the cabin top, spreading his laugh out across the water—laughing at the girl, at the guys, at George, at me sucking my bleeding thumb, at the captain back at the pier and the bicycle rider and the service station guys and the five thousand houses and the Big Nurse and all of it. Because he knows you have to laugh at the thing that hurt you just to keep yourself in balance, just to keep the world from running you plumb crazy." McMurphy knows there is a painful side (this is something the narrator has doubted up until this moment), but he has a balanced view about it: "He won't let the pain blot out the humor no more'n he'll let the humor blot out the pain." The laughter becomes infectious and takes on cosmic proportions in this moment of epiphany:

> It started slow and pumped itself full, swelling the men bigger and bigger [size, it will be remembered, is the metaphor used repeatedly to signify self-reliant strength and dignity]. I watched, part of them, laughing with them—and somehow not with them. I was off the boat, blown up off the water and skating the wind with those black birds, high above myself, and I could look down and see myself and the rest of the guys, see the boat rocking there in the middle of those diving birds, see McMurphy surrounded by his dozen people [his disciples], and watch them, us, swinging a laughter that rang out on the water in ever-widening circles, farther and farther, until it crashed up on beaches all over the coast, on beaches all over all coasts, in wave after wave after wave.

After this moment of transformation, this Pentecost, the group radiates a new aura of self-assurance that is immediately apparent to the loafers on the dock: "They could sense the change that many of us were only suspecting; these weren't the same bunch of weak-knees from a nuthouse that they'd watched take their insults on the dock this morning."

Bromden, in particular, is greatly strengthened by this experience and restored to a sense of harmony with nature, from which the machines have separated him for so long. "I noticed vaguely that I was getting so's I could see some good in life around me. McMurphy was teaching me. I was feeling better than I'd remembered feeling since I was a kid, when everything was good and the land was still singing kid's poetry to me." But this strength that Bromden and the others have acquired has been tapped from McMurphy; so at the same time Bromden remarks on the positive change within himself, he also remarks on the exhaustion apparent in McMurphy, whose face reveals him as "dreadfully tired and strained and *frantic*, like there wasn't enough time left for something he had to do. . . ." This is the sacrificial hero evidencing the cost of his sacrifice and a sense of urgency concerning his mission.

### "No More Rabbits"

The day after the fishing trip, Big Nurse has her next maneuver underway: she will try to discredit McMurphy by persuading the patients his motives have been entirely selfish and mercenary. Kesey frequently uses irony in the mouth of Miss Ratched. Early in the novel she calls McMurphy a "manipulator," just as her own powers as a manipulator are being forcefully revealed. Now she insists he is not "a martyr or a saint," just as he is indeed proving himself to be a kind of martyr or saint. But for a while her insinuations about his selfish motives have the desired effect. Even Bromden has doubts when McMurphy uses him to win unfairly a bet concerning lifting the control panel. All doubts are allayed, however, when McMurphy takes George's side against Washington, one of the black aides: "right at that time all of us had a good idea about everything that was going to happen, and why it had to happen, and why we'd all been wrong about McMurphy." McMurphy precipitates the fight "sounding more tired than mad," and everybody could hear "the helpless, cornered despair" in his voice. This is a premeditated act, done almost reluctantly from a sense of duty. McMurphy has weighed the consequences.

That he acts out of a sense of responsibility is emphasized shortly after this when Bromden and McMurphy are taken to Disturbed as a result of the fight. Bromden is struck by the faces there, which reveal a need and a hunger for help, and he wonders "how McMurphy slept, plagued by a hundred faces like that, or two hundred, or a thousand." During the mental struggling of

Part 2, McMurphy had mentioned in answer to Harding's question about what he saw in his dreams that he saw "nothing but faces, I guess—just faces." These and other references to faces are used to clarify McMurphy's motivation. Near the end this motivation is made explicit when Harding says it is the weak (the patients) who drive the strong (McMurphy) into seemingly crazy acts of self-sacrifice and when Bromden says it was the patients' need and not simply defiance of Big Nurse that determined his actions: "It was us that had been making him go on for weeks, keeping him standing long after his feet and legs had given out, weeks of making him wink and grin and laugh and go on with his act long after his humor had been parched dry between two electrodes." McMurphy eventually gives us his own distinctive facial expression as a sacrifice for others. When he is brought back to the ward after the lobotomy, Bromden says, "There's nothin' in the face," and Scanlon agrees that it is "too *blank*."

Part 4 resolves the main themes and patterns of imagery. Bromden's salvation is complete enough that he can withstand the test of shock treatment: "It's fogging a little, but I won't slip off and hide in it. No . . . never again. . . . this time I had them beat." When he smashes the control panel through the window to obtain his freedom, "the glass splashed out in the moon, like a bright cold water baptizing the sleeping earth." Bromden's recovery and rebirth are central because he is a special representative figure. He has been there longer than any of the other patients; he was the farthest gone of any capable of recovery; and he is the most closely identified with nature. Member of an ethnic minority, he represents those most subject to victimization; but, significantly, he is the one with the most potential strength. And in addition to Bromden, Harding demonstrates that he too has found himself through McMurphy's example.

There is another spectacular laughing scene when the girls and the liquor are smuggled into the hospital itself. This laughing scene is a modulation of the one on the fishing boat and is necessary as a part of the falling action of the plot, in order to demonstrate that the patients are now able to laugh within the stronghold of the Combine as well as in the open freedom of nature. The laughter signifies the defeat of Miss Ratched: "Every laugh was being forced right down her throat till it looked as if any minute she'd blow up like a bladder." As the laughter swirled around her, the "enamel-and-plastic face was caving in. She shut her eyes and strained to calm her trembling, concentrating. She knew this was it, her back to the wall." McMurphy's last defiant act, ripping open the Big Nurse's uniform and exposing her breasts, "bigger than anybody had ever even imagined, warm and pink in the light," is a final attempt to release the natural from the perverted restrictions of a regimented and mechanistic system. Miss Ratched returns in a new white uniform, but "in spite of its being smaller and tighter and more starched than her old uniforms, it could no longer conceal the fact that she was a woman." Yet McMurphy himself is defeated; his work as savior is consummated by the sacrifice of himself, but his saving mission succeeds. Even after he is gone, his "presence" is "still tromping up and down the halls and laughing out loud in the meetings and singing in the latrines."

### "The Juggernaut of Modern Matriarchy"

By skillfully drawing upon proven conventions within the literary tradition—a timeworn yet timeless pattern of myth, a conscious and elaborate manipulation of images, a standard conflict-and-resolution plot with hero and villain—Kesey has created a novel that in terms of the social or cultural tradition is highly unconventional. His degree of formal skill is noteworthy among recent novelists and gives *Cuckoo's Nest* a significant place in recent fiction. Most critics acknowledge this formal excellence, but some are troubled by the novel's treatment of women and blacks. The rising popularity of the book coincided with the rising influence of the women's movement, and this situation has produced the principal controversy regarding the novel. Many of the women in *Cuckoo's Nest* are portrayed as domineering, manipulative, and emasculating. Miss Ratched is the principal offender, but her characteristics are echoed in the woman who leads the group desiring the dam, in Bromden's mother, in Billy's mother, and, to some extent, in Harding's wife. The only woman treated sympathetically aside from the prostitutes is the Japanese nurse. Harding announces the novel's primary view of women when he says, "We are victims of a matriarchy here, my friend, and the doctor is just as helpless against it as we are."

Many feminists have expressed guilt for having actually enjoyed the novel when they first read it prior to "liberation." One woman in a symposium on *Cuckoo's Nest* said, "It's the real dinosaur vision of the relationships between the sexes. It reinforces a large number of negative stereotypes that are very present in our culture anyway. They slide in so noiselessly because we're taking such pleasure in the different, more human liberation with which we identify, that we are not even aware of them, and that's why I use the word 'dangerous' about the novel." Leslie Horst argues that the novel portrays women who violate social expectation as unnatural and evil, while those who are pliable and fit the male view, as do the prostitutes, are portrayed as good. The message is that good women cannot be threatening or powerful. "Not only is the portrayal of women demeaning, but considerable hatred of women is justified in the logic of the novel. The plot demands that the dreadful women who break rules men have made for them become the targets of the reader's wrath." Elizabeth McMahon argues that "The Big Nurse happens also to be the Big Victim when viewed with an awareness of the social and economic exploitation of women." She suggests that Kesey should have been sympathetic and understanding toward Big Nurse's point of view. Ruth Sullivan provides a Freudian interpretation in which Miss Ratched is Big Mama, McMurphy is Big Daddy, and the patients are Little Sons; it is an Oedipal triangle marked by a man-woman power struggle. The sons are taught that mature women are dangerously intent on emasculating men. Raymond Olderman finds that Kesey's "flat portrayal of women and of blacks is more stereotypic and uncomfortable than funny or fitting with his cartoon character pattern. It borders too much on the simplistic." In a particularly caustic attack on the novel, Robert Forrey insists that "The premise of the novel is that women ensnare, emasculate, and, in some cases, crucify men."

*Cuckoo's Nest* puts into sharp relief some important issues concerning feminism and literature, serving as a special case in this regard. Many feminists concede that the novel is artistically successful but are outraged by the sexism they see in it. This raises questions about whether the problem lies with Kesey or with a narrow feminism. And these questions lead to considerations about the author's freedom: to what extent does programmatic feminism infringe upon artistic freedom?

The antifeminist charges have naturally generated counterarguments. Ronald Wallace argues that such charges are based on two faulty assumptions: "first, that the novel is a romance, and second, that McMurphy is its hero, fully embodying its values." He says *Cuckoo's Nest* is not a romance but a comedy. It does have the typical romantic antitheses: self/society; primitive/civilized; freedom/control; heart/mind. But its final wisdom is that of high comedy and its primary method is reversal of expectation and inversion of values. "To fault Kesey for his treatment of women and blacks is to miss the comedy of a device that has informed comic art from Aristophanes to Erica Jong, the reversal of traditional roles." The reversal of human and mechanical and traditional male-female roles is a comic indication of the world being out of joint.

Another counterargument is based on an interpretation of the novel as tragedy. That it is read as romance, comedy, tragedy, satire, and several other things is a tribute either to its richness as an object of criticism or to the ingenuity of critics. In any case, Michael Boardman argues persuasively that *Cuckoo's Nest* has tragic power and is related to the great tragedies of all ages because it portrays a conflict that is not merely between individuals but is inner. As in Shakespeare's tragedies, the struggle between Big Nurse and

McMurphy becomes a fight between two opposed principles in McMurphy's being. McMurphy, like Hamlet, must become something other than what he was before the disaster or tragic victory. According to this argument, the antifeminine element that some readers have found objectionable is "local" rhetoric designed to allow the reader to experience McMurphy's tragedy as moving and significant. "For the dramatic requirements of the story," says Boardman, "Nurse Ratched had to be very nearly an incarnation of evil, unthinking or otherwise. For Mac's struggle to seem important, the forces opposing him must not be too 'understandable,' and never sympathetic. . . . A little understanding, where villains are concerned, often courts disaster; with Big Nurse, as with Iago, the moral terms of the struggle need to be clear in order to prevent confusion." Consequently, to have made Big Nurse more "human," more understandable, as McMahon suggested Kesey should have done, would have been to attenuate the force of the tragic action.

Ronald Billingsley acknowledges that women serve as antagonists for the men in the novel but insists that the real conflict is not one between men and women. "It would be a serious mistake," he says, "to read the novel as the work of a misogynist. Big Nurse and her emasculating ilk are no more truly feminine than the Acutes and Dr. Spivey are truly masculine. Like machines, these women are neuter, asexual devices that respond to *power*." Statements from the novel such as the following support this interpretation: Big Nurse walked past McMurphy, "ignoring him just like she chose to ignore the way nature had tagged her with those outsized badges of femininity, just like she was above him, and sex, and everything else that's weak and of the flesh." Miss Ratched is a villain not because she is a woman, but because she is not human. McMurphy's ripping open of her shell-like uniform is not a revengeful attack on a castrating bitch: it is a symbolic gesture indicating that the human must be liberated from the machine if the oppression of the Combine is to be eliminated.

Kesey himself feels that the charges of sexism in *Cuckoo's Nest* are unwarranted. He insists his motives, conscious or unconscious, were not those attributed to him by feminist critics. Some biographical information is pertinent to the controversy. One of the Kesey tapes records a conversation at a party in which Kesey is telling about his experiences working at the hospital. Another man who did similar work is present. They both agree that the white nurses were usually hard, tough, and trying to prove something. The black nurses were different. The nurse in "The Kicking Party" and Big Nurse are undoubtedly shaped largely out of Kesey's experiences with nurses as an aide. The kind Japanese nurse in *Cuckoo's Nest* perhaps had her origin in the black nurses he knew. Consequently, Big Nurse may reflect to some extent a "pre-Liberation" female personality of the late 1950s—the woman feeling

much alone in asserting herself in a male world and therefore finding it necessary to be overly aggressive and domineering in order to prove her worth.


## Responses and Evaluation

*Cuckoo's Nest* is notable for the variety of interpretive responses it has
evoked. As was mentioned above, it has been treated as comedy, most extensively by Ronald Wallace, who believes it is structured on the fertility ritual
described by F. M. Cornford in *The Origin of Attic Comedy*. The basic conflict
is between two archetypal characters, the *alazon* and the *eiron*, the boastful,
self-deceived fool and the witty self-deprecator who pretends ignorance in
order to defeat his opponent. In addition to acting as *eiron*, McMurphy functions as "A Dionysian Lord of Misrule" who "presides over a comic fertility
ritual and restores instinctual life to the patients." Raymond Olderman
interprets the novel as a romance centering on the waste-land theme, in
which McMurphy is "a successful Grail Knight, who frees the Fisher King
and the human spirit for a single symbolic and transcendent moment of
affirmation." Michael Boardman's interpretation of the novel as tragedy was
mentioned in the preceding section. Sheldon Sacks also categorizes it as a
"narrative tragedy," pointing out that McMurphy makes choices leading to
the lobotomy. "The protagonist's monstrous doom is consequently seen as a
victory, and his human quality, though in all conventional ways mundane,
unlovely, self-seeking, as one we must newly conceive of as great."

A number of critics have been interested in *Cuckoo's Nest* as a western
novel reflecting characters, language, and values associated with the American frontier. Richard Blessing says, "Essentially, the McMurphy who
enters the ward is a frontier hero, an anachronistic paragon of rugged individualism, relentless energy, capitalistic shrewdness, virile coarseness and
productive strength. He is Huck Finn with muscles, Natty Bumppo with
pubic hair. He is the descendant of the pioneer who continually fled civilization and its feminizing and gentling influence." According to Blessing,
McMurphy mirrors the classic and popular patterns of American manhood.
As a logger, associated with cowboys, he reminds us of Paul Bunyan, Pecos
Bill, the Lone Ranger, and the Marlboro man. He is also linked with other
American heroic types: the gambler, hustler, confidence man, and the
phallic hero of traveling-salesman and locker-room stories. Ronald
Billingsley fits the novel into the tradition of southwest humor, noting the
element of exaggeration, the tall-tale character, the regional dialect, the
bawdy language and racy stories, the emphasis on physical strength, and the
oral style. And he explains that "the tall tale comic tradition can be utilized

not only for humor, but also for rich character portrayals, social criticism and the explication of significant themes." These vernacular western and folk elements are significant in *Cuckoo's Nest* and are even more apparent in *Great Notion*. They originate in Kesey's family background, his life in Oregon, and his temperament and personality. He admires frontier values, and Gerald Graff is correct in suggesting that underlying the ostensibly iconoclastic mood of *Cuckoo's Nest* is nostalgia, "nostalgia for a period in which the pitting of a heroic protagonist against a hostile, persecuting bourgeoisie corresponded roughly to social fact."

Popular culture manifests itself in the novel in ways besides allusions to folk heroes. The Big Nurse's ward is described as having "that clean orderly movement of a cartoon comedy"; the patients' conversation is "like cartoon comedy speech" and their world is "like a cartoon world, where the figures are flat and outlined in black, jerking through some kind of goofy story that might be real funny if it weren't for the cartoon figures being real guys." The way characters grow big or small in Bromden's perspective resembles a visual technique often used in cartoons. Terry Sherwood believes the novel demonstrates a noteworthy use of popular culture in a serious novel. He points out that, as in comic strips, *Cuckoo's Nest* turns on the mythic confrontation of Good and Evil. He suggests that Bromden's transformation is like that of Freddy Freeman (he means Billy Batson) to Captain Marvel; McMurphy and Bromden are like the Lone Ranger and Tonto. Kesey has a keen interest in comic books and popular culture and took them seriously before Popular Culture associations and conferences became common. At Perry Lane he talked about comic-book superheroes as the honest American myths. He once said in an interview, "A single *Batman* comicbook is more honest than a whole volume of *Time* magazines." Discounting the exaggeration and shock effect of this statement, we are still left with a kernel of truth about his attitude toward comic books and popular culture. They function significantly in the development of theme and characterization in *Cuckoo's Nest*, and he makes deliberate use of them (e.g., Captain Marvel and Wolfman) in *Great Notion*.

In a letter to Whitney Daly describing his pleasure at seeing his first novel in print, Kesey said, "But my book is good, and has as much integrity as I am able to muster without losing my ability to laugh, and if you've hit the one solid punch dead center they can never take that away from you." Our final consideration is, how solid and dead center is that punch? Peter Beidler has suggested one respect in which the punch scores tellingly: self-reliance. This is a quality most Americans think they have or wish they had. It has been an important theme in American literature from the beginning (Puritans, Franklin, Emerson, Thoreau, Whitman, Hemingway), and a novel that celebrates it effectively is bound to make an impact. Beidler says self-reliance "is made up in part of self-confidence (knowing that you *can*), in part of self-trust (knowing that *you* can), in part of self-consciousness (*knowing* that you can), and in part of self-control (acting on the knowledge that you can). Those who are self-reliant are usually not bound by authority or tradition, are independent in thought, and are courageous and tenacious in pursuit of their goals." Self-reliance is usually accompanied by optimism. Kesey once said he gets weary of people "who use pessimism to avoid being responsible for all the problems in our culture. A man who says, we're on the road to disaster, is seldom trying to wrench the wheel away from the driver. I prefer the troublemaker. He tells them he doesn't like the way they're running the show, that he thinks he could do better, that the fact is he's going to *try!*" McMurphy has the kind of self-reliance Beidler describes, and it is precisely what the patients need. Contemporary readers want to be shown that it works, and they want to be shown that the weak can become strong, the cowardly brave, and the impotent potent: *Cuckoo's Nest* does these things.

The question remains as to how convincingly it does them. Terry Sherwood thinks the novel sentimentalizes and oversimplifies moral problems: "Kesey believes in the comic strip world in spite of himself. . . . He forgets that the comic strip world is not an answer to life, but an escape from it. The reader finds Kesey entering that world too uncritically in defense of the Good." Others are disturbed by the way that self-reliance is asserted; they find it merely a matter of jokes, games, obscenity, and verbal disrespect, and doubt that throwing butter at walls, breaking windows, stealing boats, and doing what comes naturally is really the answer for achieving lasting sanity and self-esteem. They feel the novel's "yes" to life is anarchic and that too much emphasis is placed on the sexual and scatological as weapons against the impersonal and repressive aspects of society. Bruce Wallis has pointed out that it is not the Combine that generates the evil Kesey observes, but the evil that generates the Combine. The flaws in the system result from anterior flaws in the people who created and maintain it. The philosophy of the novel, in attacking the system, is attacking the symptom instead of the disease.

If the message of *Cuckoo's Nest* is that emotional stability and human dignity are to be achieved simply through vulgar and anarchic rebellion against authority, then the novel has questionable worth despite its humor and its engaging battle between freedom and oppression. If its saving laughter is nothing more than defiant ridicule or irresponsible escape, then it has little to contribute to solving the puzzling but all-important question of the proper relationship between society and the individual. If Kesey believes that the answer to the dehumanizing abuse of technology is to give reign to sensual impulse, then getting back in touch with the natural world can mean little more than being close to nature the way an animal is. There is a disturbing adolescent tendency persistent in Kesey to equate the scatological with freedom, vitality, manliness, and naturalness. Perhaps it partly originated in his exposure during an impressionable period to Beat literature, life in North Beach, and the nascent counterculture of Perry Lane. It undoubtedly results partly from his rural background, the coarser elements of which he may have exaggerated as a stance toward the attractive but rather intimidating intellectual and cultural sophistication he encountered in coming to California. Whatever its source, it is apparent in *Cuckoo's Nest*. It is possible, however, to interpret the novel by viewing the obscenity as a means rather than an end. McMurphy is a coarse and vulgar personality, but the victory wrought by him is not merely a triumph of coarseness and vulgarity. His crude strength and cocky self-centeredness are manifestations in caricature of an underlying moral strength and a salutary self-respect. His example should not be taken at face value; it is symbolic on an unconventional, almost cartoon level of values that are conventional in the most positive and universal sense: self-reliance, compassion for the weak, hope, perseverance, self-sacrifice, and harmony with nature.

M. GILBERT PORTER

# Musical Messages in Kesey's Novels: You Can Tell a Man by the Song that He Sings

*To my mother and father—*
*Who told me songs were for the birds,*
*Then taught me all the tunes I know*
*And a good deal of the words.*
— Dedication/*Sometimes a Great Notion*

As the Tutelary Spirit of *Sometimes a Great Notion*, Kesey describes in the epigraph to chapter six the tricky feat of performing a duet with an echo:

> "Row, row, row your boat, gently down the stream. . . ."—and just as you start on your merrily-merrilies, the echo comes in, "Row, row, row . . ." right on cue. So you sing with the echo. But you must be careful in choosing your key or your tempo; there is no changing of the pitch if you start too high, no slowing down of the tempo if you start too fast . . . because an echo is an inflexible and pitiless taskmaster; you sing the echo's way because it is damned sure not going to sing yours. And even after you leave this mossy acoustical phenomenon to go on with your hiking or fishing, you cannot help feeling, for a long time after, that any jig you whistle, hymn you hum, or song you sing is somehow immutably tuned to an echo yet unheard, or relentlessly echoing

From *Connecticut Review* 12, no. 2 (Summer 1990). © 1990 by Board of Trustees, Connecticut State University.

a tune long forgotten—. . .—and sometimes as you sing, you cannot help feeling that the unheard echoes and tunes forgotten are echoes of other voices and tunes of other singers . . . in that kind of world.

This passage focuses on two important matters: One is the enigmatic way that we all participate in the mysterious deterministic forces that shape our lives, a recurrent theme in Kesey's work. The other is the prominence that Kesey assigns to music in his text and in his experience. Kesey's world is filled with tunes, lyrics, players and singers, and Kesey himself makes joyful noises on the guitar, flute and his Thunder Machine, a 1962 Thunderbird converted to a musical instrument, which Kesey calls "a kind of Modern Jazz Quartet of junk." What follows here is a sampler of the way Kesey's awareness of and love for musical forms enhance his fiction, from background sounds for verisimilitude to musical allusions and leitmotifs to establish character or theme.

The laughter that McMurphy brings into the Cuckoo's Nest, for example, carries with it a musical tone: "that laughing sound hovers around him," Bromden observes, "the way the sound hovers around a big bell just quit ringing. . . ." McMurphy even introduces himself to the ward with a bit of balladry: "'My name is McMurphy, buddies, R. P. McMurphy, and I'm a gambling fool.' He winks and sings a little piece of a song: '. . . and whenever I meet with a deck of cards lays . . . my money . . . down,' and laughs again." This line is from "A Roving Gambler," a song that functions here to identify McMurphy as a risk-taker. The tattoo of aces and eights—the "deadman's hand"—on his shoulder confirms later that the risks he is willing to take involve high stakes indeed—his life for the lives of the inmates.

McMurphy dislikes the Muzak-style tape that plays incessantly in the day room because its characterless homogeneity is for him emblematic of what the ward tries to do to people, to neutralize all individual differences. The tape resonates in the ward as the theme music of conformity for the Big Nurse's rare "successful Dismissal": "it brings joy to the Big Nurse's heart, something that came in all twisted different is now a functioning, adjusted component, a credit to the whole outfit and a marvel to behold." "*I wish*," McMurphy shouts in outrage, "*some idiot in that nurse's hothouse would turn down that frigging music!*"

McMurphy's songs, by contrast, insist on individual differences and serve to limn his character and to personalize his relationships with others in the Cuckoo's Nest. Early in the morning of his first day in the hospital, McMurphy fills the corridors with song, taking impish joy in several verses of "The Wagoner's Lad": "'My horses ain't hungry, they won't eat your hayay-aeee.' He holds the note and plays with it, then swoops down with the rest of the verse to finish it off. 'So fare-thee-well, darlin', I'm gone on my way'," and "Hard livin's my pleasure, my money's my own, an' them that don't like me, they can leave me alone." In this scene, McMurphy sings both to express his vital good spirits and to indicate his disdain for place and policy. Later in the corridor, as Washington sidles around spilled wax toward an angry Big Nurse, McMurphy whistles, with pointed allusion to the Harlem Globetrotters, "Sweet Georgia Brown" as comic accompaniment to the aide's evasive shuffle. After shocking Nurse Ratched with his whale shorts, McMurphy accompanies her hasty retreat to the Nurses' Station with another verse from "The Roving Gambler" to remind her of his style and independence: "'She took me to her parlor, and coo-oo-oold me with her fan'—I can hear the whack as he slaps his bare belly—'whispered low in her mama's ear, I luh-uhvv that gamblin' man'." The song reverberates incongruously along walls that usually give off only a deadly mechanical hum.

In response to McMurphy's success in the second TV vote and his subsequent growing brashness, Big Nurse punitively assigns the big redhead to latrine duty, but, as Bromden observes, McMurphy takes his toilet duties lightly and mitigates the unpleasantness with music: "The most work he did on them was to run a brush around the bowls once or twice apiece, singing some song loud as he could in time to the swishing brush. . . ." Big Nurse is not pleased with the result: "She walked along shaking her head and saying, 'why this is an outrage . . . an outrage . . .' at every bowl. McMurphy sidled right along beside her, winking down his nose and saying in answer, 'No, that's a toilet bowl . . . a *toilet* bowl'." With his new Indian friend, however, McMurphy is gentle and understanding. As a way of getting Bromden to relax and open up to him, McMurphy sings him a silly hillbilly song: "'Oh, does the Spearmint lose its flavor on the bedpost overnight?'," a number that leads Bromden to reveal that he can speak and induces a chuckle in him that will culminate in the liberating and salvific laughter of the climactic fishing episode. These musical notes are entered with a light touch, but they add dimension to both character and scene in *One Flew Over the Cuckoo's Nest.*

*Sometimes a Great Notion* carries even greater musical reference, from the title, the epigraph and the dedication to its own chorus of voices, popular-song allusions, live bands, jukebox tunes and a disputation over jazz, bop and blues.

Kesey's employment of the multiple point-of-view provides an antiphony of sound in the novel, and these various voices offer contrasting choral refrains of yea and nay. Lee's Old Reliable voice, clamoring for him to "Watch out," bounces off "Hank's bell ringing," Hank's private, joyful response to nature, work and life. Boney Stokes's jeremiads—"Our day is

ending, our skies are turning black" —have to contend with Old Henry's gay
reveilles—"Wake it an' shake it. Wag it an' shag it! . . . Le's get out there an'
take the shade offn the ground" —and his fierce calls to battle—"We'll *whup*
it! We'll *whup* it!" Indian Jenny, however, invokes aid from natural and supernatural sources to effect her revenge on Henry for his sexual rejection of her:
"('*Oh clouds,*' Jenny chants, '*Oh rain* . . . come against the man I say
. . .')." The geese call "Guh-luke . . . ?" Molly the hound bells "BAYOOHR
. . . !" A composite voice of the town reflects on weather and woes: "Got
troubles with the old lady? It's the rain. . . . Got a deep hollow ache bleeding
cold down inside the secret heart of you from too many deals fallen
through? . . . That there, brother, is just as well blamed on the rain. . . ." Yet
the Real Estate Hotwire intones assurances to the town, "Prosperity *round*
the bed," and Brother Walker promises that "the Lord is merciful." Jonas's
feeble assurance, "Blessed Are the Meek, for They Shall Inherit the Earth.
Matt. 6," is displaced rudely by Henry and Hank's theme, "NEVER GIVE
A INCH." The loggers stridently curse Hank and his defiance: "*goddamn you
anyhow, Hank Stammmmper!*" The jukebox at the Snag bubbles appropriate
lines of commiseration: "*To try an' fergit I turn to the wine . . . / An empty bottle
a broken heart / An' still you're on my mind.*" The old wino boltcutter captions
the waffle of voices with one jaded comment—"Horseshit," an item that Joe
Ben has learned with his boundless faith to transform into the stuff of realized dreams. Joe's optimistic voice has the effect of harmonizing the other
discordant voices as he defends Lee, supports Henry, encourages Hank, and
entertains everyone. With his goblin grin and irrepressible good spirits, Joe
Ben bounces through the life of Wakonda singing his simple song of affirmation: "Oh yeah . . . Oh yeah . . . Oh yeah." More grandly, the orchestration of sounds is extended by Lee's introduction of classical music into the
mix. Hank's nightly checking of the tension on the cables along the
retaining wall sound to Lee's educated ear like the opening notes of
"Beethoven's Fifth, 'Whack whack whack *thongggg!*' Dum dum dum *dong!*"

The strains of Beethoven are a rare classical interlude here, for the
main motifs are conveyed in lines from country and western music or
popular songs. The title and epigraph of the novel are taken from "Good
Night, Irene," by Huddie Ledbetter and John Lomax. The lines "Sometimes
I get a great notion / To jump in the river . . . an' drown" point up the
impulse to defeatism and suicide that is anathema to Old Henry, Hank and
Joe Ben, but that is attractive to Lee and fatal to Myra and Ben. The west-
ering spirit that compelled the restless Stamper clan to follow the sun from
Kansas to Oregon is captured early in the narrative in the folk ballad of jour-
neyers: "I'm goin' down . . . that long dusty road," from Woody Guthrie and
Lee Hays' "Going Down the Road." As Henry and Hank dump the wooden

box containing Jonas's body into the bay during the antecedent action of the early 1940s, the voice of Eddy Arnold comes from the radio of a nearby pickup: *"There'll be smoke on the water, on the land an' the sea,/ When our Army and our Navy overtake the en-ah-mee"* ("Smoke on the Water," by Earl Nunn and Zeke Clements), a World War II tune that suggests that the international conflict of values has its counterparts in the local community and in the Stamper family. Hank Snow's rendition of "I'm Movin' On" comes first from the jukebox in the Snag—*"I'm movin' on,/ Just hear my song"*—and later from Joe Ben's tiny transistor radio—*"Mister engineer take that throttle in hand/ Cause this rattler's the fastest in all the land,/ so keep movin on. . . ."* The song serially accents movements both geographical and thematic: As the Stamper clan gathers for a strategy meeting in the meadhall-like house on the river, Evenwrite is returning from Portland with his damaging information from union officials about the WP contract, Draeger drives from Eugene toward Wakonda for his surprising encounter with Hank and his never-give-a-inch tactics, and Lee botches his suicide in New York and heads for his destiny-changing rendezvous with his big brother: the biggest move of Lee's very transient life.

Lee's actual homecoming and his immersion in childhood memories are signified on his first day in the woods by the music heard during the lunch break from Joe Ben's radio: *"Come home, come home,/ It's suppertime./ I'm going home at last."* Jimmy Davis's song captures Lee's rare feelings of nostalgia for his Oregon past, but the subsequent misunderstanding with Hank over choker-setting and spar-rigging brings Lee back to his vindictive present, and Joe's radio picks up that mood in the next song: *"Ah got a radiation burn,/ On my pore pore heart."* The struggle between the two brothers has its larger counterpart in the conflict between the union brotherhood and Hank, an antagonism that comes to a boil in the fight with Biggy Newton in the Snag. Bandsmen Rod and Ray prime the crowd for the evening's match with a lively version of "Under the Double Eagle," touting American glory in battle, and they characterize the feigned amenities between Hank and his neighbors—and Biggy—just before the fight with the ersatz sweetness of "Candy Kisses": *"Candy kisses, wrapped in pay-per, Mean more to you, than any of mine. . . ."* After his victory over Biggy, Hank lies battered and asleep under the tender ministrations of Viv, who sings gently to him "Buckeye Jim," the children's lullaby that frames the chapter: *"Way* up yonder, top of the sky . . . *blue*-jay lives in a silver eye. Buckeye Jim, you can't go. . . . go weave an' spin, you can't go. . . . Away up yonder, top o' the sky. . . ."* Hank dreams, we are told, "that he is at the top of his class and nobody is trying to pull him down. . . ." Viv's song tells of yearning for impossible transcendence beyond strife and underlines the pressure on Hank as the man at the top who finds the pressure deeply wearing on his spirit despite his obstinate resistance. Viv also uses song to comfort the anguished spirit of Hank when he becomes atypically frightened by the gabble of geese, and disoriented in the confrontation with his own reflection in the rain-splattered window the night before the disasters in the state park. While Hank submits gladly to the calming effect of Viv's gently massaging hands on his battered back, she sings him some soothing escapist verses from a North Carolina children's ballad, "The Bird Song":

> *Wild Geese flying through the air*
> *Through the sky of blue-oo . . .*
> *They're now a-floating where the south sun glows*
> *So why not me and you. . . .*

When Hank persists in his isolation from the town, the subject of the final conversation between Viv and Draeger in the Snag on Thanksgiving day, the jukebox plays two tunes in the background. One echoes the recent estrangement between Hank and Viv (Hank Williams's "Why Don't You Love Me"): *"Why don't you cuddle up . . . an' console me,/ Snuggle up . . . an' comfort me,/ Pacify my heart jes' one more time?,"* and the other *"Ah cast a lonesome shadow/ An' Ah play a lonesome game"*—emphasizes Hank's never-give-a-inch rugged individualism as well as Draeger's description of what Hank is risking: "complete—*total*—alienation. . . ."

The character of Viv and her relations to Hank and Lee are several times suggested by music. As she moves gracefully and pleasurably through her household duties, she hums her satisfaction with her work in a line from "The Battle Hymn of the Republic": "Mine eyes have seen the glory of the coming umming umm," and her singing of "All the Pretty Little Horses," which the exhausted Lee hears through the wall on his first night at home, comes to him as "an answer that he couldn't quite interpret":

> *. . . when you wake, you'll have cake*
> *And all the pretty little horses . . .*

Later, after the fight at the Snag and while Viv is singing "Buckeye Jim" to victorious Hank, envious Lee begins to intuit an answer from Viv's horse song as "The last three weeks wheel around his bed in full carrousel gallop. . . . He lies dreamily in the center of the wheeling display, trying to decide which steed he will be riding tonight. After some minutes of careful scrutiny he chooses 'That one there!'—a high-prancing filly with slim flanks and sleek withers and a flowing golden mane. . . ." The filly he has chosen sleeps next door with his brother; she can join him only in his dreams—and in his plans. Setting and theme music here, then, place Viv firmly at the center of the two brothers' lives.

The actual fistfight over Viv that develops between Hank and Lee is prefigured by a shouting match over music, an argument, following the hunt, that grows out of Lee's assertion to Hank that "the *one* edge that the West Coasters must concede to the East was that it boasted far greater opportunities to hear good music." Hank denies the claim and to support his case plays records by Joe Williams, Fats Domino, Joe Turner, and Fats Waller, the "old blues and boogie and bop" that, as Hank says, "had some man to it." Lee counters with Dave Brubeck, Jimmy Giuffre, Cal Tjader, and finally John Coltrane, whose "Africa Brass" is to Lee "Jazz black as it comes, black balls dragging the ground. . . ." Hank's music is bluesy, joyous and celebrative. Lee's music is protest music, a cry of outrage in the night. Hank defines Lee's music as "crap," as "exactly the sorta dismal manure" that Myra would go for. To Hank's ear the sounds are self-pitying and self-destructive. Lee denies this, but later, alone in his room, he bitterly admits to himself that "he is right, it is the very sort of manure Mother would buy. He is right and cursed right and damn him for it damn him to everlasting hell!" This pent-up poison is finally released in the fight with Hank on the riverbank under Viv's anxious observation.

Like the personal conflicts, the elemental conflicts are also given musical accompaniment. On the last day of cutting, as Old Henry, Hank and Joe Ben work under pressure with the old-fashioned logging methods but with joy in their isolation and their teamwork, Joe Ben's radio crystallizes their camaraderie and their temporary freedom from strife with the union and the community:

> *I know you love me*
> *An' happy we could be*
> *If some folks would leave us alone. . . .*

With the rain, the flooding tide, and the rising wind, however, things quickly turn ugly. A tree slabs and takes off Henry's arm, the runaway log pins Joe Ben and then drowns him, and Hank watches powerlessly as his family, his contract, and his life seem to be collapsing around him. Joe Ben's radio plays two songs through this sequence. One is *"Leaning, Leaning,/ Safe and secure from all alarms . . . ,"* an old protestant hymn that testifies to Joe Ben's fundamentalist faith. It does so ironically, however, for the happy little man who believed himself snug in God's pocket dies there, but dies laughing, his optimism intact until the very end. The other song is the Burl Ives version of "The Doughnut Song": *"As you walk through life you will have no cares/ If you walk the lines and not the squares. . . .* When you go through life make this your goal. . . . Watch the doughnut, not the hole." This dime-store philosophy urging cautious optimism and conservatism sounds in secular counterpoint to the sacred hymn of faith, both plumping for an easy affirmation belied by the grim reality here of fate's indiscriminate bludgeoning and nature's ferocity. The last song in the novel also accentuates an ironic contrast. As the juke box in the Snag plays Johnny Redfeather singing nostalgically of "Swanee," that placid old southern stream, Hank, Lee and Andy are battling the turbulent waters of the Wakonda Auga trying to deliver their log booms to the mill.

Although some music in the novel is unidentifiable (for example, Viv's satisfied postcoital humming after her first lovemaking with Hank), and some is used to place the novel in time (Lee's scanning of the song titles on the jukebox in the Snag), and some is simply a function of profession (Ray, the guitarist, whistling the introduction to Hank Thompson's "A Jewel Here on Earth"), most musical references are carefully placed to delineate character, to point up ironic contrasts, to enlarge theme, to enhance the texture of the tale. And what does this artistic employment of music reveal about the man within the artist? That music has helped to shape his sensibilities since childhood. That he is keenly attuned to the rhythms and melodies and lyrics of the life around him. That he is closer to the street than to the concert hall. That music functions for him as a powerful medium to document human wretchedness, to nurture resilience, to accompany joy and sorrow, and to inspire affirmation in the face of formidable evidence for negation. That he shares, therefore, the sentiments of the Grateful Dead, his favorite band, that music will lead us to the light:

> I spent a little time on the mountain,
>   Spent a little time on the hill.
> Things went down we don't understand,
>   But I think in time we will.
>   One way or another,
>   One way or another
>   One way or another,
>   This darkness got to give.

The creative alliance of fiction and music will no doubt be continued and even expanded in Kesey's work in progress, for the working title of the Alaska novel, scheduled tentatively for publication this year, is *Sailor's Song*.

BENJAMIN GOLUBOFF

# The Carnival Artist in the Cuckoo's Nest

Readers familiar with the work of the Russian formalist critic Mikhail
Bakhtin will discover in Ken Kesey's *One Flew Over the Cuckoo's Nest* plentiful
material to illustrate Bakhtin's theory of the carnivalesque. Bakhtin's "carnivalization" has been applied with profit in Medieval and Renaissance studies;
only recently has it been brought to bear upon American texts. Yet Bakhtin's
carnival spirit is as much present in Kesey's novel as in Cervantes or Rabelais,
and to recognize this is to discover elements of *Cuckoo's Nest* that have been
overlooked by the novel's many commentators. For example, virtually
nothing has been said in the abundant critical work on *Cuckoo's Nest* about the
carnival imagery which pervades the novel at its simplest level. It is this
imagery which most clearly invites readers to a reappraisal of *Cuckoo's Nest* in
the light of Bakhtin's ideas.

Images of carnival life begin with the first poker game McMurphy
plays with the inmates. There we learn that among the various jobs
McMurphy held before coming to the ward was "a season on a skillo wheel
in a carnival." This is how McMurphy, the gambler, has learned how to
"know what the mark *wants*, and how to make him think he's getting it." One
of McMurphy's "marks" is Dr. Spivey, the befuddled psychiatrist who
presides at the "Group Therapy" sessions on the ward. McMurphy has
conned the doctor into believing that the two of them are old schoolmates.

From *Northwest Review* 29, no. 3 (1991). © 1991 by *Northwest Review*.

"And in the course of our reminiscing" Dr. Spivey tells the meeting, "we happened to bring up the carnivals the school used to sponsor—marvellous noisy gala occasions." The doctor and McMurphy have been wondering, he continues, "what would be the attitude of some of the men toward a carnival here on the ward." Their attitude, it turns out, is largely favorable. The schizophrenic Cheswick even stands up and proclaims the merits of the plan: "Lots of therapeutics in a carnival. You bet." The Big Nurse, of course, doubts the therapeutic value of the carnival and ultimately quells the plan, but carnival imagery persists in the novel.

Harding, the effeminate and college-educated inmate, describes the effect of Electro-Shock Therapy to McMurphy as "a wild carnival wheel of images, emotions, memories . . . the barker takes your bet and pushes a button. . . . Pay the man for another spin, son, pay the man." The secret party on the ward which brings Kesey's novel to its climax can be seen, in its quality of giddy and temporary misrule, as the reemergence of the carnival idea discussed in the therapy meeting. The party is the culminating attempt to undermine the authority of Nurse Ratched. It is orchestrated by McMurphy, whom the narrator, Chief Bromden, has already characterized as "a carnival artist." The title suits McMurphy well, and it calls attention to the artistry of what Bakhtin helps us to identify as a "carnivalized" novel.

Bakhtin's theory of the carnivalesque is set forth in *Problems of Dostoevsky's Poetics* (1929) and *Rabelais and his World* (1940). The theory is derived from the European tradition of folk carnivals extending from the Roman saturnalia to medieval and Renaissance feasts and rituals of misrule. Coexisting with the official rites and feasts of the Church, carnival "offered a completely different, nonofficial, extraecclesiastical and extrapolitical aspect of the world, of man, and of human relations . . . a second life outside of officialdom." Carnival, for Bakhtin, points up the relativity of "officialdom" as it celebrates the cyclical renewal of time and nature:

> All the symbols of the carnival idiom are filled with this pathos of change and renewal, with the sense of the gay relativity of prevailing truths and authorities. We find here the characteristic logic, the peculiar logic of the "inside out" (*à l'envers*), of the turnabout, of a continual shifting from top to bottom of . . . numerous parodies and travesties, humiliations, profanations, comic crownings and uncrownings.

Grounded in the cycles of nature's becoming, and opposed to the canons of prevailing authority, carnival is for Bakhtin "the true feast of time"; it reinforces for its celebrants "the collective consciousness of their eternity, of their earthly, historic immortality as a people, and of their continual renewal and growth."

In the medieval and Renaissance tradition that Bakhtin describes, the carnival does not manifest itself principally in verbal forms. Rather, carnival consists of "*syncretic pageantry* of a ritualistic type . . . an entire language of symbolic concretely sensuous forms. . . ." Yet, according to Bakhtin, the spirit of carnival "is amenable to a certain transposition into a language of artistic images that has something in common with its concretely sensuous nature; that is, it can be transposed into the language of literature." This "transposition" Bakhtin speaks of as "the carnivalization of literature." "Carnivalization" begins for Bakhtin around the second half of the seventeenth century with the disappearance of the concrete forms of folk carnival. The displaced forms and tropes of carnival are transposed to seriocomic genres of literature—genres of "multi-toned narration" characterized by "the mixing of high and low, serious and comic."

The seriocomic *Cuckoo's Nest* can be identified as a "carnivalized" novel for a number of reasons. It blends elements of high and popular culture with the easy familiarity of the carnival spirit. The carnival trope of crowning and uncrowning gives shape to Kesey's narrative. The novel's curious pattern of allusions may be interpreted as carnivalesque parody. These allusions parody not only the nineteenth-century American texts they evoke, but also the critical authority which presented those texts to readers of the sixties. Leslie Fiedler, it will be seen, is the butt of Kesey's travesties. Most immediately, what Bakhtin defines as "carnival laughter" may be seen as a powerful thematic element in Kesey's novel.

Bakhtin describes carnival laughter as "universal in scope; it is directed at everyone, including the carnival's participants." Carnival laughter often takes aim at authorities and sacred texts. (This will explain the essentially comic quality of the allusions in Kesey's novel.) Crucially, for Bakhtin, carnival laughter acknowledges the pathos of change in time and nature:

> Laughter embraces both poles of change, it deals with the very process of change, with *crisis* itself. Combined in the act of carnival laughter are death and rebirth, negation (a smirk) and affirmation (rejoicing laughter). This is a profoundly universal laughter, a laughter that contains a whole outlook on the world.

Carnival laughter is always ambivalent, then, in its recognition of cyclical change, death and rebirth.

*One Flew Over The Cuckoo's Nest* is an ambivalent comedy of death and renewal. The period of misrule it describes culminates with the death of

McMurphy and what must be read as the rebirth of Chief Broom. The Chief's escape is a rebirth insofar as his fog hallucinations have given way to clarity by the end of the novel; he has reclaimed memories of his own history hitherto erased by the conditions of the ward, and he has chosen to speak again after his twenty years' silence. When he throws the control panel through the window of the tub room to make his escape, the Chief notices how the broken glass lies in the moonlight "like a bright cold water baptizing the sleeping earth." The Chief's rebirth, or new baptism, has been fostered by the climate of carnivalesque privilege which McMurphy has created on Nurse Ratched's ward. And in the Chief's account of it, this is the privilege of laughter.

"I forget sometimes what laughter can do," the Chief says early in McMurphy's stay on the ward. For the men on the ward laughter does much indeed. It helps restore the Chief to speech and identity. It establishes a comic solidarity among the inmates, and exposes Nurse Ratched and her policies as susceptible to derision. Most importantly, it gives the men a new wry perspective on their lot in the hospital. "Man, when you lose your laugh you lose your *footing*," McMurphy says to the grim inmates. In his joking campaign against the Big Nurse, he gives the men at least a temporary comic footing from which to view their life on the ward. All the most telling scenes describing McMurphy's battle with the Nurse—the World Series revolt, the fishing trip, the party on the ward—are scenes of laughter.

The Chief tells us that McMurphy's is "the first laugh I've heard in years. . . . Even when he isn't laughing, that laughing sound hovers around him, the way the sound hovers around a big bell just quit ringing." While McMurphy's laughter marks momentary victories over the Nurse and the policies of the hospital, it is as often directed at himself and his condition of limitation and powerlessness. In other words, his laughter bears that ambivalent mixture of affirmation and negation which Bakhtin associates with the laughter of the carnival.

The Chief understands that McMurphy "knew you can't really be strong until you see a funny side to things. . . ." But he wonders if his hero might not be "blind to the other side, if maybe he wasn't able to see what it was that parched the laughter deep inside your stomach." On their return from the fishing trip, where the party has incurred various wounds, the Chief finally realizes the ambivalent quality of McMurphy's laughter:

> He knows you have to laugh at things that hurt you just to keep yourself in balance, just to keep the world from running you plumb crazy. He knows there's a painful side; he knows my thumb smarts and his girlfriend has a bruised breast and the

doctor is losing his glasses, but he won't let the pain blot out the humor no more'n he'll let the humor blot out the pain.

This is the laughter that presides over Kesey's tale of death and rebirth. The laughter is, in Bakhtin's words "gay, triumphant, and at the same time mocking and deriding. It asserts and denies, it buries and revives."

Connected to the role of ambivalent laughter in Bakhtin's version of the carnivalesque is the ritual of crowning and uncrowning. Through this action the carnival spirit enacts its subversion of established authority:

> The primary carnivalistic act is the mock crowning and subsequent decrowning of the carnival king. . . . Under this ritual act of decrowning a king lies the very core of the carnival sense of the world—the pathos of shifts and changes, of death and renewal. . . . Crowning/decrowning is a dualistic ambivalent ritual, expressing the inevitability and at the same time the creative power of the shift-and-renewal, the joyful relativity of all structure and order, of all authority and all (hierarchical) position.

In the European tradition of carnival that Bakhtin surveys in his work on Rabelais, mock priests and bishops were installed to celebrate parodic liturgies. At banquets and bean feasts ephemeral kings and queens (*rois pour rire*) presided by lottery. Each ruled for the duration of the feast and was decrowned at the end. Because of its wide currency as a folk practice, and because of the "image of constructive death" it conveys, Bakhtin maintains that "the ritual of decrowning has been the ritual most often transposed into literature."

Not much elaboration is required to identify McMurphy as a carnival king. Crowned and uncrowned during his tenure on the ward, McMurphy expresses for the inmates the "joyful relativity" of the hierarchy in which they live, and leads them through a ritual of change and renewal. The ritual begins when McMurphy first meets the inmates of the ward. "Which one of you claims to be the craziest?" McMurphy wants to know. "Who runs these card games? . . . Who's the bull goose loony here?" As president of the Patients' Council, Harding seems to hold this title, and much of part one of the novel describes how McMurphy supplants Harding as the inmates' leader. He does this by engineering the World Series revolt and thus winning his bet about breaking the Big Nurse's composure. As part one of the novel closes and the men abandon their chores to cheer an invisible baseball team on a blank TV screen, it is as clear from the inmates' new solidarity as from the Nurse's rage that McMurphy has been installed as lord of misrule.

As the ward's new "bull goose loony," McMurphy secures the loyalty of the inmates and directs their laughter at the forms and policies of hospital life. He orchestrates disruptions of the Big Nurse's regime and, as is forshadowed in his initial question to Harding, he now runs the card games. It is significant that so much of McMurphy's activity as bull goose loony involves games of chance, for such games, according to Bakhtin, have a special meaning in the carnival sense:

> The images of games were seen as a condensed formula of life and of the historic process: fortune, misfortune, gain and loss, crowning and uncrowning. . . . At the same time games drew the players out of the bounds of everyday life, liberated them from usual laws and regulations, and replaced established conventions by other lighter conventionalities.

Imagery of games and chance are persistent in *Cuckoo's Nest*. There is McMurphy's history at the skillo wheel, and the innumerable games of blackjack and stud poker he institutes on the ward. Memorable as well is the Monopoly game McMurphy plays with the hallucinating Martini: "Hold it a minute. What's thum other things *all* over the board?" And finally there is the Chief's vision of loaded dice during Electro-Shock Therapy. These games of chance figure the inmates' liberation from the conventions of the ward even as they suggest McMurphy's crowning and uncrowning as carnival king.

McMurphy presides as a *roi pour rire* through the body of the novel. His carnival artistry, culminating in the fishing trip and the ward party, continues to undermine the authority of the Big Nurse and to redeem the inmates from what Harding has described as their condition of docile "rabbithood." McMurphy's uncrowning comes about in the circumstances of violence and sacrifice with which the novel concludes. When the ward party has been discovered and the no longer virginal Billy Bibbit has been shamed into suicide by Nurse Ratched, McMurphy attacks the Big Nurse. For this action he is sent to the Disturbed ward and eventually given a lobotomy. In the novel's penultimate scene, the Chief suffocates the post-operative McMurphy in a weeping embrace.

McMurphy's is clearly what Bakhtin calls a "constructive death"— "destruction and uncrowning are related to birth and renewal." After McMurphy's death, of course, the inmates cease to be inmates. "Everything was changing," the Chief tells us. "Sefelt and Frederickson signed out together Against Medical Advice, and two days later another three Acutes left, and six more transferred to another ward." The Chief himself, restored to speech and identity, escapes to revisit the scenes of his childhood. Even Harding has ceased to be a "rabbit." He makes his departure just the way he had said he wanted to: "right out that front door, with all the traditional red tape and complications." In their last conversation, McMurphy had returned to Harding the mantle of leadership he claimed from him on their first meeting: "You can be bull goose loony again, buddy, what with Big Mack outa the way." The return of the title suggests that for Harding, especially, McMurphy's uncrowning enables a constructive liberation.

McMurphy's tenure as lord of misrule or carnival king frees the inmates from the hospital and returns them, if not to sanity, at least to a condition of creative self-sufficiency. But McMurphy has not destroyed the authorities against which he has taught the inmates to rebel. At the end of the novel the Big Nurse has come back into control of the ward. Billy Bibbit is dead. And the forces of mechanistic conformity which the Chief identifies as the "Combine" still obtain in the world of the novel. The only difference is that the inmates no longer fear the Nurse's authority and the Chief no longer fears the Combine.

According to Bakhtin, the spirit of carnival opposes but does not destroy official authority. The tradition of European folk carnival never replaced the civil and ecclesiastical authorities that it mocked. "The aim" of carnival symbolism, says Bakhtin, "was to find a position permitting a look at the other side of established values, so that new bearings could be taken." So the ritual of McMurphy's crowning and uncrowning allows the inmates an alternative to the hierarchy of the ward, showing them the "joyous relativity" of the established values it represents, without tearing down or replacing those values.

The theory of "carnivalization" also helps to explain the generic instablity of *Cuckoo's Nest*: the uneasy coexistence in the novel of disparate generic elements that has long engaged Kesey's critics. Discussion has focused primarily on the curious blending of high- and pop-cultural elements in the novel. There are, on the one hand, the reflections of Cooper and Twain and Melville which permeate the book, and which will be discussed more fully later. On the other hand, *Cuckoo's Nest* is conspicuously informed by the tropes and vision of American comic books and TV shows. The stammering Billy Bibbit has become, under the scrutiny of Kesey's critics, a figure who recalls both Melville's Billy Budd, and Captain Marvel's alter ego, Billy Batson. According to the Chief, the ward is "like a cartoon world, where the figures are flat and outlined in black, jerking through some kind of goofy story. . . ." The hospital's library, we learn, is well stocked with comic books, and Harding joins many of the novel's critics in suggesting that McMurphy and the Chief find comic-book parallels in the Lone Ranger and Tonto.

Terry G. Sherwood has assessed the comic-strip vision of *Cuckoo's Nest* and discovered in it the novel's principal flaw: a moral "simplification" based on a too "clear-cut opposition between Good and Evil. . . ." This simplified moral vision, according to Sherwood, allows Kesey to ignore the more complex problems of characterization suggested by his references to the American romance:

> Kesey rejects the profounder symobolism of Melville, frightening in its incomprehensible mysteriousness, for the delimited symbolism of the comic-strip super-hero. Our sympathy with these "unrealistic" and superhuman heroes is always reserved. We cannot expect psychological fullness from them.

Sherwood is correct in observing that the comic-book qualities of Kesey's heroes weaken the moral vision of the book, but it is a mistake to say that these popular-culture elements constitute a "rejection" of the symbolism of American romance. It is more accurate to say that the high- and popular-culture elements of the novel exist together in a carnival dialogue.

The first principle of carnival for Bakhtin is familiarity, the free mingling of disparate types that takes place during carnival time. He maintains that in seriocomic European literature:

> Carnivalization constantly assisted in the destruction of all barriers between genres, between self-enclosed systems of thought, between various styles, etc.; it destroyed any attempt on the part of genres and styles to isolate themselves or ignore one another; it brought closer what was distant and united what had been asunder.

*Cuckoo's Nest* is a novel that describes a nurse inflating herself like a comic book monster. Its protagonist is "the cowboy out of the TV set." The narrator hears "cartoon comedy speech" and hallucinates Disney scenes. That these elements should obtain in a novel that also evokes Melville and Twain may be a rejection of moral complexity, but it is also a wonderfully comic acknowledgment of the "joyous relativity" behind cultural distinctions of high and low.

Kesey's handling of his high-culture materials is consistently comic, and this the critics who have searched the novel for allusions have downplayed. From *Cuckoo's Nest* have been sifted references to *The Last of the Mohicans, Moby Dick, Huckleberry Finn,* and "The Waste Land," as well as to Hemingway, Faulkner, Burroughs, and Thoreau. Much has been made, for example, of the symbolism of the fishing trip, and of McMurphy's white-whale undershorts. (He got them from a "Literary major" at Oregon State: ". . . she said I was a symbol.") Several writers have also called attention to the way in which McMurphy and his faithful Indian companion parallel the black and white outcast pairs famously described in Leslie Fiedler's *Love and Death in the American Novel*. But no one has illustrated the comic logic behind these allusions with the clarity that Bakhtin's carnival spirit provides.

Carnivalization allows us to recognize the allusions in Kesey's novel as essentially parodic. For Bakhtin, parody is a central component of the carnival sense. In his work on Rabelais he surveys the *parodia sacra*—parodies of sacred texts—by which the carnival spirit of the Middle Ages satirized ecclesiastical authority. In the study on Dostoevsky the issue of parody is described in these terms:

> In carnival, parodying was employed very widely, in diverse forms and degrees: various images (for example, carnival pairs of various sorts) parodied each other variously and from various points of view; it was like an entire system of crooked mirrors, elongating, diminishing, distorting in various directions and to various degrees.

The peculiar logic of carnival parody is the logic of inversion. Carnival life is "life turned inside out . . . *Monde à l'envers*." "Also characteristic is the utilization of things in reverse: putting clothes on inside out . . . trousers on the head . . . and so forth."

The world of *Cuckoo's Nest* is eminently a world of "things in reverse." Recall the notes in mirror writing that McMurphy leaves for Nurse Ratched to discover when she inspects the latrines with a dentist's mirror. The roll sheet for the men on the ward "is listed alphabetically backwards to throw people off. . . ." The novel's most disturbing image of upsidedown-ness is revealed in the Chief's visions under Electro-Shock Therapy. In this disjointed monologue the Chief recalls how his father and uncle exhumed his grandmother's corpse from its pauper's grave and hung it in a tree: "High high high in the hills, high in a pine tree bed, she's tracing the wind with that old hand. . . ." Throughout the novel things low are brought high and poles are reversed, very much in the carnival's "peculiar logic of the 'inside out,' of the turnabout, of a continual shifting from top to bottom."

This peculiar logic of the turnabout is what gives Kesey's allusions to "high-culture" texts their distinctive parodic flavor. Even in some of his one-liners the turnabout is evident. Describing the Big Nurse's position on Electro-Shock Therapy, Harding tells McMurphy that she is "one of the few with the heart to stand up for a grand old Faulknerian tradition in the treatment of the rejects of sanity: Brain Burning." When Candy, one of the hookers McMurphy knows from Portland, arrives for the ward party, he spies her at the window and says: "She walks like beauty, in the night." Thus Byron and Faulkner make their appearances in the novel in inverted posture.

One parodic moment in the novel that its critics have consistently overlooked occurs that night in the dormitory when the Chief first speaks. When he finishes his whispered account to McMurphy of how the Combine and his mother worked to rob the Chief's father of his size and strength, he lies silently and watches McMurphy in the next bed:

> He didn't say anything after that for so long that I thought he'd gone to sleep. . . . I looked over at him and he was turned away from me. His arm wasn't under the covers, and I could just make out the aces and eights tattooed there. . . . I wanted to reach over and touch the place where he was tattooed, to see if he was still alive. . . . That's a lie. I know he's still alive. I want to touch him because he's a man. That's a lie too. . . . I want to touch him because I'm one of those queers! But that's a lie too. I just want to touch him because he's who he is.

This exchange takes place on the night before the fishing trip and constitutes an inverted mirror image of "The Counterpane," chapter four of *Moby Dick*, where Ishmael and Queequeg meet before the voyage of the Pequod. All the elements of Melville's famous chapter are present in this dormitory scene, and all are presented in an inverted condition.

In both scenes the white man and the native are in bed together. But in *Cuckoo's Nest* the point of view belongs to the indian rather than to his white bedfellow. In Kesey's novel, the Chief breaks his long silence just as Ishmael, in "The Counterpane," speaks up at last after being frightened to silence by the harpooneer's approach to the bed. As the Chief admires the aces and eights on McMurphy's arm, it had been Ishmael who remarked on the markings of the native: ". . . this arm of his tattooed all over with an interminable Cretan labyrinth of a figure. . . ." And where Chief Broom desires to touch the white man and rejects the homoerotic dimension of the situation, it had been Ishmael who, awakening in Queequeg's embrace, wrestled to get out of his "bridegroom clasp." The episode in *Cuckoo's Nest*, then, is a striking inversion of "The Counterpane," and one presented through the "distorting mirror" of the carnival spirit.

For many readers after 1960, of course, Melville's "Counterpane" has become an emblem of Leslie Fiedler's famous *hierogamos*: "the pure marriage of males—sexless and holy . . . in which the white refugee from society and the dark skinned primitive are joined till death do them part." Fiedler's *Love and Death in the American Novel* appeared in 1960 while Kesey was auditing Malcolm Cowley's writing class at Stanford, and it is reasonable to assume that Kesey was aware of Fiedler's ideas by the time he finished *Cuckoo's Nest* in the spring of 1961. It is certain that in his handling of the partnership between McMurphy and the Big Chief, Kesey achieves a strikingly parodic inversion of Fiedler's myth of the good companions.

"Parody," says Bakhtin, "is the creation of a *decrowning double;* it is that same 'world turned inside out'." McMurphy and the Chief, then, are comic doubles of those light- and dark-skinned pairs of men through whom Fiedler described the "archetype" or "model story . . . haunting almost all our major writers of fiction." As such, Kesey's characters act to decrown the authority of a vision of American literature that was gaining academic currency when *Cuckoo's Nest* first appeared.

That Fiedler's terms are particularly at issue in the novel is suggested early in part one when Harding first points out Chief Broom to McMurphy: "There's your Vanishing American, a six-foot-eight sweeping machine, scared of its own shadow." It seems Harding has been reading Fiedler's discussion of James Fenimore Cooper, for it is there that Fiedler brands Chingachgook as "nature's nobleman and Vanishing American" and assigns him a place in the "model story" of the *hierogamos.* Just as the Vanishing American is transformed by Kesey into a mute and schizophrenic Columbia Indian, so the general terms of Fiedler's *hierogamos* are inverted in parody.

For Fiedler, the partnerships of dark and light in Cooper, Melville, and Twain enact for the American imagination an "inner escape from a world of blameless, sexless, females." *Cuckoo's Nest* is also an avatar of the old antimatriarchal strain in American fiction; recall, for example Harding's remarks about "matriarchy" and the "pecking party." And *Cuckoo's Nest* participates as plainly in "the American Dream of guilt remitted" by the dispossessed dark races as does any of the texts on which Fiedler preached the *hierogamos.* It is specifically in the relations between McMurphy and Chief Broom that Kesey's parody of the "sacred marriage" obtains.

First of all, Kesey rearranges the terms through which the world of physical nature is understood by the partners in the *hierogamos.* Early in McMurphy's stay on the ward, the Chief goes sweeping by the new inmate's bed and notices a smell he'd almost forgotten after twenty years in the hospital. The ward smells of "Pablum and eye-wash, of musty shorts and socks . . . but never before now, before he came in, the man smell of dust and dirt from the open fields, and sweat, and work." For the Chief, this white man is always associated with the forces of nature: ". . . McMurphy was a giant come out of the sky to save us. . . ."

As he restores the Chief to identity and speech, McMurphy becomes a representative of the free and unmediated life of the outdoors: "McMurphy was teaching me. I was feeling better than I'd remembered feeling since I was a kid, when everything was good and the land was still singing kid's poetry to me." Presiding over the fishing trip McMurphy becomes, like Melville's harpooneer and Cooper's good indians, a genius of the hunt, initiating the tenderfoot Chief into a struggle with nature. All this, of course, parodies Fiedler's account of the "model story" in which the white partner is the tenderfoot who "reaches out to the uncorrupted sources of natural life . . ." represented by the native partner.

Fiedler's color scheme is inverted in other ways as well. In Fiedler's model story, the native partner sometimes acts as "a substitute father" to the white, educating him and leading him through the dangers of the frontier. In *Cuckoo's Nest*, the Chief consistently associates McMurphy with his own father whom he sees, like his white companion, as another sacrifice to the Combine. McMurphy's role as a stand-in father is perhaps most clearly suggested by his efforts to cure the Chief of his delusion of having lost his physical stature: "Look here, Chief . . . You growed a half a foot already." Much as Nigger Jim had done for Huck Finn, McMurphy supervises and encourages the Chief's growth to self-sufficient manhood.

And finally, in the classic American novels which, for Fiedler, present the *hierogamos*, it is usually the dark partner who dies for the white: Chingachgook for Natty, Queequeg for Ishmael. In *Cuckoo's Nest*, the white man dies to free the indian, sacrificing his life to ensure the freedom of his companion. Like Ishmael upside-down, Chief Broom alone survives to tell the tale of his pale-faced savior.

The inversion of Fiedler's *hierogamos* in *Cuckoo's Nest* is a parodic activity which may be called carnivalesque in both its aims and means. Bakhtin's "decrowning doubles" or carnival pairs are conspicuous inhabitants of Kesey's novel, mocking and mirroring the figures of the American "model story." Moreover, for Bakhtin the rituals of carnival bring about for their participants "the realization that established authority and truth are relative." Despite the near-hegemony it would enjoy through the midsixties, Fiedler's version of the American novel is, like any critical formulation, a purely relative one. *Cuckoo's Nest* must be seen as one of the earliest statements of dissent against Fiedler's critical authority, celebrating as it does the "joyous relativity" of his categories for the American novel.

"Writers," Kesey has said, "are trapped by artificial rules. We are trapped in syntax. We are ruled by an imaginary teacher with a red ball-point pen. . . ." Fiedler's rules for the American novel, like the Big Nurse's rules for life on the ward, are artificial rules. McMurphy, the "carnival artist," reveals for the inmates the relative quality of the ward's regime through his laughter and through his being crowned and uncrowned as a king of misrule. So the parodic allusions in this "carnivalized" novel stand Fiedler's rules on their head, permitting Kesey's readers "a look at the other side of established values, so that new bearings could be taken."

# Chronology

1935      Ken Elton Kesey born in La Junta, Colorado, 17 September.

1946      Family moves to Springfield, Oregon.

1956      Marries Faye Haxby.

1957      Graduates from University of Oregon.

1958      Finishes "End of Autumn" (unpublished novel).

1959      Enters creative writing program at Stanford on a Woodrow Wilson Fellowship.

1961      Volunteers fro government drug experiments and works as a psychiatric aide at Menlo Park VA Hospital. Finishes "Zoo" (unpublished novel).

1962      *One Flew over the Cuckoo's Nest* is published.

1963      Stage version of *One Flew over the Cuckoo's Nest* comes out.

1964      *Sometimes a Great Notion* is published. Embarks on a cross-country bus trip with the Merry Pranksters filming "The Movie."

1965        Arrested in April for possession of marijuana.

1966        Arrested in January for possession of marijuana. Flees to Mexico. Returns in late fall and is arrested.

1967        Convicted and spends June to November in the San Mateo County Jail and later at the San Mateo County Sheriff's Honor Camp.

1968        Moves to Pleasant Hill, Oregon. Tom Wolfe's *The Electric Kool-Aid Acid Test* is published.

1969        Lives in London from March to June, doing some work for *Apple* (The Beatles music label).

1971        Coedits (with Paul Krassner) *The Last Supplement to the Whole Earth Catalog.*

1973        *Kesey's Garage Sale* is published.

1974        *Spit in the Ocean*, no. 1, including "The Thrice-Thrown Tranny-Man or Orgy at Palo Alto High School" and the first part of *Seven Prayers by Grandma Whittier* is published.

1976        *Spit in the Ocean*, no. 2, including second part of *Seven Prayers* is published. "Abdul and Ebenezer" is published in *Esquire*.

1977        *Spit in the Ocean*, no. 3, including third part of *Seven Prayers* is published.

1978        *Spit in the Ocean*, no. 4, including fourth part of *Seven Prayers* is published.

1979        *Spit in the Ocean*, no. 5, including "Search for the Secret Pyramid" and fifth part of *Seven Prayers* is published.

1980        *The Day After Superman Died* is published.

1981        *Spit in the Ocean*, no. 6, including sixth part of *Seven Prayers* is published. Takes a trip to China to cover the Beijing Marathon.

1982    "Running into the Great Wall" is published in *Running*.

1986    *Demon Box* is published.

1989    *Caverns*, by O.U. Levon (Kesey and the Thirteen members of his graduate writing seminar at the University of Oregon) is published.

1990    *The Further Inquiry*, a screenplay examining Neal Cassady and the 1964 voyage of the bus *Further*, with 150 color photographs by Ron "Hassler" Bevirt, is published.

1990    *Little Tricker the Squirrel Meets Big Double the Bear* (children's book) is published.

1991    *The Sea Lion* (children's book) is published.

1992    *Sailor Song* is published.

1994    *Last Go Round* (with Ken Babbs) is published.

# Contributors

HAROLD BLOOM is Sterling Professor of the Humanities at Yale University and Henry W. and Albert A. Berg Professor of English at the New York University Graduate School. He is the author of over 20 books, including *Shelley's Mythmaking* (1959), *The Visionary Company* (1961), *Blake's Apocalypse* (1963), *Yeats* (1970), *A Map of Misreading* (1975), *Kabbalah and Criticism* (1975), *Agon: Toward a Theory of Revisionism* (1982), *The American Religion* (1992), *The Western Canon* (1994), and *Omens of Millennium: The Gnosis of Angels, Dreams, and Resurrection* (1996). *The Anxiety of Influence* (1973) sets forth Professor Bloom's provocative theory of the literary relationships between the great writers and their predecessors. His most recent books include *Shakespeare: The Invention of the Human*, a 1998 National Book Award finalist, and *How to Read and Why*, which was published in 2000. In 1999, Professor Bloom received the prestigious American Academy of Arts and Letters Gold Medal for Criticism.

TERRY G. SHERWOOD is a literary scholar and critic who has published several essays on contemporary fiction including an essay—reprinted in different journals—on Kesey's use of comic strip themes and methods. Sherwood has taught English at the University of Victoria, B.C.

TONY TANNER is a literary scholar and critic who has published several manuscripts on contemporary fiction. His publications include *City of Words*, *Conrad: Lord Jim*, *Saul Bellow* and *The Reign of Wonder.*

RAYMOND M. OLDERMAN has been a professor of English at Miami University, Ohio. His publications include *Beyond the Waste Land: The American Novel in the Nineteen-Sixties*.

BRUCE E. WALLIS has been a professor of English at the University of Victoria, B.C. His essays have appeared in the *University of Toronto Quarterly* and in *Short Fiction*. He has also published a full length manuscript on Byron.

STEPHEN L. TANNER has been a professor of English at Brigham Young University. His articles and essays have appeared in *American Literature, Shakespeare Quarterly, Studies in Romanticism, Essays in Literature, English Language Notes*, and *Southwest Review*. He has also published a full length manuscript on Paul Elmer More.

JOHN WILSON FOSTER is a literary scholar and critic whose essays on contemporary fiction have appeared in such journals as *Western American Literature* and *Critique*.

BARRY H. LEEDS has been a professor of English at Central Connecticut State College. His publications include *The Structured Vision of Norman Mailer* and the critical study, *Ken Kesey*.

Professor of English and associate Vice Provost at the University of Missouri-Columbia, M. GILBERT PORTER has also published two books on Kesey: *The Art of Grit: Ken Kesey's Fiction* (University of Missouri Press) and *One Flew Over the Cuckoo's Nest: Riding to Heroism* (Twayne, 1988).

BENJAMIN GOLUBOFF is a literary scholar and critic whose studies of American travel writing have appeared in *ATQ, American Studies, New Orleans Review*, and *Northwest Review*.

# Bibliography

Allen, Henry. "A '60's Superhero, After the Acid Test," *Washington Post*, June 9, 1974, pp. L1–L3, cols. 4, 1–6.

Barsness, John A. "Ken Kesey: The Hero in Modern Dress," *Bulletin of the Rocky Mountain Modern Language Association 23* (1969): 27–33.

Blaisdell, Gus. "SHAZAM and the Neon Renaissance," *Author & Journalist 48* (June 1963), 7–8.

Blessing, Richard. "The Moving Target: Ken Kesey's Evolving Hero," in *Journal of Popular Culture 4* (1971): 615–27.

Boardman, Michael M. "*One Flew over the Cuckoo's Nest: Rhetoric and Vision.*" *Journal of Narrative Technique 9* (1979): 171–83.

Boyers, Robert. "Attitudes Toward Sex in American 'High Culture,'" *Annals of the American Academy of Political and Social Science 376* (1968): 36–52.

Carnes, Bruce. *Ken Kesey*, Boise State University Western Writers Series, no. 12. Boise, Idaho: Boise State University, 1974.

Falk, Marcia L. "A Hatred and Fear of Women?," *New York Times*, December 5, 1971, p. 5.

Field, Rose. "War Inside the Walls," *New York Herald Tribune*, February 25, 1962, p. 4.

Fiedler, Leslie A. "Making It with a Little Shazam," *Book Week*, August 2, 1964, pp. 1, 10–11.

Foster, John Wilson. "Hustling to Some Purpose: Kesey's *One Flew over the Cuckoo's Nest*," *Western American Literature 9* (Summer 1974), 115–29.

Gaboriau, Linda. "Ken Kesey: Summing up the '60's; Sizing up the '70's," *Crawdaddy*, no. 19 (December 1972), pp. 31–39.

Havemann, Carol Sue Pearson. "The Fool as Mentor in Modern American Parables of Entrapment: Ken Kesey's *One Flew over the Cuckoo's Nest*, Joseph Heller's *Catch-22* and Ralph Ellison's *Invisible Man*." Diss., Rice University, 1971.

Hoge, James O. "Psychedelic Stimulation and the Creative Imagination: The Case of Ken Kesey," *Southern Humanities Review 6* (Fall 1972), 381–91.

Knapp, James O. "Tangled in the Language of the Past: Ken Kesey and Cultural Revolution," *Midwest Quarterly 19* (1978): 398–412.

181

Levin, Martin. "A Reader's Report," *New York Times Book Review*, February 4, 1962, p. 32.

———. "Life in a Loony Bin," *Time* 79 (Feb. 16, 1962), 90.

Lish, Gordon. "What the Hell You Looking in Here for, Daisy Mae? An Interview with Ken Kesey," *Genesis West* 2, no. 5 (1963): 17–29.

Martin, Terrence. "*One Flew over the Cuckoo's Nest and the High Cost of Living*," *Modern Fiction Studies* 19 (Spring 1973), 43–55.

Maxwell, Richard. "The Abdication of Masculinity in *One Flew over the Cuckoo's Nest*," in *Twenty-seven to One: A Potpourri of Humanistic Material*. Ogdensburg, N.Y.: Ryan Press, 1970.

Mills, Nicholaus. "Ken Kesey and the Politics of Laughter," *Centennial Review* 16 (Winter 1972), 82–90.

Olderman, Raymond M. *Beyond the Wasteland: A Study of the American Novel in the Nineteen-Sixties*. New Haven, CT: Yale University Press, 1972, pp. 35–51.

Peden, William. "Gray Regions of the Mind," *Saturday Review* 45 (April 14, 1962), 49–50.

Pratt, John Clark, ed. *One Flew over the Cuckoo's Nest: Text and Criticism*, New York: Viking Press, 1973.

Sassoon, R.L. Review of *One Flew over the Cuckoo's Nest*, *Northwest Review* 6 (Spring 1963), 116–120.

Schopf, William. "Blindfolded and Backwards: Promethean and Bemushroomed Heroism in *One Flew over the Cuckoo's Nest* and *Catch-22*," *Bulletin of the Rocky Mountain Modern Language Association*, vol. 26, pp. 89–97.

Sherman, W.D. "The Novels of Ken Kesey," *Journal of American Studies* 5 (August 1971), 185–96.

Sherwood, Terry G. "*One Flew over the Cuckoo's Nest* and the Comic Strip," *Critique* 13, no. 1 (1972), 96–109.

Smith, William James. "A Trio of Fine First Novels," *Commonweal* 75 (March 16, 1962), 648–49.

Tanner, Stephen L. "Salvation Through Laughter: Ken Kesey and the Cuckoo's Nest," *Southwest Review* 57 (Spring 1973), 125–37.

Tanner, Tony. "Edge City (Ken Kesey)," in *City of Words: American Fiction 1950–1970*. New York: Harper & Row, 1971.

Waldmeir, Joseph J. "Two Novelists of the Absurd: Heller and Kesey," *Wisconsin Studies in Contemporary Literature* 5 (Autumn 1964), 192–204.

Wallis, Bruce E. "Christ in the Cuckoo's Nest: or, the Gospel According to Ken Kesey," *Cithara* 12 (November 1972), 52–58.

Witke, Charles. "Pastoral Convention in Virgil and Kesey," *Pacific Coast Philology* 1 (1966), 20–24.

Wolfe, Tom. *The Electric Kool-Aid Acid Test* (1968). New York: Bantam Books, 1969.

Zaskin, Elliot M. "Political Theorist and Demiurge: The Rise and Fall of Ken Kesey," *Centennial Review* 17 (Spring 1973), 199–213.

# Acknowledgments

"*One Flew Over the Cuckoo's Nest* and the Comic Strip" by Terry G. Sherwood from *Critique*, Vol. 13, No. 1 (1970): 97–109, © 1970 by *Critique*. Reprinted with permission.

"Edge City (Ken Kesey)" from *City of Words: American Fiction 1950-1970* by Tony Tanner, © 1971 by Tony Tanner. Reprinted by permission of HarperCollins Publishers, Inc.

"The Grail Knight Arrives: Ken Kesey, *One Flew over the Cuckoo's Nest*" by Raymond M. Olderman from *Beyond the Waste Land: A Study of the American Novel in the Nineteen-Sixties* by Raymond M. Olderman, © 1972 by Yale University. Reprinted with permission.

"Christ in the Cuckoo's Nest: or, the Gospel According to Ken Kesey" by Bruce E. Wallis from *Cithara*, Vol. 12 (November, 1972): 52–58, © 1972 by St. Bonaventure University. Reprinted with permission.

"Salvation Through Laughter: Ken Kesey & the Cuckoo's Nest" by Stephen L. Tanner from *Southwest Review*, Vol. 58, No. 2 (Spring 1973): 125–136, © 1973 by Southern Methodist University Press. Reprinted with permission.

"Hustling to Some Purpose: Kesey's *One Flew Over the Cuckoo's Nest*" by John Wilson Foster from *Western American Literature*, Vol. 9, No. 2 (August 1974): 115–130, © 1974 by the Western Literature Association. Reprinted with permission.

"*One Flew Over the Cuckoo's Nest:* 'It's True Even If It Didn't Happen'" by Barry H. Leeds from *Ken Kesey* by Barry H. Leeds, © 1981 by Frederick Ungar Publishing Co., Inc. Reprinted with permission.

"The Plucky Love Song of Chief 'Broom' Bromden: Poetry from Fragments" by M. Gilbert Porter from *The Art of Grit: Ken Kesey's Fiction* by M. Gilbert Porter, © 1982 by University of Missouri Press. Reprinted with permission.

"*One Flew Over the Cuckoo's Nest*" by Stephen L. Tanner from *Ken Kesey* by Stephen L. Tanner, © 1983 by G. K. Hall & Company. Reprinted with permission.

"Musical Messages in Kesey's Novels: You Can Tell a Man by the Song that He Sings" by M. Gilbert Porter from *Connecticut Review*, Vol. 12, No. 2 (Summer 1990): 13–20, © 1990 by Board of Trustees, Connecticut State University. Reprinted with permission.

"The Carnival Artist in the Cuckoo's Nest" by Benjamin Goluboff from *Northwest Review*, Vol. 29, No. 3 (1991): 109–122, © 1991 by *Northwest Review*. Reprinted with permission.

# Index

The" (Porter), 101–21
Poet, Bromden as, 103–11
Politics, and hustling, 67–78
Popular culture, 129, 149, 167
  and comic strip, 1, 3–13
Porter, M. Gilbert, 101–21, 153–60
*Problems of Dostoesvky's Poetics*
  (Bakhtin), 162, 169
Prostitutes, 44, 75, 88, 93, 97, 98, 141,
  170
Puppet show, 9
Pynchon, Thomas, 26, 44

*Rabelais and His World* (Bakhtin), 162,
  165, 169
Racial relations, 7–8, 85
Rand, Ayn, 1
Rape, and Nurse's Aides, 85
Rawler, suicide of, 92
Religion, and Miss Pilbow, 95–96
  *See also* Christ imagery
Revolutionary allegory, 73–74
Romance elements, 43–44, 148
Ruckly, 39, 57, 131, 136
  and faces, 117–18

Sacks, Sheldon, 148
"Salvation Through Laughter: Ken
  Kesey & the Cuckoo's Nest"
  (Tanner), 55–66
Sandy, 88, 97
Scanlon, 139, 144
Sefelt, 70, 118, 166
  and Christ imagery, 48, 75, 138
  and faces, 119
  and sexuality, 12
Self
  annihilation of, 27–31
  mystery of, 35–45
Self-reliance, 149–50

Sexism. *See* Feminism
Sexuality, 150
  and Bibbit, 12
  and Big Nurse, 42, 56, 65–66, 77, 84,
    110, 144–45, 147
  and Bromden, 11–12, 86, 96–97
  and hands, 86–87, 88
  and Dale Harding, 9–10, 11–12
  and Vera Harding, 89
  and McMurphy, 10, 11–12, 84–85,
    86, 87–88
  and Miss Pilbow, 95–96
  and prostitutes, 88
  and Sefelt, 12
Sherwood, Terry G., 3–13, 149, 150,
  168
Snyder, Gary, *Earth House Hold*, 33
*Sometimes a Great Notion* (Kesey),
  19–23, 153–54, 155–60
Songs, 4–5, 154–55
Spivey, Doctor, 85, 86, 112, 124
  and carnival imagery, 161–62
*Stranger in a Strange Land* (Heinlein),
  30
Strong men, as theme, 132
Structure, 56–66, 130
Sullivan, Ruth, 124, 146
Swimming pool episode, 92, 118
Synecdoche, and Bromden, 103, 111,
  112–21

Taber, Mr., 6, 49, 115, 136
Tanner, Stephen L., 55–66, 123–51
Tanner, Tony, 15–34
Thoreau, Henry David, 168
Tolkien, J. R. R., 1
Tonto, Bromden as, 8, 12, 149, 167
Totalitarianism, 72
  *See also* Modern machine culture
Townbred girl, 4, 5
"To You" (Whitman), 28